W9-BOO-798

HOW TO
SPEAK
MONEY

HOW TO
SPEAK
MONEY

What the Money People Say—And What It Really Means

John Lanchester

W. W. NORTON & COMPANY

New York • London

For information about special discounts for bulk purchases, please contact
W. W. Norton Special Sales at specialsales@wwnorton.com or 800-233-4830

Manufacturing by RR Donnelley, Harrisonburg, VA
Book design by Chris Welch
Production manager: Anna Oler

ISBN 978-0-393-24337-6

W. W. Norton & Company, Inc.
500 Fifth Avenue, New York, N.Y. 10110
www.wwnorton.com

W. W. Norton & Company Ltd.
Castle House, 75/76 Wells Street, London W1T 3QT

1 2 3 4 5 6 7 8 9 0

For Mary-Kay Wilmers

The ideas of economists and political philosophers, both when they are right and when they are wrong, are more powerful than is commonly understood. Indeed the world is ruled by little else. Practical men, who believe themselves to be quite exempt from any intellectual influence, are usually the slaves of some defunct economist. Madmen in authority, who hear voices in the air, are distilling their frenzy from some academic scribbler of a few years back. I am sure that the power of vested interests is vastly exaggerated compared with the gradual encroachment of ideas.

—John Maynard Keynes, *The General Theory of Employment, Interest and Money*

Sugar: You own a yacht? Which one is it? The big one?
Joe: Certainly not. With all the unrest in the world, I don't think anybody should have a yacht that sleeps more than twelve.

—Billy Wilder and I. A. L. Diamond, *Some Like It Hot*

Contents

Preface

n relation to economics, governments are like Jack
Nicholson's marine colonel in the Aaron Sorkin movie *A Few
Good Men*: "You want the truth? You can't handle the truth!"
Their assumption seems to be that we can't be trusted to face
facts and cope with uncomfortable realities about how the world
works. And—let's be honest—there's probably something in that.
Although we the people will never admit as much, we would on the
whole prefer to be spared difficult truths. As a character remarks
in Martin Amis's novel *The Information*, "Denial was so great.
Denial was the best thing. Denial was better even than *smoking*."
Unfortunately, in this case, denial won't work. When the economic
currents running through all our lives were mild and benign, it
was easy not to think about them, in the way that it's easy not to
think about a current when it's drifting you gently down a river—
and that, more or less, is what we were all doing, without realizing
it, until 2008. Then it turned out that these currents were much
more powerful than we knew, and that instead of cosseting us and
helping us along, they were sweeping us far out to sea, where we'd
have no choice but to fight against them, fight hard, and without

any certain sense that our best efforts would be enough to get us back to shore and safety.

That in essence is why I've written this book. There's a huge gap between the people who understand money and economics and the rest of us. Some of the gap was created deliberately, with the use of secrecy and obfuscation; but more of it, I think, is to do with the fact that it was just easier this way, easier for both sides. The money people didn't have to explain what they were up to, and got to write their own rules, and did very well out of the arrangement; and for the rest of us, the brilliant thing was, we never had to think about economics. For a long time, that felt like a win-win. But it doesn't any longer. The current swept too many of us out to sea; even when we got back to land, those of us who did, we can remember how powerful it was, and how helpless we felt. It's a gap we need to close—both at the macro level, in order for us to make informed democratic decisions; and at the micro level, in terms of the choices we make in our own lives.

A big part of this gap is almost embarrassingly simple: it's to do with knowing what the money people are talking about. On the radio or the TV or in the papers, a voice is going on about fiscal and monetary this or that, or marginal rates of such-and-such, or yields or equity prices, and we sorta-kinda know what they mean, but not really, and not with the completeness that would allow us to follow the argument in real time. "Interest rates," for instance, is a two-word term that packs in a great deal of knowledge of how things work not just in markets and finance but across whole societies. I know all about this type of semiknowledge, because I was completely that person, the one who sorta-kinda knew what was being talked about, but not in enough detail to really engage with the argument in a fully informed, adult manner. Now that I know more about it, I think everybody else should too. Just as C. P. Snow said, in the late 1950s, that everyone should know the second law of thermodynamics,* everyone should know about interest rates, and why they matter, and also what monetarism is, and what GDP is, and what an inverted yield curve is, and why it's scary. From that starting point, of language, we begin to have the tools to make up an economic picture, or pictures. That's what I want this book to do: to give the reader tools, and my hope is that after reading it you'll be able to listen to the economic news, or read the money pages, or the *Wall Street Journal*, and know what's being talked about and, just as importantly, have a sense of whether you agree or not. The details of modern money are often complicated, but the principles underlying those details aren't; I want this book to leave you much more confident in your own sense of what those principles are. Money is a lot like babies, and once you know the language, the rule is the same as that put forward by Dr. Spock: "Trust yourself. You know more than you think you do."

---

* An RMBS is a residential mortgage–backed security. Its details are complicated and take a bit of explaining—it's a type of pooled debt based on people's mortgages, turned into something that investors can buy and sell. These things that can be bought and sold come in several different tranches, with different levels of safety and accordingly variable yields to the investor. Mezzanine is the riskiest and therefore the highest-yielding tranche of this debt. So that's a vanilla mezzanine synthetic RMBS. It's not rocket science, but it's also not *The Cat in the Hat.*

Part I

THE LANGUAGE OF MONEY

1

The most important mystery of ancient Egypt was presided over by a priesthood. That mystery concerned the annual inundation of the Nile floodplain. It was this flooding that made Egyptian agriculture and therefore civilization possible. It was at the center of their society in both practical and ritual terms for many centuries; it made ancient Egypt the most stable society the world has ever seen. The Egyptian calendar itself was calculated according to the river, and was divided into three seasons, all of them linked to the Nile and the agricultural cycle it determined: *akhet*, or the inundation, *peret*, the growing season, and *shemu*, the harvest. The size of the flood determined the size of the harvest: too little water, and there would be famine; too much, and there would be catastrophe; just the right amount, and the whole country would bloom and prosper. Every detail of Egyptian life was linked to the flood: even the tax system was based on the level of the water, since that level determined how prosperous the farmers were going to be in the subsequent season. The priests performed complicated rituals to divine the nature of that year's flood and the resulting harvest. The religious elite had at their disposal a rich, emotionally satisfying mythological system; a subtle, complicated language of symbols that drew on that mythology; and a position of unchallenged power at the center of their extraordinarily stable society, one that stayed in an essentially static condition for thousands of years.

But the priests were cheating, because they had something else too: they had a Nilometer. This was a secret device made to measure and predict the level of floodwater. It consisted of a large, permanent measuring station sited on the river, with lines and markers designed to predict the level of the annual flood. The calibrations used the water level to forecast levels of harvest from Hunger up through Suffering to Happiness, Security, and Abundance, to, in a year with too much water, Disaster. Nilometers were a, perhaps *the*, priestly secret. They were situated in temples where only priests were granted access; the Greek historian Herodotus, who wrote the first outsider's account of Egyptian life, in the fifth century BC, was told of their existence, but wasn't allowed to see one. As late as 1810, thousands of years after the Nilometers had entered use, foreigners were still forbidden access to them. Added to accurate records of flood patterns dating back for centuries—accessible only to the priests, because only they could read and write—the Nilometer was an essential tool for control of Egypt. It had to be kept secret, because otherwise the ruling class and institutions would have given up too much of their authority.

The world is full of priesthoods. The Nilometer offers a perfect paradigm for many kinds of expertise, many varieties of religious and professional mystery. Many of the words for deliberately obfuscating nonsense come from priestly ritual: mumbo jumbo from the Mandinka word *maamajomboo*, a masked shamanic ceremonial dancer; hocus-pocus from *hoc est corpus meum* in the Latin mass. On the one hand, the elaborate language and ritual, designed to bamboozle and mystify and intimidate and add value; on the other, the calculations that the pros make in private. Practitioners of almost every métier, from plumbers to chefs to nurses to teachers to police, have a gap between the way they talk to each other and the way they talk to their customers or audience. Grayson Perry is very funny on this phenomenon at work in the art world. "As for the language of the art world—'International Art English'—I think obfuscation was part of its purpose, to protect what in fact was probably a fairly simple philosophical point, to keep some sort of mystery around it. There was a fear that if it was made understandable, it wouldn't seem important."[1] Sometimes, this very gap is what attracts people to a trade in the first place—politics, for instance, is all about the difference between public and private.

To the outsider, economics, and the world of money more generally, looks a lot like the old Nilometer trick. In the *Economist* not long ago, I read about a German bank that had observers worried. The journalist thought that, despite the worry, the bank would probably be OK, because "holdings of peripheral euro-zone government bonds can be gently unwound by letting them run off." What might that mean? There's something kooky about the way the metaphor mixes unwinding and holding and running off—it's like something out of a screwball comedy. That's inappropriate, given that what that phrase really means, spelled out, is this: the bank owns too much debt from euro-zone countries such as Greece, Italy, Spain, Portugal, and Ireland, but rather than selling off that debt, what the bank will do instead is wait for the loan period of the debt to come to an end, and then not buy any more of it. In this fashion the amount of such debt owned by the bank will gradually decrease over time, rather than shrinking quickly through being sold. In short, the holdings will be gently unwound by letting them run off.

There's plenty more where that came from. When you hear money people talk about the effect of QE2 on M3, or the supply-side impact of some policy or other, or the effects of bond yield retardation, or of a scandal involving forward-settling ETFs, or MBSs, or subprime and Reits and CDOs and CDSs and all the other panoply of acronyms whose underlying reality is just as complicated as they sound—well, when you hear those things, it's easy to think that somebody is trying to con you. Or, if not con you, then trying to put up a smoke screen, to obfuscate and blather so that it isn't possible to tell what's being talked about, unless you already know about it in advance. During the recent credit crunch, there was a strong feeling that a lot of the terms for the products involved were deliberately obscure and confusing: it was hard to take in the fact that CDSs were on the point of taking down the entire global financial system, when you'd never even heard of them until about two minutes before.

And sure, yes, some of the time the language of finance is obscure, and has the effect of hiding the truth. (One of my favorite examples came from the financial derivatives that played a role in the 2008 implosion: "a vanilla mezzanine RMBS synthetic CDO.")* More often, though, the language of money is complicated because the underlying realities are complicated, and need some explication and analysis before you can understand them. The language isn't immediately transparent to the well-intentioned outsider. This lack of transparency isn't necessarily sinister, and has its parallel in other fields—in the world of food and wine, for instance. A taste or smell can pass you by, unremarked or nearly so, in large part because you don't have a word for it. Then you experience the thing and realize the meaning of the word at the same time, and both your palate and your vocabulary have expanded. In respect

---

* An RMBS is a residential mortgage–backed security. Its details are complicated and take a bit of explaining—it's a type of pooled debt based on people's mortgages, turned into something that investors can buy and sell. These things that can be bought and sold come in several different tranches, with different levels of safety and accordingly variable yields to the investor. Mezzanine is the riskiest and therefore the highest-yielding tranche of this debt. So that's a vanilla mezzanine synthetic RMBS. It's not rocket science, but it's also not *The Cat in the Hat.*

of wine, that's how those of us who take an interest learn, for instance, to tell grape varietals apart: one day you catch the smell of gooseberries from a Sauvignon Blanc, or red currants from a Cabernet, or bubble gum from a Gamay, or cow shit from a Syrah, and from that point on you can recognize that varietal, and you know what people are talking about when they talk about those flavors. Our palate and our vocabulary grow simultaneously; we learn a new taste at the same time as we learn a new word for a taste. The smell of a corked bottle of wine, for instance, is something, once it's pointed out to you, that you never forget (and usually realize you have drunk a zillion times in the past, knowing something wasn't quite right but not knowing exactly what). You don't need to know that what you're smelling is 2,4,6-trichloroanisole to remember the smell of corking forever.

So this is how I think it works: As you learn to name things, you learn to taste and remember them. That might sound like a double benefit, a win-win: but there is a catch here, a potential problem. We can use our food vocabulary to talk about food with other people, to enter a dialogue with—well, with anyone; or almost anyone. This is the social aspect of food language, and it's very powerful within the community whose members know what they are talking about. But it's also a potential problem. The words and references are really useful only to people who've had the same experiences and use the same vocabulary: you're referring to a shared basis of sensory experience and a shared language. People who don't have those things are likely to think you are producing the thing that smells like Shiraz, and they don't mean it as praise. Sometimes, there are referents we don't understand. People who like fancy dark chocolate often talk about "red fruit" notes in the flavors; I like fancy dark chocolate, but for the life of me I can't taste red fruit in it. I'd go so far as to say that the fact that it doesn't taste at all like red fruit is one of the things I like about it. "Underripe bananas" is a smell that's sometimes said to be present in good olive oil. Eh? I can't taste those tastes in those substances, because I've never had the experience of recognizing them; that doesn't necessarily mean that the people who can taste them are bluffing, just that they have a vocabulary of specific sense references that I don't. (Just to complicate the matter, sometimes, actually, they are bluffing.) This is the loss involved in learning about taste: as you learn more about the match between tastes and language, you risk talking to fewer and fewer people—the people who know what these taste references actually mean. As your vocabulary becomes more specific, more useful, more effective, it also becomes more exclusive. You are talking to a smaller audience.

The language of money works like that too. It is powerful and efficient; but it is also both exclusive and excluding. The qualities are intimately linked. To take the hypothetical example I mentioned earlier, of someone talking about the effect of QE2 on M3—when an economist talks like that, she isn't just being deliberately bamboozling and obstructive. The fact is that it's complicated to explain what QE2 is and how it works. There's a certain kind of explanation that you come across in complicated subjects, for instance, science, where you read it, and can kind of follow it while you're reading it, and then can remember it for maybe five or ten seconds after you stop reading, and then about two minutes later you've forgotten it. There's nothing else to do except read it and follow it and try to work through it in your head again. And maybe again. And who knows, maybe again, again. That's not because you're thick; it's because the subject is genuinely complex. There are lots of things like that in the world of money, where the explanation is hard to hold on to because it compresses a whole sequence of explanations into a phrase, or even just into a single word.

I talk about a number of these terms in the lexicon that follows, but for now, just to stick with the example of QE2, what we're talking about is the government buying back its own debt from participants in the market. These are banks and companies—in theory, but I think not much in practice, individuals too. Once the government has bought back that debt, well, there's no particular benefit to that: it's like borrowing money from your neighbor and then paying the neighbor back the exact same amount. Nothing has changed. The trick in this case is that the money the government uses to buy back the debt is newly created electronic money. It's money that simply didn't exist before. It's like typing 100,000 at a keyboard and magically having $100,000 added to your bank account. Then you use that newly created money to pay off your debts. That's QE. As for QE2, well, that's just the second lot of QE, put into place because the first one didn't have enough of a stimulus effect on the economy. As for M3, that's a way of measuring the amount of money in the economy. The question of how much money is moving in the economy forms an entire branch of economics in itself: it's a subject of huge argument just how much that number exactly matters. But that's what they're talking about when they talk about M3. Now, all those ideas are packed into the words "QE2's effect on M3," which money people don't need to explain to themselves, or to anyone they're in the habit of talking to. That's because everyone in that world is completely familiar with the terms. It's also because the explanation is quite complex and demanding, and it's much much easier for everyone who already understands the language to just skip it to get on to the next point in the argument. As for the majority of people, perhaps even the vastly overwhelming majority of people, who don't fully understand what QE2 and M3 are: you've already lost them. They're no longer meaningfully participating in the conversation. The argumentative Elvis has left the building.

It's important to bear something in mind here. To use the language of money does not imply acceptance of any particular moral or ideological framework. It doesn't imply that you agree with the ideas involved. Money person A and money person B talking about the effect of QE2 on M3 may well be coming from completely different economic places. Person A might be an openhanded free-spending Keynesian (don't worry, this book will tell you what that means) who thinks QE2 is the only thing saving the economy from apocalyptic meltdown. On the other hand, person B might think that QE is a certain formula for ruin, is already wreaking havoc on savers, and is well on course to turn the United States into a version of Weimar Germany. A also thinks M3 money supply is bullshit, a pure example of "voodoo economics" at its most fanciful, whereas B thinks that a disciplinarian approach to control of the money supply is the last pure hope for the survival of democracy and civilized life as we know it. In other words, they completely disagree about everything they're discussing; and yet they have a shared language that enables them to discuss it with concision and force. The language doesn't necessarily imply a viewpoint; what it does is make a certain kind of conversation possible.

I learned this for myself the hard way—or, if it's a bit too melodramatic to say it was the hard way, I learned it gradually, protractedly, and by myself. My interest in the subject grew out of a novel I was writing. One of the things that happens to you, or at any rate happened to me, as a novelist is that you become increasingly preoccupied by this question: what's the thing behind the thing? What's the story behind the evident story? The answer I often found was that the story behind the story turned out to concern money. I started to take more of an interest in the economic forces behind the surface realities of life. As a way of pursuing this interest, I wrote a few long pieces for the *London Review of Books* that reflected this increasing curiosity and the increasing knowledge that came with it. I wrote an article on Microsoft, one on Walmart, and one on Rupert Murdoch. I came to think that there was a gap in the culture, in that most of the writing on these subjects was either by business journalists who thought that everything about the world of business was great or by furious opponents from the left who thought that everything about them was so terrible that there was no interest-

ing story to be told: that what was needed was rageful denuncia-
tion. Both sides missed the complexities, and therefore the interest,
of the story—that was what I felt.

By that point I was starting to think about writing a whole
book along those lines, a book about companies and the people
behind those companies. The idea was that it would be a secret
history of the modern world, or of the powers that be in the
world, through the stories of the powerful companies that made
the world—something like that, anyway. But I'm usually thinking about more than one book at the same time, and in parallel
with that I was thinking of writing a big fat novel about London.
And then the two things converged, as things sometimes do. The
editor of the *London Review of Books*, Mary-Kay Wilmers, called
me up and suggested that I do "one of my pieces about companies" about banks; as it happened that was exactly what I had just
started to think about for the purposes of my novel. I'd realized
that you can't really write about London without starting to take
an interest in the City of London, because finance is so central
to the place London has become. So that was how I ended up getting my education in the language of money: by following the subject in order to write about it. It wasn't a crash course; I didn't
immerse myself in it up to the eyeballs and try and ingest every
single detail about economics in one go. Instead I just followed
it, for years, by reading the financial papers and financial pages,
and following the economic news. The main thing I did, every
time I didn't understand a term or idea, was try to find out what it
meant. I'd Google it or go to any of the various books I was starting to accumulate on the subject. I know it sounds like reality TV
bullshit to say it was a journey, but actually it was a journey.

A crucial part of this was that my father had worked for a bank.
His kind of banking wasn't at all the kind of fancy go-go modern
investment banking that blew up the global financial system in
2008. The type of banking my father did was the kind that involved

lending money to small businesses to get going. More than once, driving around Hong Kong in my childhood, he would point out a factory or a business where he'd been the person who said yes and approved the initial loan that got the business started. There were no vanilla mezzanine synthetic RMBSs in his work. But the fact that he worked in the world of money had an effect on my sense that it was and is comprehensible. A lot of people don't have that. They feel prebaffled, put off or defeated in advance, by everything to do with money and economics. It's almost like a magnetic repulsion from the subject. I didn't have that. I had permission to understand it if I wanted to. I know it sounds weird, but I've come to think that a lot of people don't feel they have that permission.

Even with the permission, there were times when the whole process felt a little bit like learning Chinese—figuring out the meaning, word by word. A typical sentence would be something like this: "Economists are concerned that although the RPI is still comfortably in positive territory, stripping out the effects of noncore inflation reveals strong deflationary pressures." When I started learning about money, my reaction to that would have been: "You what?" But then I learned first what the RPI is and then why, as part of the way economists view inflation, they would regard it as "comfortable" if it was positive; and I came to understand the linked issue of why deflation terrifies them so much; and then what noncore inflation is; and then what it means to take that number out of the overall inflation figure; then, bingo, I understood the sentence. Multiply that example by hundreds and hundreds of times, and that was how I learned to speak money. After you read this book, I hope that you will too.

The feeling of learning something and communicating that learning at the same time was, from the writing point of view, what was exciting about economics. I knew that I didn't know more than I knew, and I was absolutely and definitively no expert. At the same time I also felt that was keeping me closer to readers who share the same sense of being curious, and intrigued, and slightly baffled, and having to figure out this stuff as they went along. I saw what I was doing as being an intermediary, the person who stood between the experts and the broader public. I knew exactly the right amount to be occupying that intermediary role. And yet all the time, without fully realizing it, my understanding of the vocabulary and the ideas behind it was growing, and I was slowly and inexorably becoming one of Them.

When I say Them I don't mean to sound as if I'm suffering from paranoia about evil alien lizard overlords. All I mean by Them is one of the people who speak money; who, quite simply, understand the language. By that I don't mean I understand all of it all the time, but I understand enough of it to know when I don't understand: in other words when a concept or piece of vocabulary is new, I know that it's new. I can remember vividly the moment I realized I became one of Them. It was at a political magazine lunch that also functioned as an off-the-record briefing by the then chancellor (the British equivalent of the US Treasury secretary). He gave a short talk, and then there were questions from the other guests. The chancellor seemed sane and competent and reassuringly calm—this was a point in 2009 in which it felt as if the initial crisis phase of the credit crunch was only just over, and might flare back up at any moment. But that wasn't my main memory of the event. What I really took away from it was this weird, oddly demoralizing realization: I thought, oh shit, I understood that. This is a disaster! I've crossed over. I've become one of Them, and that means I'm not going to be able to write about money any more.

That turned out to be wrong—I manifestly have kept writing about it. But it is a little different now. Perhaps I shouldn't admit this, but it is harder. The difficulty is in communicating across the gap between the moneyists and everyone else, now that I know just how concise and powerful and plainly useful that language can be. It's not that different from, say, plumbers: if they're talking about their expertise, it's much simpler if they don't have to keep pausing to explain j-bends and ABSs and orbital welds. Same with any field of expertise. But imagine if plumbing became a national problem, a national emergency—which of course is exactly what it would become, if the national sewage system stopped working. Then, although we could all remember happier times when we didn't have to speak plumbing, we would have a reason to learn. But the plumbers would still have a tendency to talk to each other in their own technical language, if we let them, just because it's more efficient that way. Economists are no different. I saw this at close range at one of the most interesting and radicalizing events I've ever taken part in, Kilkenomics, billed as "the world's first ever festival of comedy and economics," in Kilkenny in the autumn of 2010.

The festival was the brainchild of two brilliant Irishmen, the economist David McWilliams and the comedy producer Richard Cook. The thinking behind it went something like this: Ireland had been bankrupted by its government's stupid decision to stand behind the debts of the country's insolvent banks. The consequences in terms of economic collapse were already severe—job losses, pay cuts, tax rises, emigration, a spike in the suicide rate—and were likely to become more so. The economic miracle of the Celtic Tiger had turned into a disaster. Ireland was in a strange mood, a mixture of resignation and fury, alternating between the two feelings so quickly it was almost as if there was a bizarre new hybrid emotion: blazingly furious philosophical resignation. In that atmosphere Cook and McWilliams—McWilliams having been one of the very few Irish economists to have predicted the crash—decided that since the only two things you could really do about the current predicament were laugh or cry, why not laugh? And why not, since Kilkenny was already the site of an internationally famous comedy festival, do it in Kilkenny? Hence, Kilkenomics: the world's first-ever festival of comedy and economics, which is still running as an annual event. Every event at the festival mixes comedians together with economists. The idea behind that was brilliantly simple: what the comedians do is force the economists to stop talking entirely to each other and engage the audience instead. It was extraordinary to see how effective this was; you could see it in the body language of participants onstage. As the economists got into their stride, they would, entirely unconsciously, begin to turn towards each other and away from the audience. At that point one of the comedians would make a joke, often along the lines of not knowing what the fecking hell the economists were talking about, and everyone would laugh, and the economists would remember where they were and turn back to reengage with the audience.

It was revealing to see how much the economists did actually want to engage with the public. On the audience's side there was a pressing need to understand the predicament, and on the experts' side, just as pressing an urge to explain it. This is where the question of the language became so important. The economists' tendency to turn towards each other was based on the fact that they spoke the same language and could use it to communicate so effectively—so, if you'll forgive the pun, economically. It was actually the language, the seductive power of it, that was encouraging them to talk mainly to each other. One of the events at Kilkenomics was a brilliant panel game in which two teams, both of them with one comedian and one economist, played a game in which the moderator held up a word, then the comedians guessed what it meant, before the economists gave an explanation of what it really was. It was very funny, and it also offered a real education in this issue of just how important the language of economics is.

This doesn't mean that the economists agreed, by the way—not at all. All the money language did was give a vocabulary in which to be clear about their disagreements. The disagreements in economics aren't just about technicalities: they're usually based on profound divergences in moral analysis. In economics, though, the morality is buried below the surface of what you're talking about.

Morality and ethics are too basic, too fundamental to be given direct expression in economics. The language of money doesn't express any implied moral perspective. Judgments of what's right and wrong are left out. This can make the language seem abrasive, even shocking, to people who habitually speak a different kind of discourse. Since much of the language of public life has an implied moral and political load, this makes money-speak very distinctive. "Welfare scroungers" has a different spin from "benefit claimants," who don't sound at all the same as "the working poor," even if these are all the same people, and the benefit they're claiming is called "job seeker's allowance," where once it was known as "unemployment benefit" in an attempt to provide a heavy nudge (and to placate right-wing headline writers). Your "asylum seeker" is my "refugee"; your "entitlements" are my "pensions." Aristotle was right when he said that man is a political animal; our language is one of the most political things about us.

Compared with these styles of public discourse, there's something amoral and stripped-down about the language of money. It sets out to be less an expression of politics, and more a tool for discussing them. Morality is left out, or left to one side, or parked elsewhere for the duration of the discussion. Some people, especially on the political left, find that intensely alienating, as if the language of money involves an inherent kind of betrayal, an absence of other sorts of value. When job losses are being discussed, for instance, or cuts to benefits, or reductions in pension rights, it's sometimes as if there's a desire for disapproval and outrage to be registered not just at the level of argument but with the very words themselves, as if the language itself should storm the barricades in protest at the thought of any of those bad things being advocated or permitted. I understand that, I really do. And at the same time there's a bracing quality to talking about the technical details, the practical meat of the subject, without the outrage.

Mind you, having said that, some of the time the amorality is real, and deep, and troubling. Some of the people who speak money do genuinely not give a shit about anything other than money. They think that poor people are poor because they are lazy or stupid or weak, and that rich people are rich because they are hardworking, intelligent, and strong, and that all the evident inequalities and injustices in the world result from those unpalatable facts. But that's interesting, in a way, no? It would be better if the people who think that actually say it, and try to argue for it. At the moment we in the English-speaking world have a political and economic direction of travel that embodies the trends towards baked-in, permanent inequality, without the conversation in which people in favor of the arrangement spell out their views.

In any case, I have to admit that this amoral quality is one of the things I like about the language of money. Our public life is dominated by hypocrisy, by people holding back from saying exactly what they mean because they don't want to offer targets for opponents or the media, especially targets for the form of fake outrage that figures in so much of our public discourse. There's less of that in the language of money; it is not, in general, hypocritical. As a result, it gets to the real matter under discussion with commendable speed—once you have the linguistic tools to join the conversation.

2

f the language of money is so useful, so effective at communicating ideas economically, how come it seems so off-puttingly difficult, so closed and excluding? How come we don't learn it automatically as we grow up, the way we learn the language that we actually speak?

The answer isn't just to do with the difficulty of the ideas involved in economics and money. Many fields of thought have ideas that are far more difficult to understand, but that don't have the same sense of a linguistic perimeter around them. In physics, for instance, there are an enormous number of ideas of a complexity so great that they can't really be grasped at all in ordinary language, but are available only to someone with an advanced level of math. Even then they are very hard to understand. The great physicist Richard Feynman, who knew his subject as well as anyone who's ever lived, and who explained it better than anyone who ever lived, said in *The Character of Physical Law*, "I think I can safely say that no one understands quantum mechanics." But you can still get a sense of what these fields of thought are about. Take the very obscure and difficult field of quantum chromodyamics. (As it happens, that was Feynman's speciality.) I haven't really got a clue what that is. But even if you don't know anything about physics, you can tell that it is about quantum things; even if you don't know that quantum physics concerns the study of very very very very small things, where nonintuitive and anti-commonsense rules apply, you still probably know that it's weird modern physics stuff. As for the "chromo" bit, that's something do with color. "Dynamics" concerns movement. So even without knowing anything about it, you can tell quantum chromodynamics is the study of weird modern physics to do with color and movement. (As it happens, the color is metaphorical—it's a random, whimsical name given to a range of mathematical properties.) The large hadron collider? Well, it's large and it collides hadrons, whatever they are. Again, you can get the gist.

For many concepts in the world of money, that isn't true. Often, there's no way to break a term down and work out more or less what it means. "Consumer surplus," for example, sounds like a surplus of consumers. It isn't. Bulls think the price of something is going to go up, and bears think the price is going to go down—but why? Why is it that way around? What is a confidence interval: is it a gap during which you don't feel confident about something? Who is Chocfinger? Does he really have a chocolate finger?

To explain why the language of money is complicated in this particular counterintuitive way—why it is difficult to parse—I am going, with apologies, to introduce a newly coined term of my own. That term is "reversification." I mean by it a process in which words come, through a process of evolution and innovation, to have a meaning that is opposite to, or it least very different from, their initial sense. Take the term "Chinese wall," much used in the world of finance. This is a classic example of reversification. In real life, a Chinese wall is a very big, very real physical wall in China, built to keep out marauding barbarians. (Actually it's a whole set of linked walls, built over several centuries, and is the focus of its own field of historical scholarship—but let that pass for now.) It's so big that it is sometimes said to be the only man-made object visible from space, which isn't true—many other man-made entities are visible, and the wall itself is very hard to spot—but the legend is at least a tribute to its extraordinary scale. In the world of money, though, the term "Chinese wall" means an invisible dividing line inside a financial institution that prevents people from sharing information across it, in order to avert conflicts of interest. In theory, banks are full of Chinese walls, such as the one dividing analysts, who study companies and sell the conclusions they reach as advice, from the investment bankers, who offer services to those same companies. In practice, Chinese walls tend to be highly permeable, especially in times of stress and/or opportunity. In other words, it is the opposite of the actual Chinese wall. In considering the financial use of the term, we would all do well to bear in mind something said by the investor Vincent Daniel, in speaking to Michael Lewis: "When I hear 'Chinese wall,' I think, 'You're a fucking liar.'"[2]

So that's "reversification": a term being turned into its opposite. In this case it is the pressures of capitalism that are responsible, because those forces have led to the creation of institutions that have within them different departments, which—if the system is to function without conflicts of interest— shouldn't really be there. What the banks themselves say is that we can trust them because managing conflicts of interest is what they do, all day and every day; it's at the heart of their work. The answer to that is obvious in the size of the scandals and disasters that have been uncovered since the crash of 2008—I say uncovered, because most of the practices involved took place in the years of the boom that preceded the bust, and would not have come to light without the downturn. The Libor scandal, which has seen many banks fined billions of dollars, is one of the scandals. The scandal over the selling of residential mortgage–backed securities, which currently has JPMorgan Chase looking at a fine of $13 billion, is another. The unfolding Forex scandal, which resembles Libor in that it is another example of banks manipulating what were supposed to be authoritative benchmark rates, is a third. All of these scandals have in common not just a failure to manage conflicts of interest but a blatant exploitation of customers and manipulation of markets. The Chinese walls to protect customers were worse than nonexistent; they provided opportunities for the banks to make money by exploiting people who trusted them. Not only did not exist; they provided opportunities to exploit them. That's reversification.

Another example is the term "hedge fund." This baffles and bamboozles outsiders, because it's very hard to understand what these Bond villains—which is what hedge funders are in the public imagination—have to do with hedges. The story of how the term made its journey is a good one, and it has a lot to tell us about the language of money and the pressures brought to bear on it by the forces of financial innovation. In fact, I'm not sure that there is a purer example of reversification at work than in "hedge fund."

Here's what happened. The word "hedge" began its life in economics as a term for setting limits to a bet, in the same way that a hedge sets a limit to a field. That's what a hedge is for: demarcating an area of land. The word "hedge" is Anglo-Saxon, turning up for the first time in the eighth century and cognate with other northern European terms to denote an enclosure. We can safely suppose that this was in the first instance a question of property and ownership. Six hundred years later, "hedge" became a verb, meaning to enclose a field by making a hedge around it. Three hundred years after that, it started to show up in its monetary sense, in the Duke of Buckingham's 1671 play *The Rehearsal*, a parody of the Restoration fashion for heroic moralistic drama, in which the prologue taunts potential critics:

> *Now, Critiques do your worst, that here are met;*
> *For, like a Rook, I have hedged in my Bet.*

The word "rook" there is being used in its now obsolete sense of, to quote the *Oxford English Dictionary*, "A cheat, swindler, or sharper, esp. in gambling." So it's apparent that hedging was a technique already being used in gambling (especially by crooks) during the seventeenth century. The idea is that by putting a hedge around a bet, you delimit the size of your potential losses, just as a real hedge delimits the size of a field. At its simplest, a hedge is created when you make a bet, and at the same time make another bet on the other side of a possible outcome. While you're restricting your potential winnings by setting an upper limit to them, you are also guaranteeing that you will not lose money. The area of possible winnings and possible losses is hedged around and clearly defined. Say you've made a bet at the start of the season, that the Green Bay Packers will make it to the Super Bowl, at odds of 20 to 1. You put down ten bucks. They make it to the conference championship, where they're playing the San Francisco 49ers. At this point you decide to hedge your bet by putting some money on the 49ers to win. The 49ers are 3 to 1 to win the game. You put $10 on them; this now means that you're guaranteed a profit, whatever the outcome. If the Packers win, you win $200, plus the initial $10 you bet, minus the $10 you bet on the 49ers, so you end up with $200 in your pocket. If the 49ers win, you win $30, and get back the $10 you bet on them, but lose the initial $10 you put on the Packers, so you end up with $30 in your pocket. Sure, the second bet, on the 49ers, draws some money from your potential winnings if the Packers come out ahead, but if you didn't make that bet, and the 49ers win, you'll lose $10.

The bigger winnings from the unhedged bet might look tempting—but remember, in the hedged version, the bettor cannot lose. Any financial structure in which you can make profit and are guaranteed not to lose money is going to have many ardent fans. Bear in mind that this example is as simple as it gets, and many of the examples of hedging in gambling are a lot more complex than that. Gamblers will often bet on a "point spread," the difference between the winning team and the losing team, and will bet a specific amount for each point of difference: $10 a point in a game of football, say. As the game draws closer, or even after it begins, a point-spread bettor will often make another bet in the opposite direction, for the same reason: to delimit the extent of any possible losses, at the cost of also limiting the extent of possible wins.

What's generally agreed to have been the first hedge fund developed a more sophisticated evolution of the techniques used by gamblers hedging their bets. It was the creation of the American investment manager Alfred Winslow Jones. A *Fortune* magazine article about Jones used the term "hedge fund" for the first time. I like the title of the piece: "The Jones Nobody Keeps Up With."[3] At the time the story came out, in 1966, his fund had just gone up 325 percent in five years.

Jones was an interesting man, and had an interesting life. He was born in Melbourne in 1900 and moved to America at the age of four. After graduating from Harvard in 1923, he sailed around the world on a tramp steamer, then joined the US foreign service, where he served as vice consul in Berlin during Hitler's rise to the chancellorship; then he went to the Spanish Civil War as an official observer for the Quakers; then he took a PhD in sociology at Columbia University. The subject of his thesis was class distinctions in modern American life. He turned the thesis into a book, *Life, Liberty, and Property: A Story of Conflict and a Measurement of Conflicting Rights*. (Quite an irony: the man who invented hedge funds was fascinated by the question of social class in America.) On the basis of the book, Jones was hired as a writer by *Fortune* magazine, where he began to take an interest in the world of money. After the war he left *Fortune* to set up as a freelance writer and came across the subject of number-based forecasting. He wrote a piece about it, "Fashions in Forecasting," in 1949. Having looked at these techniques and concluded there was something in them, he then decided, at the age of forty-eight, to establish an investment partnership designed to give them a try. He chose a partnership structure, limited to a small number of members, as a way of getting around the rules on how collective investments were regulated; he chose to pay himself 20 percent of the profits, on the basis that this was what Phoenician sea captains paid themselves after a successful voyage (no, really); he used borrowed money to magnify the impact of his choices; and his investments were hedged. That's to say, he bet on some things going up, "going long," as it's called, and simultaneously on other things going down, "going short." He used mathematical techniques to try and ensure that all movements in the market would be taken account of by this mixture of long and short "positions" and produce a positive outcome, whatever happened. As the official history of the partnership states,

His key insight was that a fund manager could combine two techniques: buying stocks with leverage (or margin), and selling short other stocks. Each technique was considered risky and highly speculative, but when properly combined together would result in a conservative portfolio. The realization that one could use speculative techniques to conservative ends was the most important step in forming the hedged fund. Using his knowledge of statistics from his background as a sociologist, Jones developed a measure of market and stock-specific risk to better manage the exposure of his portfolio.

It is important to note that Jones referred to his fund as a "Hedged Fund" not a "Hedge Fund" because he believed that being hedged was the most important identifying characteristic. Many "hedge funds" today are unregulated investment partnerships with performance compensation structures, but some of them may not actually be hedged.[4]

The classic hedge fund technique, as created by Jones, is still in use: funds employ complex mathematical analysis to bet on prices going both up and down in ways that are supposedly guaranteed to produce a positive outcome. This is "long-short," the textbook hedge fund strategy. But as that enjoyably sniffy note from the Jones company points out, many hedge funds don't in fact follow classic hedging strategies. As it's used today, the term "hedge fund" means a lightly regulated pool of private capital, almost always doing something exotic—because if it wasn't exotic, the investors could access the investment strategy much more cheaply somewhere else. There will almost always be a "secret sauce" of some sort, proprietary to the hedge fund; it is usually a complicated set of mathematical techniques. Does that sound straightforward? It shouldn't. Most hedge funds fail: 90 percent of all the hedge funds that have ever existed have closed or gone broke. Out of a total of about 9,800 hedge funds worldwide, 743 failed or closed in 2010, 775 in 2011, and 873 in 2012—so in three years, a quarter of all the funds in existence three years earlier disappeared. The overall number did not decrease, because hope springs eternal, and other new funds kept being launched at the same time.

In a sense hedge funds provide a model of how capitalism should work: people risking their own money, being rewarded when they are right, and losing out when they are wrong, and none of it costing the ordinary citizen anything in bailouts or subsidies. Mind you, the sense in which they are losing "their own money" is broad, because hedge funds, ever since the days of Alfred Jones, have depended heavily on leverage, in other words on money borrowed from other people. So as long as we understand that hedge funds losing their own money includes the money of people who have lent them money, then it still holds that the only people whose money they're risking is themselves and consenting adults. (For an explanation of the pro-hedge argument, see Sebastian Mallaby's *More Money Than God: Hedge Funds and the Making of a New Elite*.)

Hedge funds are more lightly regulated than other types of pooled investment, the idea being that access to them is restricted to people who know what they are doing and can afford to lose their money. They're expensive, too: a standard fee is "2 and 20," i.e., 2 percent of the money is charged in fees every year, and also 20 percent of any profit above an agreed benchmark. I wonder how many "hedgies," stroking their Ferraris while sipping Cristal at the end of the financial year, remember to raise a glass to the Phoenician sea captains. There are no hedges to be seen, not even in the far distance.

A hedge is a physical thing; it turned into a metaphor; then into a technique; then the technique was adopted in the world of high finance, and became more and more sophisticated and more and more complicated; then it turned into something that can't be understood by ordinary use of the ordinary referents of ordinary language. And that is the story of how a hedge, setting limits to a field, became what it is today: a largely unregulated pool of private capital, often using enormous amounts of leverage and borrowing to multiply the size of its bets.

This is reversification in its full glory. The force that has taken a simple, strong old word—"hedge"—and turned it into an entirely new thing, which is more or less the opposite of a hedge, is the force of economic innovation. It is, to put it differently, capitalism. Reversification is a force that can often be found in the world of money, and it's one of the things that make that language baffling to outsiders. "Securitization" doesn't immediately make its meaning apparent. But a good instinctive guess would be that it has something to do with security or reliability, with making things safer. Right? No, wrong. Securitization is the process of turning something—and in the world of finance it can be pretty much anything—into a security. In this context, a security is any financial instrument that can be traded as an asset. Pretty much anything can be securitized; indeed, pretty much anything is. Mortgages are securitized, car loans are securitized, insurance payments are securitized, student debt is securitized. During the Greek economic crisis of 2011, there was talk that the Greek government might try to securitize future revenue from ticket sales at the Acropolis. In other words, investors would hand over a lump of cash in return for an agreed yield; the underlying source of the money repaying the loan would be those tourists forking out for the privilege of wandering around the ancient monument taking photographs of each other. Another example of an exotic security is the "Bowie Bond," in which future royalties from David Bowie's assets were sold to raise a lump sum of $55 million. What Bowie was in effect saying at the time the bonds were issued in 1997 was, "I have a lot of money coming in over the next ten years from my back catalogue, but I'd rather have the cash now and not have to wait."

This sounds OK: if Ziggy Stardust wants to stock up on shiny jumpsuits and needs his $55 million now, why not? And indeed, there is nothing inherently malign about securitization, just as there isn't about most of the processes invented by modern finance. Like so many of those processes, however, securitization can be put to malign use. In the case of securitization, that happened on a huge scale in the run-up to the credit crunch, when certain kinds of loans began to be securitized on an industrial scale. It happened like this: an institution lends money to a range of different borrowers. Then the institution bundles the loans into securities—say, a pool of ten thousand mortgage loans, paying out an interest rate of 6 percent. Then it sells those securities to other financial institutions. The bank that made the loans no longer gets the revenue from its lending, but instead that money flows to the people who've bought the mortgage-backed securities. (These are the RMBSs—the residential mortgage–backed securities—which I've mentioned a couple of times already.) Why is this malign? Because the institution that initially lent the money no longer has to care whether or not the borrower is going to be able to pay the money back. It takes the risk of the loan only for the amount of time between making the initial house loan, and the moment when it has sold the resulting security—which can be a matter of days. The bank has no real interest in the financial condition of the borrower. The basic premise of banking—that you lend money only to people who can pay it back—has been broken. In addition, the risk of that loan, instead of being concentrated in the place where it came from, has been spread all around the financial system, as people buy and trade the resulting security. In the credit crunch, securitization fueled both "predatory lending," in which people were lent money they couldn't possibly pay back, and the uncontrollable dispersal and magnification of the risks arising from those bad debts. So securitization has nothing to do with making things more secure. There's no way of knowing that from looking at the word "securitization" in itself. That's reversification at its least appealing.

It might be said, I suppose, that, just like "hedge fund," "securitization" is a word that we know at once we don't know: you look at it and think, eh? So at least you can say that the bafflement factor is right up front. But reversification is just as often at work with words that look as if they have a plain meaning whose ordinary sense should be obvious. "Leverage," for instance. "Leverage" is a word we can all understand immediately in its physical sense: using a lever to move an object, usually one too heavy to move without assistance. In the world of money, though, "leverage" has a range of meanings, none of them immediately obvious, but most of them involving the use of borrowed money. In consumer and company finance, leverage is borrowing: the most common form in most people's lives is a mortgage. You use your monthly income to lever a large amount of money from a bank, and use that money to buy a house: so a monthly income of say $3,000 is leveraged to buy a house costing $150,000. Or you use the same monthly income to borrow money to fund a lifestyle that would otherwise, if you weren't borrowing money, be available only to someone with an income significantly bigger than yours. You can see how the word made its journey, while at the same time thinking that the term has turned into something so unlike an actual lever that it is close to being its opposite. On the one hand, a manual process involving lots of physical force; on the other, the use of borrowed money. (It occurs to me as I write that the physical sense crops up less and less in our lives, and the economic sense more and more. I can't remember the last time I encountered a real lever, whereas the economic kind is what I used to buy my house.) To complicate things further, leverage has a special sense in banking, in which it is used to measure the ratio between how much capital a bank has, and the size of its assets. Leverage in this sense is the simplest measure of how safe a bank is, because the level of equity is the difference between a bank being solvent and a bank being broke. Again, you can see how the word made its journey, because the ratio of say twenty parts assets to one part equity is a little bit like the other kind of financial leverage, in which a relatively smaller amount of money is used to borrow a much larger sum, and that in turn is a little bit like an actual lever because it's using a small thing to have the effect of a big thing—but this is nonetheless an example of reversification at work. A lever has been turned into something that is not a lever.

A "bailout" is slopping water over the side of a boat. It has been reversified so that it means an injection of public money into a failing institution. Even at the most basic level there's a reversal—taking something dangerous out turns into putting something vital in. "Credit" has been reversified: it means debt. "Inflation" means money being worth less. "Synergy" means sacking people. "Risk" means precise mathematical assessment of probability. "Noncore assets" means garbage. And so on. These are all examples of how processes of innovation, experimentation, and progress in the techniques of finance have been brought to bear on language, so that words no longer mean what they once meant. It is not a process intended to deceive. It is not like the deliberate manufacture and concealment of a Nilometer. But the effect is much the same: it is excluding, and it confines knowledge to a priesthood—the priest-hood of people who can speak money.

The bafflement that people feel at the language of money contains a note of outrage—it shouldn't be this complicated!—and a note of self-doubt—I should be able to understand on my own! Both are misplaced. The language isn't impossibly complicated, but it isn't transparent, and nobody understands it automatically and innately. Once you learn it, though, the world does start to look different.

3

At some point in the 1840s, a French liberal thinker called Frédéric Bastiat made a trip to his capital city and had an epiphany:

On entering Paris, which I had come to visit, I said to myself— here are a million human beings who would all die in a short time if provisions of every kind ceased to flow toward this great metropolis. Imagination is baffled when it tries to appreciate the vast multiplicity of commodities that must enter tomorrow through the barriers in order to preserve the inhabitants from falling a prey to the convulsions of famine, rebellion and pillage. And yet all sleep at this moment, and their peaceful slumbers are not disturbed for a single instant by the prospect of such a frightful catastrophe. On the other hand, eighty departments have been laboring today, without concert, without any mutual understanding, for the provisioning of Paris. How does each succeeding day bring what is wanted, nothing more, nothing less, to so gigantic a market?

What, then, is the ingenious and secret power that governs

the astonishing regularity of movements so complicated, a regularity in which everybody has implicit faith, although happiness and life itself are at stake? [5]

His answer: the free market. This was a lightbulb moment for Bastiat, a glimpse of the complexity that can develop from a simple starting point.* All those fundamental needs supplied, all those goods bought and sold, all those provisions transported at the expense of cash and effort and ingenuity, all those transactions made, and all of it constituting a mechanism that functions so effectively that the good citizens of Paris don't even notice how dependent they are on it—and the whole mechanism created just by allowing people to trade freely with each other. Economists have a shorthand reference to this epiphanic insight into the power of markets: they call it "Who feeds Paris?"

For most people with an interest in economics, there's a revelatory moment resembling Bastiat's. The bravura opening of Adam Smith's *The Wealth of Nations*, the founding text of economics, has a description of a pin-making factory that is very like Bastiat's moment of awakening in Paris. The eureka moment isn't always to do with the power of markets, though that's a pretty good starting point, since the balance of wants and needs manifested in a functioning market is an extraordinary thing: the contents of Aladdin's cave, all on sale at an ordinary store near you, and brought there by nothing more than market forces. Or it can be some form of change that prompts the thought, a change to do with the kind of people

---

* Bastiat (1801–1850) was a strikingly clear-minded early advocate of what came to be known as liberal economics, whose central idea is that the state should get out of the way of free trade. He would be a lot more famous if he wasn't French, since the French are highly distrustful of the whole notion of liberal economics and tend to see it as an Anglo-American cross between a conspiracy and a mistake.

who live in a place, or who do a certain kind of job, or something more fundamental, like the disappearance of an entire industry or the change in character of an entire city, an entire country. The forces at work behind these changes are economic. A curiosity about these forces is the starting point of economics.

The subject begins with the way people behave, and moves to the question of "why": economics is, in the words of Alfred Marshall, one of the great modern founders of the subject, "the study of mankind in the ordinary business of life." That sounds lofty, and suspiciously broad—which is exactly what it is. The most famous tag ever given the field of economics was Thomas Carlyle's magnificent put-down, "the dismal science." That's a good zinger, but it isn't fair. For one thing, it isn't at all clear that economics actually is a science—many people in the field like the idea that it's a science, and refer to it as a science, but that's more a claim than a statement of fact. The conservative philosopher Michael Oakeshott wrote about the main areas of the humanities as "conversations": poetry, history, and philosophy were conversations that humankind had had with itself, and that anyone could join in, just by paying attention and studying and thinking. Economics, it seems to me, is a conversation in that Oakeshottian sense, rather than a science like the hard physical sciences. That said, there are areas of economics that come very close to science, in which experiments are made and can be measured and repeated. These experiments are largely in the field of microeconomics, which is the study and analysis of how people behave. Microeconomists look at things like the way in which people consume free supermarket samples of jam, or rate wine in blind tastings, or use online dating services. A lot of what they find is useful, even entertaining, even fun, in its way. And that's the other reason Carlyle was wrong. Economics isn't dismal. It has dismal bits to be sure, and the whole idea of reducing the complexity and diversity of human behavior to shared underlying principles can sound joyless. In public life, economists are often to be found playing the role of people who explain why something is unaffordable, or why some group of people have lost their jobs, or why some other group has to work longer for less pay. But that's an accidental manifestation of what economics really is: the study of human behavior in all its forms, and the attempt to discern principles and rules underlying the chaotic multiplicity of all the things we do. Psychology looks at people from the inside. Economics looks at them from the outside. Human beings aren't dismal, and neither is economics.

The attempt to study human behavior on this scale is a large undertaking, and it follows that economics is a large field. There are lots of different tribes within it. Nothing annoys economists more than the assumption that they are all essentially the same. An economist working as a risk analyst for an investment bank is very different from an academic economist whose main interest is the developing world and whose PhD thesis was, say, a study of water wells in Nigeria; a number cruncher poring over industrial output data at the Treasury is doing something very different from a microeconomist trying to design an experiment that studies cognitive mistakes in people's filling out of insurance claim forms. More generally, economists get very annoyed at the widely held thought that they are all macroeconomists; that's a view that's held even by people who don't know exactly what a macroeconomist is or does. Macroeconomists are the guys whose field was born out of the study of the Great Depression, and the attempt not to repeat it: they look at whole economies, up to and including the planetary level. They're the people who are often seen as being at fault in not having predicted the credit crunch and the Great Recession that followed. The queen's famously good question at the London School of Economics (LSE)—"Why did nobody see it coming?"—is a macroeconomic question. But that's by no means what most economists do and are.

I've made a bit of a shuffle here, by switching from the question of how to speak money to economics as a subject. I should point out that just as most economists aren't macroeconomists, quite a lot of them have absolutely no interest in money. I don't mean at the personal level: I mean they have no interest in money as a subject. In large parts of the discipline, or disciplines, of economics, money had come to be seen as no longer interesting at a theoretical level. Money had been solved. It was a way of keeping score of things being exchanged, but the real points of interest lay beyond and through it: it could be regarded as transparent, as safely ignorable. That seems pretty amazing now, with the benefit of hindsight, when we have seen a convulsion inside the function of money that took the entire global financial system to the edge of the abyss, with consequences that are bitterly present in many of our lives more than half a decade later. You could even say that large parts of the economic profession resembled the British defenses at Singapore, with their guns pointed in the wrong direction.

There's no consensus inside economics about the importance of money. There's no consensus about anything, really, not even on how important the credit crunch and subsequent Great Recession were. "Who cares?" an academic economist at the LSE said to me, apropos exactly this point. "What happens to hundreds of millions of very poor people in South Asia and sub-Saharan Africa is a lot more important. So we in the West are going to have a difficult decade or two—so what?"

This lack of consensus doesn't just apply to the overall conclusions that people reach; it also touches on the very subjects of discussion, the terms of debate themselves. Economists and people who speak money argue all the time about things like inflation, not just in terms of what to do about it and its practical consequences but actually in terms of the very essence of what it is and how it works and how best to define it. Here is the range of views, as summarized by Wikipedia:

Some economists maintain that high rates of inflation and hyperinflation are caused by an excessive growth of the money supply, while others take the view that under the conditions of a liquidity trap, large injections are "pushing on a string" and cannot cause significantly higher inflation. Views on which factors determine low to moderate rates of inflation are more varied. Low or moderate inflation may be attributed to fluctuations in real demand for goods and services, or to changes in available supplies such as during scarcities, as well as to changes in the velocity of money supply measures—in particular the MZM (money zero maturity) supply velocity. However, the consensus view is that a long sustained period of inflation is caused by money supply growing faster than the rate of economic growth.

That's an amazing spread of views to exist around something as fundamental to practical economics as inflation, bearing in mind that this is a subject right at the core not just of government economic policy but of the actual experience of daily life. I experienced it about an hour ago: Starbucks has just raised the price of its double espresso from £1.75 to £1.90. That's easy to understand. Coffee the drink must be more expensive because coffee the commodity is more expensive, right? No, not in this case. Two years ago coffee was trading at $2.10 a pound, whereas this month it's at $1.07.*

---

* Some complexities are concealed in this figure. There are a zillion different ways of counting the price of coffee as a commodity: at the farm gate and off the dock in New York, as a daily price or as a futures contract, by the pound or by the ton, in ground form or in beans, robusta or arabica, and within arabica as the different varieties of Colombian mild, other mild, or Brazilian natural. The numbers I'm quoting here are the International Coffee Organization's average price of all the different types of beans. Note that as the cost of beans goes up, the cost of your cup might actually go down, if your favorite café switches from the more expensive, subtler arabica beans to the cheaper,

This means that the price of the one and only ingredient in my coffee has fallen by nearly 50 percent, but at the same time the price of the drink has gone up 11.2 percent! Not fair! The power at work here is the all-purpose, all-weather factor we're discussing, inflation, which has raised the cost of everything involved in transporting and making the coffee and running the stores and paying the staff—at least, that's what Starbucks would claim. It's sort of comforting, or at least I find it sort of comforting, to reflect on the fact that inflation is mysterious in its essence as well as in disconcerting practical manifestations like the price of this drink.

As for money itself, that's a subject of immense difficulty, again not just on the practical level but in its essence and nature. There's a standard definition of money in economics, or at least of the uses of money, as serving a triple function: a store of value, a medium of exchange, and a unit of account. But the real uses of money are more mysterious than this makes them sound, and its evolution is more mysterious too. There are sometimes arguments in science about whether specific breakthroughs are better defined as discoveries or as inventions: are the findings of mathematics discoveries of entities that preexist, or are they creations of the human imagination? Or both? Money is like that too. Did we invent it, or is it somehow inherent in transactions between people—implying that there is a "moneyness" in exchanges, which money then abstracts and turns into an exchangeable thing-in-itself? (The popularity of this view was one of the reasons many economists had stopped being interested in money: the transactions were more interesting than the tool through which they were transacted.)

The historical fact of money's invention or discovery is lost to us, but it does look as if the standard economists' account of how

---

stronger robusta variety. This happened in lots of places during the great coffee-bean price spike of 2010–11, so if you started noticing a few years ago that your morning espresso was making you gibber, that's probably the reason.

money came to be is almost certainly wrong. That account features barter as the basic economic process: I have a pile of yams, you have a spare portion of goatskin; I need to make a covering, you need to eat; so we swap. This is barter, the beginning of economics. Another time, I have some more yams, and you have another goatskin; you're still hungry, but I'm fine for covering, thanks. Yet you would still like to eat. So what we do is agree that some shells on the ground are worth the equivalent of the pile of yams; in future, I will be able to come to you and exchange the shells for the yams you owe me, or for some other agreed quantity of some other agreed thing. Behold! We have just invented money. Then we realize: maybe we don't need the money tokens at all; maybe all we need to do is keep score of who owes what to whom, and we can carry on exchanging things backwards and forward, with each other and with other people, keeping track of the value of what we have exchanged by means of a notional quantity of those same shells, as a way of keeping score of who is owing what to whom. Gasp! We've just invented credit! So the sequence has gone: barter, money, credit, and we're now ready for the development of something like a modern economic system.

The trouble with this account is that there is absolutely no evidence for its ever having occurred. In real-life examples from anthropology, it looks as if credit in reality comes first: people agree to exchange goods and services on a credit basis even in the most "primitive" societies, long preceding the invention of money.[6] Credit isn't that complicated an idea for us humans: we get it. The interwoven, interdependent nature of our existence makes us very quick to understand the circulating reciprocalities involved in the idea of credit. We invent money afterwards, for trading with people outside the circles we already know. As for barter, which is where the whole notion of money is supposed to have come from: it's vastly less common. The standard economic account of the invention of money has no evidence to back it up in the historical or anthropological record.

Even once we get a grip of this story, though, we still haven't come close to capturing the deep weirdness of money in its modern manifestation, as digital bits moving from screen to screen that combine complete ephemerality with total power over us. As Steve Jobs once said, all computers do is shuffle numbers about. But these digital ones and zeros measure the value of our labor and define a large part of our being, not just externally in terms of the work we do and where we live and what we own, but in terms of what we think, how we see our interests, with whom we identify, how we define our goals and ambitions, and often, perhaps too often, even what we think of ourselves in our deepest and innermost private being. And yet they're just ones and zeros. And these ones and zeros are willed into being by governments, which can create more of them just by running a printing press; in fact, thanks to the miracle of quantitative easing, they don't even need to do that, but instead can merely announce that there is now more electronic money. We're inclined to think of money as a physical thing, an object, but that's not really what it is. Modern money is mainly an act of faith—an act of credit, of belief.

One of the lessons of the credit crunch was that this credit, this belief, can be vulnerable. A moment came when it wasn't clear, even to people at the heart of the system—the high priesthood of money itself—that the ones and zeros were worth what they were supposed to be worth. If people and companies couldn't pay their debts, then all the accumulated credits in the financial system weren't worth their nominal value; and if that was the case, then, as George W. Bush so eloquently put it, "this sucker could go down." Even after the financial system recovered from its near-death experience, it has proved hard to forget that moment of noncredit, and to let go of that sense of appalled wonder. Andy Haldane, director of stability at the Bank of England (great job title: perhaps each and every one of us should have a personal director of stability), made a study of modern derivative transactions and found that some of them involve up to a billion lines of computer code. That is beyond comprehension, not in a metaphorical way, but as a plain fact: no human can understand and parse a financial instrument of that complexity. None of us really understands how the labor of humans and the movement of goods and exchange of services can be turned into purely financial transactions that involve a "black box" financial instrument a billion lines long. We just have to take it on credit. One of the best books written about money is a history of it by the economist and economic historian John Kenneth Galbraith. It begins with a wonderfully bracing line: "The reader should proceed in these pages in the knowledge that money is nothing more or less than what he or she always thought it was—what is commonly offered or received for the purchase or sale of goods, services, or other things."[7] That, by refusing to engage with the problem, is a potent acknowledgment of its scale. In effect the great man is saying, "Money? I've no idea what that stuff really is."

This, I think, is an important part of what is interesting about the language of money, and about the field of economics, and maybe even about people. There's so much we don't know, not just on a superficial level but at the deepest levels too. That is why the language is so useful, and so important: it delineates the thing we're talking about, in order to leave us clear to agree or disagree, to make up our minds or to fail to make them up, and come to the conclusion that while we can see the problem, we don't entirely know what we think about it. At the present moment, economic news hasn't been far from the front pages for more than about forty-eight hours anywhere in the Western world at any point in the last six years. The subject has dominated politics and loomed over ordinary lives; the specifics of what policies to follow have been at the subject of extensive analysis everywhere, from the news media to international summits to the blogosphere to the kitchen table. The subject under discussion, economics, purports to be a science. It is an extremely well-staffed and well-funded field of study, employing tens of thousands of people in both the private and the public sectors; it has extensive experience of precedents and an incomparably greater amount of data than was available to any previous students of economic problems.* And yet, as Anatole Kaletsky wrote in the London *Times* on 4 April 2013, all the main questions remain open:

> In a recession, should governments reduce budget deficits or increase them? Do zero-interest rates stimulate economic recovery or suppress it? Should welfare benefits be maintained or cut in response to high unemployment? Should depositors in failed banks be protected or face big losses? Does economic inequality damage or encourage economic growth? . . . What all these important questions have in common is that economists cannot answer them.

This is an amazing state of affairs. For some, it is the moment to give up on economics as a discipline, to throw up the hands and announce that the whole subject is bollix. (And maybe to throw open the window too, and announce, "I'm as mad as hell and I'm not going to take it anymore.") This impulse is easy to understand, and has given birth to some good polemics, such as Steve Keen's *Debunking Economics: The Naked Emperor of the Social Sciences*. And indeed, there are times when faced by an institutional arrogance among some economists—a semi-autistic refusal to see the human context of their own subject, a blindness to their own short-

---

* This point is a bigger deal than one might think. I've already mentioned Alfred Marshall once, and will be coming back to him shortly, but he's relevant in this context too, because his attempt to found the subject of economics on a mathematical and empirical basis involved an enormous amount of work simply to gather data. Today there's an astounding amount of data freely available over the Internet to anyone who's interested. Marshall and other early economists spent thousands of hours working to get hold of facts that are now accessible in minutes to anyone with a network connection.

comings and the limits to their own knowledge—when it's tempting to go along with the refuseniks. But it's more tempting still, I
would suggest, to swap perspectives on the question. The lack of
definitive conclusions isn't a weakness in the field; it's what's interesting about it. The chaotic lack of consensus arises because economics is "the study of mankind in the ordinary business of life."
When is anyone going to reach any final verdicts about that? The
nature of the difficulty was touched on by Keynes, quoting a remark
made to him by Max Planck, the German scientist and theoretician
who made the intellectual breakthrough that led to the birth of
quantum physics. That means Planck was one of the most brilliant
mathematician-physicists the world has ever seen.

> Professor Planck of Berlin, the famous originator of the
> Quantum Theory, once remarked to me that in early life he
> had thought of studying economics, but had found it too diffi-
> cult! Professor Planck could easily master the whole corpus of
> mathematical economics in a few days. He did not mean that!
> But the amalgam of logic and intuition and the wide knowl-
> edge of facts, most of which are not precise, which is required
> for economic interpretation in its highest form, is, quite truly,
> overwhelmingly difficult for those whose gift mainly consists
> in the power to imagine and pursue to their furthest points
> the implications and prior conditions of comparatively simple
> facts which are known with a high degree of precision.[8]

Keynes's point—which was also Planck's point—is that in economics, the mathematics can't be relied on to do all the work. The
"amalgam of logic and intuition and the wide knowledge of facts,
most of which are not precise," makes the field one requiring an
unusual mix of aptitudes. This of course is what is fascinating about
it: the fact that its complexity derives from the variety of human
lives. We're not simple, so why should economics be?

At this stage, the question arises: if economics and money-stuff is so inherently interesting, why do people hate it so much? Why does the field feel so alienating to outsiders? The answer I think is to do with a wrong turn taken by a particular segment of the economic profession, and the way that turn helped contribute to both the crisis of 2008 and the Great Recession that followed. There are two main contributing factors to the wrong turn: one of them is a tendency in the field, an apparently built-in bias towards a specific intellectual mistake; the other is the grip of one particular subspecies of economics, calcified into a narrow view of how markets and societies must function.

To take the tendency first, the factor at work here is a general predisposition to be overconfident about the discoveries of economics. It would be wonderful to find laws of human behavior, cast-iron rules that we know we can rely on, at all times and in all weathers, and that are always present under the apparently chaotic diversity of human behavior. (It's the dream of doing that which underlies one of the masterpieces of science fiction, Isaac Asimov's *Foundation* trilogy.) One of the things that readers love about works such as Stephen Dubner and Steven Levitt's *Freakonomics* is the idea that apparently simple economic principles underlie everything from the crime rate to why drug dealers live with their mothers and to which schools are fiddling their exam results. The human phenomena, so complicated and so apparently diverse, can be shown to be the product of a few fairly obvious rules. "Morality . . . represents the way that people would like the world to work—whereas economics represents how it actually *does* work."[9] Economics looks beneath the surface and sees the math at work.

It's an attractive idea—though having said that, lots of people find the program of looking through human things to seek abstract principles at work to be cold and dissociated. Still, even if you're not the kind of person to be tempted into this kind of thinking, it's still possible to see how it might be useful, and exert a gravitational tug. The problem is that there is a temptation to see the underlying principles in the wrong light: to see them as fixed laws, analogous to those of physics, rather than as guidelines, as aids to thought, as crutches and assistants. The danger is something that was clear to Alfred Marshall, the Cambridge professor who was both the first person to create a mathematical foundation for economic laws and the first person to warn of the dangers and difficulties implicit in thinking of economics in this way.

Right at the beginning of his 1890 masterwork, *Principles of Economics*, Marshall considers the example of the laws of gravity, which are precise and permanent and definite, and concludes that "there are no economic tendencies which act as steadily and can be measured as exactly as gravitation can: and consequently there are no laws of economics which can be compared for precision with the law of gravitation." In looking for a metaphor for how the laws of economics work, Marshall finds one in an interesting place: tides. We understand how tides work, and we know exactly what the phases of the moon are, and we have the historical data to show high and low tides everywhere around our coasts and up our rivers, and using all this "people can calculate beforehand when the tide will *probably* be at its highest on any day at London Bridge or at Gloucester; and how high it will be there." The crucial word is "probably." "A heavy downpour of rain in the upper Thames valley, or a strong north-east wind in the German Ocean, may make the tides at London Bridge differ a good deal from what had been expected." The point is this:

> The laws of economics are to be compared with the laws of the tides, rather than with the simple and exact law of gravitation. For the actions of men are so various and uncertain, that the best statement of tendencies, which we can make in a science of human conduct, must needs be inexact and faulty. This might be urged as a reason against making any statements at

all on the subject; but that would be almost to abandon life. Life is human conduct, and the thoughts and emotions that grow up around it. By the fundamental impulses of our nature we all—high and low, learned and unlearned—are in our several degrees constantly striving to understand the courses of human action, and to shape them for our purposes, whether selfish or unselfish, whether noble or ignoble. And since we *must* form to ourselves some notions of the tendencies of human action, our choice is between forming those notions carelessly and forming them carefully. The harder the task, the greater the need for steady patient enquiry; for turning to account the experience, that has been reaped by the more advanced physical sciences; and for framing as best we can well thought-out estimates, or provisional laws, of the tendencies of human action.

The term "law" means then nothing more than a general proposition or statement of tendencies, more or less certain, more or less definite.[10]

That, I think, is the single most important thing ever written about the laws of economics. "A general proposition or statement of tendencies, more or less certain, more or less definite": now, that can be a very useful thing, especially if it never forgets its own tentativeness and provisionality. When economists talk about models, this is the kind of thing they are supposed to have in mind: guides to clearer thinking, general propositions "more or less certain, more or less definite." Here's one example, from the work of the Nobel Prize–winning Israeli psychologist Daniel Kahneman. His first proper job as a psychologist was during his national service in the Israeli army, where he set out to study the army's techniques for assessing the quality of recruits. The soldiers were given an extensive battery of psychometric tests, followed up by an interview. One of the aims of the process was to assign the recruits to the various branches of the army: artillery, armor, infantry, and so on. Kahneman studied the existing techniques and framed them in a new way. A test of this sort, Kahneman thought, is in essence an attempt at predicting the future: how well will the persons being tested perform at the work they need to do? So now he asked a question that didn't seem to have occurred to anyone, or at least not with sufficient force: were the tests any good at that feat of prediction? The answer was no. The process was useless. Interviewers consistently made what Kahneman later came to call a "substitution": they took their evaluation of what the soldier was like, and how well he had performed in the tests and interview, and substituted that for the real question at issue, which was to predict what kind of soldier he would be. Instead of answering the question "How will he do?" the interviewers were substituting the question "What's he like?" Kahneman went to work and came up with a new model for how the assessments should be done—and he to this day advocates the technique for job interviews.

> If you are serious about hiring the best possible person for the job, this is what you should do. First, select a few traits that are prerequisites for success in this position (technical proficiency, engaging personality, reliability, and so on). Don't overdo it—six dimensions is a good number. The traits you choose should be as independent as possible from each other, and you should feel that you can assess them reliably by asking a few factual questions. Next, make a list of those questions for each trait and think about how you will score it, say on a 1–5 scale. You should have an idea of what you will call "very weak" or "very strong."

This should take about half an hour. Do each point score separately, one after the other, and then add them up.

Firmly resolve that you will hire the candidate whose final score is the highest, even if there is another one whom you like better—try to resist your wish to invent broken legs to change the ranking. A vast amount of research offers a promise: you are much more likely to find the best candidate if you use this procedure than if you do what people normally do in such situations, which is to go into the interview unprepared and to make choices by an overall intuitive judgment such as "I looked into his eyes and liked what I saw."

This technique sounds like a very blunt instrument. That's certainly what the interviewers themselves thought. They were trained and intelligent people (and they were also mainly women, who at that point weren't allowed in combat roles in the Israeli defense forces), and they resented being forced to apply this simple technique for interviews, in place of a complex and nuanced process of assessment. "You are turning us into robots!" said one of them. In response to that objection, Kahneman added another stage to the interview, after the allocation of points across six categories: "So I compromised. 'Carry out the interview exactly as described,' I told them, 'and when you are done, have your wish, close your eyes, try to imagine the recruit as a soldier, and then assign him a score on a scale of 1 to 5.'" [11]

The results were startling: the crude point-scoring process was much better than the apparently more sensitive and inflected former process had been. The tests went from being "completely useless" to "moderately useful." What's more surprising is that this is an outcome that has been repeatedly confirmed by experiment. Using a crude tool like a point score, job interviewers do a better job of predicting how interviewees will turn out in the jobs for which they're being assessed. We are not nearly as good at evaluating people in interviews as we think we are. Relying on the numbers does much better. Kahneman found another thing, though, and greatly to his surprise: the "close your eyes" intuitive score performed as well as the numerical test—which in turn performed far better than the old-school purely intuitive interview process. So intuition went from being completely useless to markedly useful, once a structured process of assessment had been introduced to help it. "I learned from this finding a lesson that I have never forgotten: intuition adds value even in the justly derided selection interview, but only after a disciplined collection of objective information and disciplined scoring of separate traits."[12] You'd think that common sense and experience and intuition would be the best guides for the interview process—but they just aren't. Your best guide is having a fixed system for awarding points; only after doing that should you use your own subjective evaluations.

This is both a metaphor for and an example of how models are supposed to work in economics. The questions in the structured interview process don't even need to be all that well framed: what makes them effective is the structure, the grid they impose on the interviewers' thinking and assessments. That's what economic models are, or should be: guides, aids, assistants. But there's a tendency for them to undergo definition creep: from guides, aids, assistants to axioms, rules, laws. On the lecture platform, economists will often say things like "My model shows . . ." The striking thing about that is the idea that a model can show something. A model can imply, suggest, guide, hint, invite us to conclude; but it can't in that strong sense "show." In economics, models are spoken of as being made of physics when in truth they are made of Lego. They have that degree of provisionality and tentativeness and, importantly, rebuildability. There's a permanent invitation to take them apart and put them together again in a form that works better. People in the business know this perfectly well. They're not stupid. But there is an inbuilt tendency for that definition creep, for Lego models to start turning into equations that have, in the great phrase of Richard Feynman, "the character of physical law."

There's a visual metaphor for the process in the form of an amazing device called the Phillips machine, the creation of a remarkable New Zealander called Bill Phillips. After a roundabout route to the world of economics via a spell in a Japanese prisoner-of-war camp, Phillips set up a workshop in a south London garage. There, using recycled Lancaster bomber parts, he botched together a machine that used the flow of water to demonstrate the functioning of the entire British economy. There was a point at which these machines, known as MONIACs—Monetary National Income Analogue Computers—were all the rage: there are about twelve of them (no one knows exactly how many were built) in places as diverse as the central bank of Guatemala, the University of Melbourne, Erasmus University in Rotterdam, and Cambridge, England, which has the only one that works. The Phillips machines/MONIACs were fine-tuned to simulate different economic conditions: the New Zealand one, for instance, was set up to match the specific dynamics of the New Zealand economy. Feel free here to make up your own joke about sheep and/or *Lord of the Rings*.

Phillips was a serious man, who partly on the basis of his machine became a professor of economics at LSE, and he had a serious specific concern in creating the MONIAC, to do with stabilizing demand inside the economy. And yet, it's hard not to see his machine as a comic allegory of what's called wrong in the model-making side of economics. It's inherently comic in the way that a Roz Chast cartoon is inherently comic. The idea that this thing can simulate something as big and complicated as an entire economy—really? And yet, that's what economic models set out to do all the time. The Federal Reserve and US Treasury are to this day reliant on models of exactly this sort; their models are built out of mathematics rather than out of bomber parts and water, but the underlying principles are the same. Credit flows and monetary supply, inflation rates and external shocks and trade imbalances and fluctuations in demand and tax changes are all modeled in an exactly analogous way.

So how should models be used in economics? One example, now not taken at all seriously by mainstream economists, is Marx's surplus theory of value. Marx was very interested in the question of where value arises from, of how commodities are exchanged for each other, and then, underlying that, of what money is. It's a very simple question but not one that had been asked with such clarity before him, and it's also, as I've been arguing, the kind of question that is no longer asked at a professional or institutional level, because the current order of things is so taken for granted. But it is a very basic and important question, or two questions: what is money, and where does its value come from?

Now, I should stress that it's almost impossible to find a modern economist who swallows Marx's surplus theory of value. As an attempt to discover the deep realities of how value is created, the surplus theory is generally seen as a dud. But as a model for thinking about relations between goods and customers, and an instruction manual for peeling off the veil of appearances and looking at the realities beneath, it is highly suggestive. It's an example of the moral underpinnings of economics, the fact that "the study of mankind of the ordinary business of life" takes us deep into questions of value, both economic and moral.

One way of talking about what has gone wrong in much of economics, especially in how the subject is taught, is to say that it has stopped engaging with questions like these. A field that began life as a branch of "moral philosophy" has turned into a playground of model building, dominated by inappropriate certainties. The particular nature of these certainties is the second way in which economics has gone wrong. They concern a set of assumptions, tied to a particular dogma about how human beings and markets work. The funny thing is, we're not all that far away from the situation described by Alfred Marshall, when he made his inaugural lecture as Cambridge professor of political economy, "The Present Position of Economics," in 1885:

> The chief fault in English economists at the beginning of the century was not that they ignored history and statistics, but that they regarded man as so to speak a constant quantity, and gave themselves little trouble to study his variations. They therefore attributed to the forces of supply and demand a much more mechanical and regular action than they actually have. Their most vital fault was that they did not see how liable to change are the habits and institutions of industry. But the Socialists were men who had felt intensely, and who knew something about the hidden springs of human action of which the economists took no account. Buried among their wild rhapsodies there were shrewd observations and pregnant suggestions from which philosophers and economists had much to learn. Among the bad results of the narrowness of the work of English economists early in the century, perhaps the most unfortunate was the opportunity which it gave to sciolists to quote and misapply economic dogmas.[13]

It's remarkable that, 128 years later, you could say almost the same thing about "the present position of economics." (A sciolist, according to the *Concise Oxford Dictionary*, is a "superficial pretender to knowledge.") Marshall's point about regarding people as constant qualities, thus attributing to them too much "mechanical and regular action," is still bang on. Although nobody would talk about socialists in that way today, it's still true that noneconomists and antieconomists have useful things to say to economists. As for the idea that lots of trouble is caused by misapplying economic dogmas: yes, yes, and again yes. The specific set of dogmas that are misapplied are generally referred to as neoliberal economics.

So what is this neoliberal economics? The shorthand answer is that it's the system that has been dominant in the English-speaking world, and in financial institutions such as the World Bank and the International Monetary Fund (IMF), for about a third of a century. The first and most prominent political exponents of the system were Prime Minister Margaret Thatcher in the UK, following her election victory in 1979, and President Ronald Reagan in the USA, following his victory in 1980. There is both a practical and a philosophical aspect to neoliberal economics. The practical aspect is the more visible, so I'll start with that. It involves policies that are designed to favor business, entrepreneurship, and the individual; to reduce the role of the state; to cut public spending; to increase the individual's possibilities and responsibilities, both for success and for failure; to promote free trade, and accordingly to eliminate protectionist barriers and tariffs; to reduce the roles of unions and collective bargaining; to minimize taxes; to pursue policies that encourage wealth creators and to trust in the process whereby that wealth trickles down to other sectors of the economy; to move enterprises from public to private ownership.

In the background of these specific policies are philosophical positions that are concerned, in the final analysis, with the role and importance of the individual. Neoliberalism sees the route to the greater collective good in the empowerment of the individual. Or maybe that's the wrong way of putting it: perhaps what it really does is to say that the individual is paramount as a moral entity; the possibilities and potential and happiness of the individual are all that really matter. If society as a whole benefits and prospers, so much the better, but the moral and practical focus of any society should be on the individual. It follows from this that the individual's potential is central to how the society, and following on from that an economy, should be structured. The economy should be arranged to allow individuals to maximize their potential. The practical promise made is that if you get government out of the way of wealth creators, the wealth they create will ultimately benefit everybody: the rich pay a lot more tax than the poor, for a start, and they spend a lot more money than the poor too, and both taxes and the money spent benefit the whole society. So it's like a magic trick: you benefit the collective good by allowing people to selfishly maximize their own gains.

What follows from this are policies that allow the rich to get richer quicker than the poor. In a free-market system, the rich will always accumulate capital and income faster than the poor; it's a law as basic as that of gravity. The promise of neoliberalism is that that doesn't matter, as long as the poor are getting richer too. A rising tide lifts all boats, as the cliché has it. It lifts the rich boats quicker, but in the neoliberal scheme of things that's not a problem. Inequality isn't just the price you pay for rising prosperity; inequality is what makes rising prosperity possible. The increase in inequality therefore isn't just some nasty accidental side effect of neoliberalism; it's the motor driving the whole economic process. During the third of a century in which neoliberalism has been the dominant economic model, almost nobody has been willing to face this reality about the philosophical underpinnings of the system. Margaret Thatcher is almost the only politician to have spelled it out with total candor: "Nations depend for their health, economically, culturally and psychologically, upon the achievement of a comparatively small number of talented and determined people."* Her frankness did not set an example, probably with good reason. It's not clear how keen electorates would have been on neoliberal-

---

* The political interviewer Brian Walden, a big fan of Thatcher's, was one of the only people who noticed the significance of her views on this question. Commenting on her in 1979, he said, "This election was about a woman who believes in inequality, passionately, who isn't Keynesian, who is not worried about dole queues." In his biography of Thatcher, Charles Moore says that in Walden's view, "if interviewers had wanted to find the truth, they should have asked her, 'Mrs Thatcher, do you believe in a more unequal society?'"

ism if they had been invited directly to face the deal they were being offered: you'll get better-off, but the rich will get a lot better-off a lot quicker—you OK with that?

There are dark undercurrents to this. I've never seen any subscriber to neoliberal economics admit the fact, but part of the way in which inequality drives economic progress—in the neoliberal system—is by making it clear that there are severe consequences for failure. Bankruptcies, dole queues, even people sleeping in the streets—all these are human tragedies, but in the neoliberal worldview, they are also reminders of what happens if you don't work hard enough. Economies need winners, as Thatcher spelled out, but this kind of economy needs losers too: they are what give the winners their fire and fuel and fear. If a single biblical text sums up this worldview, and the direction of travel in English-speaking societies since about 1980, it's this one, Mark 4:25: "For he that hath, to him shall be given."

This is the economic model that the West didn't hesitate to impose all over the world whenever developing countries hit difficulties and needed help. "The thing about organizations like the IMF is they simply don't care what your circumstances are," I was told by an Argentinian financial minister who'd dealt directly with the organization during negotiations in the early noughties. "You might have particular historic reasons why a program existed, targeting child poverty or slum sanitation or whatever, but they made it clear they had no interest in that. They were just waiting for you to stop talking so they could tell you what to do. It was the same package of solutions for everyone irrespective of local history and conditions and social problems. Just take it or leave it and shut up." That's what we in the West did abroad, dispensing aid with an attached armlock of financial reform, but to be fair, it's not so far away from what we did to ourselves as well. A different point, addressed with great force by Ha-Joon Chang in his important book *23 Things They Don't Tell You about Capitalism*, is the fact that the Western economies did not grow to dominance by pursuing a neoliberal, free-market model: during the years of their growth, every economy in the Western world pursued policies that were to various degrees protectionist. The United States, now such a strident advocate of free markets for its own exports, was during the nineteenth and early twentieth centuries the most protection-ist economy in the industrialized world. The lesson from history about development is not the same as the lesson we are teaching the developing world. In the last few decades, though, it is fair to say that we in the neoliberal West have drunk our own Kool-Aid.

Baked into this neoliberal model is a set of assumptions that embody what Marshall saw as the economist's mistaken belief in "constant and mechanical action." The crucial part of this is a faith in the power of markets. It has to be said that if you don't appre-ciate the miraculous power of markets, their astonishing ability to match buyer and seller, to meet needs, to find prices that clear themselves of goods, to satisfy wants that consumers didn't know they had, to create livelihoods in an astonishing proliferation of nooks and niches and specialisms and crafts and skills—if you don't appreciate those things, then you've probably never really "got" economics, and you're also missing out on something of the won-der and variety and complexity of human culture. Having said that, if you think that markets are magically the solution to everything and have some kind of mystical inherent ability to always be right and to self-regulate in all conditions, all weathers, all extremities, and despite all unforeseen circumstances, well then, you are prob-ably a neoliberal economist.

This received wisdom about the superiority of the neoliberal model was destroyed by the recent credit crunch. One of the dog-mas of this school is the idea that markets can solve any problem that markets create. What happened in the credit crunch was a flat contradiction of that dogma: markets created a problem that needed financial intervention from states on a historically unprecedented scale. This poses a problem for neoliberalism, and not just because of its faith in the idea that markets can self-regulate. Contained within the idea of self-regulation is the notion that markets are efficient. In this context, efficient doesn't mean quite what we take it as meaning in the rest of life. Efficient here means that markets are accurately priced in relation to all knowable relevant information. Take an imaginary publicly traded stock, Youwidgets Inc. It is the object of study by thousands, tens of thousands, of traders, analysts, and investors. Potential buyers and potential sellers frown over every potentially relevant piece of news; the company's quarterly report is given Talmud-scholarship levels of close analysis. The efficient-market theory says you can't do better, as an assessment of what that stock is worth, than what the market thinks it is worth. Note that this doesn't mean it's impossible to know better than the market: you might well have private sources of information, say, sales data that the company hasn't released yet. In that case you can certainly do better than the market's predictions about the company's performance. But you'd be running the risk of going to jail for insider dealing. What the efficient-market theory says is that it's impossible to do better than the market on the basis of publicly available information.

Most of the time, this is not just true but provably true: lots of academic research has gone into this, and the single best piece of advice you can give to any investor is to respect the power of efficient markets and invest accordingly. Don't try and beat the market.* But most of the time isn't the same as all the time, and there are obvious absurdities in the idea of a system that can be true only as long as people act on the basis that it isn't. After all, if markets were perfectly efficient, no one would bother studying prices in

---

* Book recommendation: Burton Malkiel's classic *A Random Walk Down Wall Street* lays out a thoroughly convincing explication of the thesis, with lots of practical advice for private investors.

the first place. There's a joke about an efficient-market fan walking down the street, and refusing to pick up a $100 bill lying on the pavement in front of him on the basis that, if it were really there, somebody else would have picked it up already. Efficient markets depend on most people's behaving as if markets aren't efficient. More problematically, efficient-market dogma can be taken to mean that there are no such things as price bubbles and speculative manias inside markets. Common sense tells us this is plainly ludicrous, but plenty of supersmart people don't believe in the existence of price bubbles. It comes down to theology: because prices are always rational, bubbles can't exist. The widespread adoption of this belief makes it much harder for governments to act when a bubble is developing in either stock or housing markets. Obviously it is difficult to act to prevent something if you don't believe that the thing can exist. The link between neoliberalism, efficient-market theory, and bubbles was one of the reasons for the disaster of 2008, not to mention the Great Recession and the generally negative attitudes towards economics that ensued.

There's one further way in which Marshall's argument about an overly mechanical view of people and their "constant and regular action" is still relevant. The neoliberal/efficient-market paradigm has within it a particular view of human nature. It sees people as "utility maximizers," which is a fancy way of saying that we always have a plan. We're always making calculations that further our own sense of where our advantage lies. In crude versions of this theory, the utility maximization is always about money; but the idea that we always function to our own best economic advantage in the narrowest sense is so plainly false that you don't often encounter it in the wild any more. (Mind you, there is an entire school of thought, calling itself rational choice theory, which devotes itself to the belief of utility maximization in its narrow form.) What the theory now does is define utility maximization more broadly, to allow a wider sense of what our interests are, including issues such as status and social capital. Take the question of that perennial political target of opportunity, the unemployed single mother. In a narrow version of rational choice theory, unemployed single mothers are simply doing the best for themselves economically. They are "marrying the state" because that's a better deal, in cash terms and in terms of reliability, than attaching themselves to any actually available bloke. Since the children of single parents, measured across an entire population, have higher incidence of crime as both perpetrators and victims, as well as higher incidence of mental illness, alcoholism, drug addiction, and suicide, and a lower chance of forming stable partnerships—given all these things, the single mother's choice to maximize her utility has significant negative consequences for everyone else in the society around. And all because of those greedy selfish single mothers. This translates into policies designed to make it less economically rational to be a single mother: in other words, to keep such mothers as poor as possible, without the embarrassing prospect of having them actually starve in public. And this broadly speaking is what governments successively have done. The idea is that the "cure" for single motherhood is economic stringency on the part of the state.

But what if this entire way of thinking is nonsense? The field of behavioral economics shows us that we simply aren't economically rational. It does that not through argument but through experiments that demonstrate failures in our ability to calculate accurately. We're hardwired not to be right about all sorts of calculations, including those of our own self-interest. Rational choice theory and utility maximization run headlong into behavioral economics and crashes. Or at least, it crashes if we think of it as something that is written on stone tablets, maxims that are true always and everywhere. What if utility maximization isn't that, though, but is instead a model or metaphor? What if it's a guide to thought rather than a final conclusion? In that case, thinking about the single mother, we might start to wonder what is it that makes someone choose a course that guarantees she will live under pressure and a degree of social stigma for a significant portion of her life. If we look at it that way, we might start to think about what's in it for the single mothers, not in cash terms, but more generally, in terms of patterns and meanings. Utility maximization invites us to frame actions as choices: to ask, if we think of this as a choice, what's in it for the chooser? What need is being fulfilled? In this case, I'd argue that the need is the profoundest human need of all, once sustenance and shelter and security are provided. It's a need for meaning. That's our deepest want, the most important thing in all our lives. Religion and love and work are the three primary sources of meaning in our societies, and a single mother is choosing a life that provides two out of those three. She's living in a landscape that offers few prospects for self-definition, self-actualization, or any of the routes out to prosperity available to people farther up the socioeconomic ladder. So no, I don't think that single mothers "marry the state." But I do think their choices are in some sense rational. It's always rational to choose the thing that means most.

I don't want to leave you with the impression that neoliberal economics are never an effective way of growing an economy. They are—indeed, they can be argued to be the most effective technique that we know for rapid GDP growth. But the policies don't always work, and when they do work, as I've argued, it's often at the price of sharp, arguably unsustainable levels of rising inequality. Similarly, the idea of utility maximization is a potent and effective one, as what scientists call a "first-order approximation" of human motives and behavior. It's a good rough first guess; which means it's often wrong, but equally means it's often a good place to start. The idea of efficient markets, too, is a useful tool—except when it suddenly stops working. What all of these ideas have in common is that they are tools and techniques. True believers in neoliberalism, efficient markets, and utility maximization frequently behave as if these maxims were written down on stone tablets and carried down from the mountaintop by Moses, Adam Smith, Milton Friedman, and Margaret Thatcher, and therefore that they will permanently be true, always and everywhere, irrespective of specific circumstances. This is obvious nonsense. All these things are parts of an economic tool kit, parts of which are applicable in some circumstances, and others in others. Keynes is often thought of as a narrow advocate of increased government spending on stimulus: his name has become an adjective, "Keynesian," which opponents take to mean something like "any policy that involves spending money like a drunken sailor in the desperate hope that the economy picks up, but anyway if it doesn't, at least you're buying loads of votes in the public sector." This is a caricature of Keynes's thinking, because he was, as now seems to be entirely forgotten, an advocate of austerity as well as an advocate of spending. It's just that he thought the austerity moment came during the good times. "The boom, not the slump, is the right time for austerity at the Treasury," Keynes wrote. His views about the right tools were complicated, but can be simply summarized: it's a question of picking the right tool for the right job.

> Economics is a science of thinking in terms of models joined to the art of choosing models which are relevant to the contemporary world. It is compelled to be this, because, unlike the typical natural science, the material to which it is applied is, in too many respects, not homogeneous through time. . . .
>
> Good economists are scarce because the gift for using "vigilant observation" to choose good models, although it does not require a highly specialised intellectual technique, appears to be a very rare one.[14]

Marshall would have agreed; so would another hero of mine, Charles Kindleberger, an economist who approached his subject through the prism of history rather than theory or ideology. Where others have argued about the theoretical premises of bubbles inside markets, Kindleberger did something much simpler and more useful: he wrote a history of them. There's an old joke about an economist, in the clean-up after some emergency, saying, "Well, that works in practice, but let's go and see if it works in theory." Kindleberger's mind-set was the opposite of that. This enabled him to keep a clear view of the field's salient point:

> I take the view that to be either consistently Keynesian or consistently monetarist is to be wrong. Economics . . . is a box of tools. Both the tools of Friedman and the tools of Keynes belong in the box to be taken out and applied as the problem and circumstances call for. Economists should specialize and exchange, to be sure, and some economists may wish to specialize in one mode of analysis or another; but the economist with only one model, which he or she applies to all situations, is wrong much of the time. Different circumstances, and sometimes different time horizons in the same circumstances, call for different prescriptions. The art of economics is to choose the right model for the given problem, and to abandon it when the problem changes shape.[15]

Yes—economics is about tools. And the most important of these tools, the one without which the others won't work, is language. So: shall we begin?

Part II

A LEXICON OF
MONEY

the aaaaa number A term I've just made up to denote 16,438, for the purpose of making sure it comes first in this lexicon. This number is, in the words of Melinda Gates, "the most important statistic in the world." It's the number of children under five who aren't dying every day, compared with the number who were dying daily in 1990. The change is from 12.6 million to 6.6 million deaths a year: a total of 6 million children's lives saved every year. Why isn't this a famous fact, a famous success? As Melinda Gates (that's Mrs. Bill) points out, the number of child deaths has gone down every single year for fifty years: "I challenge you to name something else that gets better on that kind of schedule."[16] Remember those really annoying ads where celebrities would click their fingers while saying, "Every time I click my fingers, a child dies"? (Prompting somebody in Ireland to shout at Bono, clicking his fingers on screen, "Stop fecking doing it then!") That could now be shown the other way around, to make the point about how many children's lives are saved: the annoying celebs could click their fingers every five and a quarter seconds to show how many lives have been saved. That's still 6.6 million child deaths too many, but surely Melinda Gates is right that the UNICEF statistic, published every year in mid-

September, matters a lot more than most of the numbers plastered all over the media every day.[17]

AAA or triple-A The highest-rated category of debt, which in practice means the rating as assessed by one of the three big credit-rating agencies, Moody's, Standard and Poor's, and Fitch. The idea of AAA debt is that it shows, in the words of S&P, "extremely strong capacity to meet financial commitments." Mistakes made by the agencies in assessing the riskiness of debt, especially in the AAA category, played a major part in the credit crisis of 2008.

A and B shares Devices used by companies to create different categories of rights among their shareholders. The most common is to separate owners with voting rights, i.e., the right to influence the decisions companies make, from owners who have a share in the business but no right to make decisions. It's very often families who use this kind of structure, to keep control of their business while also raising lots of lovely money from the public: examples are the Sainsburys at Sainsburys, the Murdochs at News Corporation, the Sulzbergers at the *New York Times*. Why would anybody invest in a company but choose to have no say in how the business is run? Because these businesses are often well run and managed for the long term, make money for their shareholders, and have the track record to prove it. There's some evidence that family-controlled businesses do better than purely public companies. The reason for that must surely be that they, if well run, have a longer-term focus and steadier nerve than companies chasing a good set of quarterly figures to keep their shareholders happy. There may also be a strong element of "survivorship bias" in the statistics, in that family firms that are less well run will be forced out of the market and/or be bought out by more efficient competitors; so the ones still in business are by definition the successful survivors.

Abenomics The name given to the policies of the Japanese prime minister Shinzo Abe, who started his second term in office in 2012. There were supposed to be three "arrows"—the Japanese are keen on archery—to the policy, involving approach to fiscal policy, reforms to the labor market, and printing money like it's about to go out of style, in an attempt to end deflation and start a beneficial level of inflation. Of these three arrows, the easiest, and therefore the only one to have been loosed, is the third: basically, the governor of the Bank of Japan has turned on the printing press and wandered off, saying, "Don't come and get me until inflation hits 2 percent." The yen has dropped, which is a good thing for Japanese industry, and inflation is showing signs of returning, which is also a good thing, though some commentators are worried that the process could quickly get out of hand. In that case Japan would be facing—to use a new term that I read just yesterday for the first time—"Abegeddon."

Policy makers in the West are fascinated by Abenomics. That's because they see a similar process of slow growth and deflation as a distinct possibility at home. Combined with the political difficulty of certain types of economic reform, the kinds that cause suffering to powerful entrenched interests, that makes the Japanese example very relevant. Add zombie banks to the mix, and the similarities are, as Dame Edna would say, spooky. Especially the similarities to Europe: deflation, check; reforms impossible, check; zombie banks, check. If Abenomics were to cure Japan's problems, then it would be a wonderfully useful model for Europe and maybe for the UK too.

"That," says a mate of mine who works for a Japanese bank, "is why they're all obsessed with Abenomics. Especially the Treasury. If you want a load of Treasury people to turn up to a talk or event, you just tell them it's about Abenomics, and they're hanging from the rafters."

Adam Smith Institute A right-wing British think tank, describing itself as "libertarian," which always argues in favor of free markets. It did influential work when Margaret Thatcher's government was in office, but the trouble with it, as often the case with this kind of ideological body, is that you always know what it's going to say: the solution to everything is deregulation and free markets.

amortization The process by which the value of something is reduced or "written down" over time on a set of accounts. If you buy a new computer for $1,200, and the rate at which it amortizes is 25 percent, after a year your computer is now worth $900. You can then put this $300 of "loss" on your company balance sheet for that year. Why would you want to do that? Because the "loss" allows you to reduce the amount of tax you have to pay. The tax rules for amortization are very complicated, as a way of stopping people from pulling accounting tricks with it—which is a sure sign that people try to pull accounting tricks with it.

arbitrage The process of using differences between prices to make what should be a guaranteed profit, by buying for one price and simultaneously selling for another. If you can buy cocoa futures in London for $1,000 a ton, and sell them immediately in New York for $1,001, that's arbitrage, and you are making a guaranteed profit. The words "guaranteed profit" are magical in finance, and so arbitrage is a beloved feature of the markets, appearing in very many complicated forms, in every imaginable cranny of every imaginable market.

asset allocation An approach to investment that has grown in popularity with modern theories of efficient markets. If it's impossible to do a better job of picking and choosing shares than the market does—which is what many studies of the stock market claim to have proved—it follows that you should save the time you spend on picking stocks and spend it instead on choosing the right areas of the market to be in. Don't think about BP versus Shell versus Exxon, think about whether you should be in oil at all; more generally, think about the balance between stocks and bonds and property and commodities, developed and emerging markets, and then allocate your assets accordingly, investing preferably via cheap pooled funds wherever possible. This balance of asset allocation is, in the modern theory of investing, the most important thing to get right.

assets and liabilities The two main categories on a balance sheet, always depicted with assets on the left, liabilities on the right. Your "equity," i.e., the stuff you actually own outright, is always equal to your assets minus your liabilities.

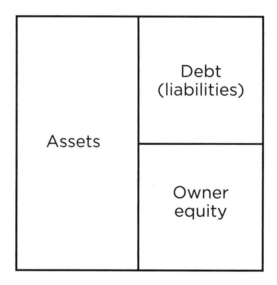

In the language of math, assets = liabilities + equity. These ideas are based on common sense, but they can also be strangely hard to get your head around. In the case of banks, for instance, customer deposits—the money we customers have put in our bank accounts—appear as liabilities: that's because it is our money and we could ask for it back at any moment. The money the bank lends to us, on the other hand, appears as a bank asset. It seems a bit weird that my mortgage is a bank asset and my cash is a bank liability, but that's the way it is.

austerity The strangest, I think, piece of political/economic vocabulary to have come along in my adult lifetime. What "austere" means in normal life is, in the words of the fifth edition of the *Concise Oxford Dictionary*, "harsh, stern; morally strict, severely simple." But that's a general quality that doesn't really mean anything tangible, which is a problem, since in this context, only the specifics matter. What we're talking about here is spending cuts. Funds are either cut or they aren't; there's nothing abstract about it. The word "austerity" reflects an attempt to make something moral-sounding and value-based out of specific reductions in government spending that cause specific losses to specific people. I think it would be useful if people made a distinction between "cuts" and "austerity," and used the latter word to mean an overall reduction in government spending as a percentage of GDP.

back end A general term to describe all the out-of-sight stuff that goes on in a business, often involving IT and logistics. It's used in banking to describe the computing and fulfillment side of the operation; it's the kind of thing you the customer hope never to notice, because if you do, it's usually a sign that something has gone wrong. Some of the most important innovations in business are in the back end: an example is bar codes, which have revolutionized all sorts of business operations in ways the customer never really sees. Malcolm Gladwell has written a brilliant piece explaining why bar codes are more important than the Internet, from a retailer's point of view.[18]

bail-in The opposite, you might have thought, of a bailout, but it's a bit more complicated than that. Instead of money being given to a troubled company to keep it in business, which is a bailout, the money is taken from people who have lent money to that company. In the case of banks (because the current examples tend to involve banks) that means that bondholders or depositors are at risk of losing money when the bank goes broke. Money they had thought was their asset, one they were free to take back and spend elsewhere, is taken from them instead. The highest-profile recent example of a bail-in was in Cyprus, where bank depositors with more than €100,000 in certain Cypriot banks lost most of their capital.[19] The European Union is planning on introducing compulsory bail-ins for bankrupt banks, to affect bondholders and larger depositors, from 2018. Some people are treating bail-ins as if they are the end of life as we know it, but the principle is a simple and fairly well-understood one that if you lend money to somebody who goes broke, you don't get all of it back. If lenders have to think about the risk they're taking when they lend money to a bank, they will want better levels of return for their risk, which will reduce the bank's profits. Banks would prefer not to be treated this way: for them it's much more pleasant and profitable if, when they go broke, the taxpayer bails them out instead.

bailout A bailout is a metaphor, and an example of reversification: a real-life bailout involves scooping water out of a boat that has sprung a leak. An economic bailout is an injection of money into a business that would go broke without it; if you look far enough back down the chain, the money usually comes from the taxpayer. Note that most of the time the money involved in a bailout needs to be paid back, because the bailouts are loans: after the crash of 2008, a number of countries received bailouts whose repayment terms were so onerous that they ended up causing new crises of their own. Note also that bailouts aren't always what they seem, and the money doesn't necessarily end up in the first place it travels to: when AIG was bailed out by the US government in 2008, most of the money went to the "counterparties," i.e., the banks for whom AIG had written insurance policies—many of which were foreign banks.

balance of payments The balance between the amount of money brought into a country and the amount going out, taking into account all economic activity, exports and imports, and movements of capital. A positive balance of payments, meaning a country is taking in more money than it is paying out, is a good thing; the opposite condition, in which a country has net transfers of money abroad, is one that obviously can't go on forever, since a country in that position will go deeper and deeper into debt. The USA's balance of payments are pretty horrible at the moment.

balance sheet An accounting convention, first recorded by the Franciscan friar Dominic Luca Pacioli in his 1494 blockbuster, *Summa de arithmetica, geometria, proportioni et proportionalità.* Pacioli didn't invent the set of accounting techniques he described, which were in use in mainly Venetian banking circles, but he was the first person to write them down. It's a remarkable fact that every business in the world uses them on a daily basis more than five hundred years later. The fundamental feature of Pacioli's system, known as double-entry bookkeeping, is that everything is recorded twice, as an asset in one place and a liability in another, and that the two sides of the balance sheet are always equal: assets = liabilities + equity.

There's a beautiful descripton of the system's impact in James Buchan's book *Frozen Desire*:

> To be able to keep books in double-entry is to have a machine for calculating the world. Understanding the technique is the work of a few days—practising it no doubt requires longer— but one feels one has mastered an ancient and far-flung language: one seems to see better into the nature of things. That soon reveals itself to be illusion. In reality, all one is seeing is a coded money value for all objects and preoccupations. Yet its influence on our thought has been almost without parallel.

Our conversation is replete with assets and liabilities, depreciations, profits and loss, balance sheets: all echoes of Luca's system. Above all, Luca laid the foundation of the modern conception of profit, not as some vague increase in possession, as in antiquity, but as something hard, even crystalline, mathematical and open to empirical test *at any time whatever* through an interlocking system of books.[20]

banking union It sounds like a small thing: getting two countries' banks to work better together by setting a standard set of rules for their operation. It has been a huge deal historically, though, and banking union was a key driver of the unification of Scotland and England, after the collapse of the Company of Scotland, and a bailout in the form of the Act of Union in 1707. But in no other country in the world has the question of banking, and the legislative framework around it, been as central as in the United States. The creation of the First Bank of the United States in 1791 was a huge deal for the new democracy, and perceived as such at the time, because it did so much to strengthen the hand of central government—to such effect, and so controversially, that the renewal of the bank's charter twenty years later, in 1811, was defeated by a single vote. The resulting chaos, especially (to quote the Federal Reserve of New York) "the lack of a central regulating mechanism over banking and credit," was so great that the Second Bank was created in 1816 by President Madison, the Speaker of the House giving as the reason for its rebirth the "force of circumstance and the lights of experience." By the end of the second twenty-year charter, controversy about its existence had not abated, and President Jackson vetoed legislation renewing the charter of the Second Bank—the issue was at the heart of his presidency. The United States finally got its permanent bank, the Federal Reserve, in 1913, not so much because of a widespread ideological change of heart as through extended experience of the practical difficulties of trying to operate a state without a central bank.

The European Union doesn't have banking union, but needs it, and proposals are being haggled over at the moment to create three crucial elements: a supervisor with responsibility for and power over European banks; a resolution framework for allowing broke banks to collapse without risking the entire financial system; and a deposit guarantee to protect all bank deposits in the euro zone up to a maximum of (probably) €100,000.

Bank of England The second-oldest central bank in the world (after the Swedish Riksbank), created in 1694 in order to raise money for a new navy, after the French destroyed the old one. It's amazing that the bank was a private company until as recently as 1946. The Bank's Monetary Policy Committee has responsibility for the monetary policy of the UK, setting the interest rates that in turn determine the interest rates for the rest of the economy; the committee is charged with meeting a target of 2 percent consumer price inflation. The Bank had responsibility for supervising financial stability taken away from it in 1997, and then (because that didn't work) given back to it in 2013, through its new body the Financial Stability Committee. The Bank of England is the UK's lender of last resort, i.e., the body that lends money to banks and financial institutions when no one else will.

There's a lot of ritual and ceremony and protocol at the Bank, which to outsiders seems a cross between Hogwarts, the Death Star, and the office of Ebenezer Scrooge. At the same time, its most important proceedings, the meetings of the Monetary Policy Committee, are surprisingly open: the results of the monthly vote on the interest rate are published, including who voted for what, and so are the committee's minutes.

bankruptcy The legally managed process for going broke. If you can't pay your debts, you can make yourself bankrupt; if someone can't pay back the money he owes you, you can make him bankrupt. The United States is unusual in having several different varieties of bankruptcy, and in most circumstances it's the debtor who goes bankrupt and chooses the "schedule" under which the process is to be managed. There's an interesting international variation in the causes of bankruptcy. In the UK the person by far the most likely to make you go broke is the tax man. In the United States, the leading cause of bankruptcy is medical bills. Death and taxes.

bankster A rude term fusing banker and gangster. It originally dates from the Great Depression of the 1930s but has had an understandable revival since the credit crunch. As Warren Buffet once said, about financial-sector conduct during a previous boom, "It was the bankers who were wearing the ski masks."

Barings The oldest investment bank, or merchant bank as they used to be called, in England. In the long list of investment bank scandals and failures of the last few decades, Barings is the only bank to have been destroyed by the actions of a single individual. The man responsible was Nick Leeson, and the fateful moment came in January 1995. Leeson had been using tiny differences between the prices of stocks in Singapore, where he was based, and Tokyo. His trades were supposed to be a form of arbitrage, exploiting small differences in the price to make guaranteed profits, but Leeson had gradually, and unauthorizedly, begun to make bigger bets on the movement of the shares. These quickly began to go wrong. He hid the trades in a secret account so that while apparently making big profits he was in reality concealing gigantic losses. Barings' supervision of his trading was shockingly negligent. Eventually Leeson bet the whole bank on the Nikkei share index going up to 19,000 but, thanks to the Kobe earthquake of 17 January 1995, instead the index went sharply downwards. Barings lost £827 million and collapsed. Leeson went to jail in Singapore and served four years of a six-and-a-half-year term before being released early because he had colon cancer. I met him once, when we were on the TV current affairs show *Newsnight* together, and liked him, though you could tell the subdued man in his forties who'd spent years in jail and recovered from cancer was a different man from the trader in his twenties who destroyed the bank. As I'm writing, the Nikkei is still at less than 14,500, so twenty years on it's still a distance below the level Leeson was betting on.

Basel III Officially the Third Basel Accord, it is an ongoing attempt to come up with a set of rules for international banking. The idea underlying Basel III is to save banks from themselves by setting up rules that make it harder for them to go broke. It is a voluntary process, with a global remit, and both of those are good things since the risks of banking are carried internationally, thanks to the interlinked and interdependent nature of financial markets. The trouble with the Basel process is twofold: it tends to focus on actions that would have prevented the last crisis, rather than on actions to prevent the next one; and it is vulnerable to lobbying from the powerful, and powerfully shameless, sector that it's attempting to regulate. At the time of writing, the financial sector has succeeded in having the timetable for implementation of Basel III extended to 2019, and also in weakening the rules on the kinds of asset that banks are allowed to count on their balance sheets as being safe.

basis point One hundredth of a percentage point. Basis points are used a lot in talking about interest rates. If an interest rate moves by 50 basis points it has moved by 0.5 percent. Referring to basis points is one of the quickest and easiest ways of pretending to know what you're talking about when it comes to money.

BBA Short for British Bankers Association, a trade group that speaks up for the banks' interests and used to run Libor, until it turned out Libor had been outrageously and illegally manipulated, so responsibility is going to be given to somebody else—we don't know whom yet, because the committee making the decision hasn't made its report. The head of the BBA often appears in the media, because senior bankers will no longer give interviews.

bear Anyone who thinks the price of something is going to go down: equity bears think equities are going down, bond bears think that bonds are going down, and so on. In real life bears are known for being unpredictable, and even an apparently docile and domesticated bear can suddenly turn nasty; in the markets, though, being bearish is more of a temperamental thing, and so the habitually skeptical and wary are sometimes known as perma-bears. The opposite of a bear is a bull.

bear market Any market that has dropped by 20 percent or more from its high point.

beggar thy neighbor In addition to a children's card game that reliably causes arguments (though that's more often called beggar my neighbor), an economic policy in which a country lowers the value of its own currency to make its exports cheaper, and at the same time follows policies that make it difficult for other countries to export to it. Beggar thy neighbor is a form of mercantilism.

behavioral economics The study of the way people make decisions and calculations, using experiments and real-life data. Instead of the big broad models used in economics, in which "rational actors" behave in ways designed to "maximize their utility," behavioral economics studies the kinds of calculations people make in real life, with a particular emphasis on things we do that are demonstrably not rational in the strict economic sense. An example is "loss aver-sion," in which people are provably more unwilling to take risks that involve losses than to take risks involving gains, even when the outcomes are, in mathematical terms, identical. The fact that people don't always behave rationally may not come as news in the wider world, but the intellectual challenge provided to conven-tional economics by behavioral economics is big and important. It's also a field that offers useful takeaways for the ordinary person, because you can catch yourself doing some of the things described by behavioral economists, such as loss aversion and "hindsight bias," i.e., the tendency to explain things that happened in terms of how they turned out, rather than how they seemed at the time.

  Some practical applications of behavioral economics are in fields such as the "nudge," which involves prompting individuals to behave in a certain way. The prompting is usually on the part of businesses or governments. Some of this is benign, some less so. Example: a famous-to-economists finding in behavioral econom-ics concerns pricing, and the fact that people have a provable bias towards the middle of three prices. It was first demonstrated with an experiment in beer pricing: when there were two beers, a third of people chose the cheaper; adding an even cheaper beer made the share of that beer go up, because it was now in the middle of three prices; adding an even more expensive beer at the top, and dropping the cheapest beer, made the share of the new beer in the middle (which had previously been the most expensive) go up from two-thirds to 90 percent. Having a price above and a price below makes the price in the middle seem more appealing. This experiment has been repeated with other consumer goods, such as ovens, and is now a much-used strategy in the corporate world. Basically, if you have two prices for something, and want to make more people pay the higher price, you add a third, even higher price; that makes the formerly highest price more attractive. Watch out for this strategy. (The research paper about beer pricing, written by a trio of economists at Duke University in 1982, was published in the *Journal of Consumer Research*. It's called "Adding Asymmetrically Dominated Alternatives: Violations of Regularity and the Simularity Hypothesis"—which must surely be the least engaging title ever given to an article about beer.)

The big book on the subject of behavioral economics is an unusual example of a book for the general reader written by the founder of a field of thought: Daniel Kahneman's *Thinking, Fast and Slow*.

Benford's law A seriously cool but quite strange law of math. It says that, in many types of random data, the number 1 is the most frequently occurring number, cropping up as much as 30 percent of the time. This is a surprisingly useful finding that is often employed to detect phoney figures in areas such as accounting and science. The math is immensely complicated, and I would love to give a full explanation of it here, but unfortunately I have to rush off now because I've just remembered I've got a thing.

Big Mac index The *Economist*'s attempt to answer the question of how expensive it is to live in different countries. Since currencies, living costs, food, rents, wages, and many other factors vary so much from place to place, how can you reliably compare the cost of living? The magazine's answer: by using the price of something that is in essence the same everywhere, the Big Mac. In economics, the thing they're trying to measure is called purchasing power parity, or PPP, i.e., how much you can buy in different places with a given amount of money. (That might sound an easy thing to measure, but establishing agreed figures for PPP in fact involves a huge international survey in which thousands of economists fan out all over the world collecting and collating data.) There used to be something called the Mars bar index, which tried to do something similar with the effect of inflation in the UK, but one of the problems with it is that Mars bars (unlike Big Macs) have changed size over time.[21]

See if, without looking at it, you can guess the most and least expensive countries in the world. Answer: Norway and Venezuela are the most expensive, and India and South Africa the least— though the Indian Big Mac is called the Maharaja Mac, and is made of chicken. If you're wondering what Norway and Venuezuela have in common, the answer is nothing, except lots of oil.

bitcoin An unregulated currency, created by someone or someones calling him, her, or themselves Satoshi Nakamoto, in 2008. It has no inherent value, so its worth depends entirely on the trust people have in it: in my view, that's the most interesting thing about bitcoin, the fact it is a built-in lesson on the arbitrary nature of money values. Bitcoins are created by "mining," i.e., by long slow computer calculations, and are stored and exchanged via digital "wallets." This number crunching burns a lot of energy, and the cost of that energy is the real cost of creating bitcoins. The currency's main use is in buying and selling things anonymously over the Internet, though there are also a few cafés and bars that take them.* The value of the bitcoin has gone up and down sharply in its short life. I'm writing this in March 2014: in the last few months the bitcoin has hit a high of over $1,200 and a low of $50. The currency lost 40 percent of its value in a single day, on 2 October 2013, when the FBI seized an illegal exchange called the Silk Road, where payment was taken in bitcoins—though it should be stressed that there is nothing illegal about bitcoins per se. In essence the bitcoin is (to quote the *Economist*) "a giant shared transaction ledger recording who owns each individual unit of the currency at any one time," in which all transactions taking place in the currency are simultaneously visible to all its users. An interesting feature of the currency is how transparent it is: all bitcoin transactions are

---

* A list of businesses that take bitcoins is available at www.spendbitcoins.com/places/.

visible, though also anonymous—the combination of those two things is unusual.*

Black-Scholes The name of the formula that made it possible to create prices in the derivatives markets; before the equation was discovered (or invented, depending on your view of what mathematics does), uncertainties about how probabilities changed made it impossible to create accurate prices for an option over time. Black-Scholes gave a way of mathematically modeling the price of the options, and led to a huge boom in the global market for derivatives. The equation is named after the two men who created it, Fischer Black and Myron Scholes.

Black Swan A term coined by the philospher-investor Naseem Nicholas Taleb for an event so rare it doesn't fit in normal models of statistical probability. As a result, institutions such as banks are grievously unprepared for this kind of very rare event. It is possible that humans are hardwired not to have a good intuitive understanding of these kinds of risks. An example would be Earth being hit by an asteroid big enough to cause global disaster, something NASA says happens every 500,000 years or so.[22] That puts the odds of its happening in a typical 80-year life at one in 6,250—which is uncomfortably high. It's very hard to know how to think about this fact.

bond A debt owed by a company, in return for money you have lent it. A bond will have a coupon, i.e., an amount of money it pays, monthly

----

* The current value of the currency is available at www.xe.com/currency/xbt -bitcoin, and the total number of bitcoins in circulation at blockexplorer.com/q/ totalbc—today, the number is 11,888,600. Bitcoin's FAQ, which I strongly recommend to anyone with an interest in the practical or theoretical questions raised by the currency, is at en.bitcoin.it/wiki/FAQ.

or quarterly or annually, and a date, at which point the bond will stop paying and you get back all the money you lent it. So you might lend Wal-Mart $5,000 for a year at a rate of 5 percent; that means the company will pay you an annual rate of 5 percent interest, probably monthly or quarterly, for a year, to a value of $250, and then give you your $5,000 back. Governments issue bonds too; that's how they borrow money. It's almost impossible to put into words just how big a deal the international market in these bonds is: they are a juggernaut, probably the single biggest force in financial markets. "Bond" is an interesting word because it is a rare example of a money metaphor that tells the truth. It is unreversified. The person raising the bond is bound by it, tied down and restrained by its obligation to repay the debt; and the borrower and lender are bound together too, their fates closely aligned, since if the borrower can't repay, the lender is in trouble as well.

bond market The international market in bonds. Ordinary members of the public hear much more about the equity market—the "stock market"—in the news and general chatter, but the bond market is much bigger and more important, in global financial terms: as an investor tells Michael Lewis in *The Big Short*, "The equity world is like a fucking zit compared to the bond market."[23]

Bretton Woods The setting for a conference in July 1944 where the Allies set out the agreement to regulate international economic relations after the war. Countries agreed to fixed exchange rates, tied to the US dollar, which in turn was tied to the ownership of actual, physical gold; the conference also agreed to the creation of the International Monetary Fund and the International Bank of Reconstruction and Development, which was to become the World Bank. The specific aim of the conference was to avoid the "beggar thy neighbor" policies between states that had played such a role in the turmoil of the twentieth century. The Bretton Woods system lasted from 1945 until President Nixon unilaterally took the USA off it on 15 August 1971, an event known as the "Nixon shock," which reintroduced free-floating currencies. Nixon's reasons for doing that were linked to the pressures on the US economy created by the Vietnam War and the growing trade deficit; his actions allowed the US dollar to drop in value, which was a help to industry and exports.

BRIC A term coined by the former Goldman Sachs economist Jim O'Neill, meaning Brazil, Russia, India, China. These are the fastest-growing emerging economies, respectively now the eighth-, ninth-, eleventh-, and third-biggest economies in the world. All of them are marked by sharp levels of recent growth accompanied by sharp levels of rising inequality.

budget A tool for managing expenditure, in which a person or company or government sets out its proposed spending for the next year. In the UK it usually takes place in March to cover the year ahead and is a huge annual fandango of an event, encumbered with pomp and tradition and an anticipatory period of "purdah" during which the chancellor, who delivers the budget, goes silent on its contents. Behind the scenes there is an enormous fight between all government departments and the Treasury. All countries have budgets, but nobody else does it with the same yearly public ritual.

Buffett, Warren A fascinating figure in a number of different ways: as an investor, he is quantifiably and provably the greatest there has ever been, not least because he doesn't invent or sell or run businesses or do anything other than make decisions about where to allocate his money. One of Buffet's axioms is "Invest in what you know," and another is "Put all your eggs in one basket, and then watch the basket"; it's advice he has followed by taking big shares in companies such as Coca-Cola, American Express, the Washington

Post Company, and Geico insurance. Through his investment holding company, Berkshire Hathaway, he has done that to an extent
that turned a $10,000 investment in his company in 1965 into more
than $50 million today, a compound return of more than 20 per-
cent a year. Nobody else comes close to that track record. And that
in turn is interesting, because modern theories of stock market
investing hold that nobody can consistently beat the market over
time; that means that Buffett is either doing something sneaky,
perhaps with leverage, or is a freak of a philosophically interesting
sort, whose achievements have serious implications for the whole
field of economics, especially the theory of efficient markets. Buffett's own view is that "there seems to be some perverse human
characteristic that likes to make easy things difficult" and that the
basic principles of investing are much simpler to grasp than people
think. That in turn raises the large question of exactly why nobody
else can do what he has done. The other interesting thing about
Buffett is that he is a brilliant writer, whose annual letters to his
shareholders, freely available on the Berkshire Hathaway website,
do a magnificent job of explaining his thinking crisply, clearly, and,
often, funnily.[24]

bull Anyone who thinks the price of something is going to go up:
equity bulls think equities are going up, bond bulls think bonds are
going up, and so on. Money people often use the word "bull" more
broadly: I heard one say, of a disgraced Irish banker, "I'm a tremen-
dous bull of the man"—this being high praise. People who deal with
bulls in real life are very cautious around them, because they're really
scary. I met a farmer who had been knocked out by a young bull who
was then kicking him along the floor of a barn towards a wall, with
the apparent intention of ramming him against the wall and killing
him; his life was saved by a farm worker who chased off the animal. I
suppose the metaphorical market bull comes from the idea that bulls
like to charge forwards. The opposite of a bull is a bear.

bullshit versus nonsense In Kingsley Amis's novel *The Old Devils* there is a brief but very thought-provoking speech by Peter Thomas, one of the book's main characters. His friend has just given a talk about how the poet Brydan, based on Dylan Thomas, didn't speak a word of Welsh but how the presence of Welsh was nonetheless very important as a subliminal presence in his work. In the pub afterwards, Peter picks him up on what he's said.

"I want to get this over to you while I remember and before I have too many drinks. When somebody tells you in Welsh that the cat sat on the mat you won't be able to make out what he's saying unless you know the Welsh for *cat* and *sat* and *mat*. Well, he can draw you a picture. Otherwise it's just gibberish."

The friend objects, but Peter presses on with his point:

"The point is it's unnecessary. They'll be just as pleased to hear how Brydan wrote English with the fire and the passion and the spirit of this, that and the bloody other only possible to a true or a real or a whatever-you-please Welshman, which if it means anything is debatable to say the least, but whatever it is it's only bullshit, not *nonsense*. Stick to bullshit and we're all in the clear."[25]

And that, for all the lightness of the context, is a very important distinction. Bullshit and nonsense are different. Bullshit is all around us; the term implies exaggeration, rhetoric, and a mild kind of untoxic falsity. It suggests that something is false but not malign. Every time someone tries to sell somebody something, a degree of bullshit is usually involved. Some words are more or less guaranteed to be bullshit: "executive," for instance, is, when used as an adjective, pure bullshit—executive chef, executive apartments, executive decision. "Exclusive" is bullshit, not least because it is used mostly about places that are open to the public, like restaurants and hotels. But the damage done by bullshit is usually fairly mild, and it can even be, if not exactly benign, then so much part of the normal process of selling that it is all just part of the dance. There's a *Big Issue* seller near where I live who holds out a copy with the line "last one"; when he sells it, he waits for the customer to walk away, then reaches into his bag and pulls out another "last one." That is bullshit, and relatively harmless—I say "relatively" rather than "wholly" because once you've fallen for the line, and then seen through it, it tends to diminish your trust in *Big Issue* sellers. The "hype cycle" around new inventions involves a near-ritualized early period of puffing, boosterism, and bullshit: as John Perry Barlow, songwriter for the Grateful Dead, once brilliantly put it, "bullshit is the grease for the skids on which we ride into the future." (I like that line because it is both an example of bullshit and a great explanation of it.) There is an enormous amount of bullshit in the world of money.

Nonsense is different: it's worse. It consists of things that are actively false, and at its worst of things that are not just not true but can't possibly be true. It is rarer than bullshit but much more toxic, and it is the difference between someone exaggerating a bit because he is trying to sell you something and someone who is consciously lying to you, or who is so far out of touch with reality that he doesn't know he's lying. In the world of money, the most recent and glaring example of nonsense was in the run-up to the credit crunch, in which broad sectors of banks and investors convinced themselves that they had invented a new category of financial instrument that guaranteed high rates of return with no risk. Since it is a fundamental axiom of investment that risk is correlated with return—that you can't make higher rates of return without taking on higher levels of risk—this is like claiming to have invented an antigravity device, or a perpetual motion machine. As the British investor John Templeton once said, "The four most expensive words in the English language are 'this time it's different.'" In everything to do with money, and in many other areas too, it's important to keep an eye out for those moments that are not just (relatively) harmless bullshit but the much more actively dangerous nonsense.

bund German government debt, used as a reference point in the world because it is the safest debt in Europe, analogous to Treasury debt in the USA.

business cycle The process in which businesses follow rhythms of expansion and contraction. There is a huge body of theory and study of why and how these cycles happen, but the most important fact is that they do. Laws of supply and demand obviously play a big part: demand for a product (bread, shoes, houses) is strong, so prices rise, so supplies grow as producers try to make money, but then they overproduce and demand weakens and the market crashes. Some businesses are more cyclical than others, and others aren't cyclical at all. Cyclical ones go up and down (house building), noncyclical ones go down and then down some more (coal mining). Important to know the difference.

business model A term that occurs with a frequency that, when you first start to read the business pages, is really annoying. I remember wishing commentators would stop using the term because it was so ubiquitous it seemed an obstacle to thought. Maybe the term's ubiquity reflects the state of business in the age of the Internet, where lots of companies try to grow traffic to their business first and then work out how to make money later—if they ever do. The word is omnipresent because this is a time when lots of companies are having to look around for business models, in a way that seems much less complicated if you manufacture something or mine something or create something. In those cases, the business model is to do the thing, then find the customers for it.

I've changed my mind on this subject, though, and now find the idea of business models a useful and clarifying one. Take Google. While the company was growing, it was very resistant to the idea that it was a media business, for three main reasons: (a) it genuinely didn't agree, (b) media businesses are closely regulated, and (c) the moneymaking prospects for media businesses are much studied and well known—the sky is not the limit, the wheel does not need to be reinvented. Google was keen instead to be seen as a new kind of technology business, one with infinite potential for growth, scalability, and profitability. What's apparent now, though, is that Google is mainly in the advertising business. Search advertising is the only one of its many impressive products that actually makes money. As one wit has said, search makes 110 percent of Google's profits—all its money, and then the 10 percent that it loses paying for all the other stuff. That advertising model reaches deep down into the core of Google's being and is starting to taint its search function, so that it brings you not necessarily the thing you most need to look for, but the link that will make it most money if you click on it.

Although there are many technical aspects to business models of the sort that people are taught when doing an MBA or similar qualification, the simple questions involved in thinking about business models are useful to almost anybody. The most basic of them is, how are we going to make money doing this? Who are our customers going to be and why will they pay for what we do? Above all, have we made sure we aren't the South Park underpants gnomes? Their business plan has three stages: stage 1 is to collect underpants, and stage 3 is to make profit—but stage 2 is just a giant question mark.[26]

buyback Something companies do when they have cash at hand and are confident about their own prospects: they buy back shares from shareholders. This has the effect of increasing the value of the remaining shares, while also giving the shareholders a welcome lump of cash. For example, say your company has 1,000 shares outstanding with 100 investors, and the shares are worth $100 each. You've had a bumper year and so decide to buy back 10 percent of them and retire them. Each shareholder sells you one share and gets $100 in cash, and now their remaining shares are worth more, because their 9 shares are now worth what 10 shares used to be worth. It might sound like a win-win, but there are pitfalls, because a company will often prefer to buy back shares when it believes those shares are undervalued—which can shade very close to a form of insider dealing, profiting the insiders who know the truth.

cajas Spanish regional savings banks, whose primary purpose was supposed to be taking people's savings and looking after them. For a while they were held up as models of locally responsive saving and lending, but during the Great Recession many of the *cajas* turned out to have lent far too rashly during the Spanish property bubble, and of the forty-seven *cajas* in business at the start of the crisis, only two remain in their original form. The *cajas* go part of the way to prove that the old-fashioned ways for banks to lose money, by lending too rashly, are just as effective as the newfangled ways involving investment banking and complex derivatives.

capitalism The subject is too big to be summed up in a lexicon entry, but one point worth stressing about it is that the thing which is supposed to be preeminent in it is capital. Not people, capital. When I wrote a book about the credit crunch, I thought that the reaction to it would be broadly divided along political lines, but I was pleasantly surprised by the amount of positive feedback I had from people on the political and economic right, many of whom, it turns out, are just as angry about the failings of global finance as anyone on the left. A big part of that is that the banks grew so powerful and so big that they were no longer capitalist institutions but rather monstrous hybrids of state sponsorship and privatized profit, ones whose main interest was in the remuneration of their own senior employees, rather than the functioning of capitalism per se. One private equity investor—a 100 percent red-meat-eating free-marketer—put it to me like this: "The banks broke capitalism."

Cato Institute A libertarian think tank, an American equivalent of the Adam Smith Institute. It is funded by the Koch brothers and has the usual libertarian views, against taxes and foreign wars, in favor of repealing antidrug legislation, and so on. The institute is named after Cato the Younger, who committed suicide in protest at the ascension to unchallenged power of Julius Caesar—an ambivalent model for a body trying to shape public opinion, I'd have thought. It always seems to me that the influence of these think tanks is stronger when their ideas aren't yet well known, and have the impact of unfamiliarity: once you know that the Cato Institute is always going to take a libertarian line on every issue, it gets a little old. I suppose the countervailing idea is that if nobody makes these arguments, they don't get made.

central banks The institutions that stand at the heart of the modern state's financial system. They set interest rates, have the power to print money to increase the amount in circulation, and play a supervisory role over the financial system. (In the UK this role was taken away in 1997 and given back in 2013.) Part of the idea of having a central bank is that it is independent from political interference; that's the theory, though the practice is often different. The three most important central banks are the US Federal Reserve, the European Central Bank, and the People's Bank of China.

CFTC The Commodities Futures Trading Commission, the body that regulates the US trade in commodities and their derivatives. It's fair to say that not many people overseas had ever heard of it before they began writing them large checks for the misdeeds of their banks in the Libor scandal: $325 million from RBS, which is 82 percent owned by the taxpayer. In its new career of kicking butt and taking names, the CFTC has also fined Barclays $200 million and UBS $700 million, with more to come as more cases work their way through the legal system.

Chapter 11 The American form of bankruptcy, generally seen as the mildest and most benevolent in the world for the person or company going bankrupt. It gives the debtor lots of room to restructure its business and to set about acquiring new funding. This reflects the reality that many troubled businesses are worth more as a going concern than they would be if they were closed down and sold off for parts—which is what many other bankruptcy regimes enforce. The American attitude to bankruptcy is remarkably forgiving and positive, which both reflects and contributes to the country's entrepreneurial culture.

Chocfinger Anthony Ward, a British commodities trader who set up a hedge fund specializing in chocolate, earned himself the nickname Chocfinger, by analogy with the Bond villain Goldfinger, who tried to take control of US gold reserves. Chocfinger didn't go as far as his namesake, but he did have many years' experience in trading cocoa and at one point even set up weather-forecasting stations in one of his company's main areas of activity, Sierra Leone, the better to predict the cocoa harvest. Chocfinger ended up controlling a significant fraction of the world's supply. At the peak of its activities, his fund, Armanjaro Trading, owned a remarkable 15 percent of the supply of cocoa. Even more amazingly, at one moment in 2010, Armanjaro took physical delivery of 241,000 tons of cocoa beans. That's an extraordinarily unusual thing to do in the commodities world, which is all about making money by trading futures and options. It must have been a memorable moment at the office: "Chocfinger, there's someone asking for you at the door. He says he has 7 percent of the planet's cocoa beans and wants to know where to put them." That one transaction left Chocfinger with enough cocoa to give everybody in the world three king-size Hershey bars each. In May 2012, the investment arm of the World Bank—which knows what it's doing, you'd have thought—bought a 6 percent stake in Armanjaro Trading, which implied a valuation for the company of between $200 million and $300 million. In 2013 the price of cocoa beans spiked upward, thanks to bad weather in one of the main growing areas, Sierra Leone. Surely good news for Armanjaro Trading, whose whole shtick concerns buying lots of cocoa, yes? Well, at the end of 2013, the fund was sold for guess how much? Go on, guess. Answer: $1. Less than the cost of a single one of those Hershey bars.

What happened? It's impossible for an outsider to know for sure, but if you're a hedge fund, and you own a lot of something, and plan to sell it, you will hedge your position and try to make money if the market moves against you. If you get the hedge wrong, and prices move outside the limits you've allowed for, you can end up losing a lot of money. My hunch would be that something like that happened to Armanjaro. Remember, pretty much all hedge funds close or go broke; this is just an unusually vivid example.

City of London A term often used as a metonymy for the UK's financial services industry, equivalent to "Wall Street" in the United States. As it happens, most of the people who work in the financial services in the UK don't work in London at all; even the ones who work "in the City" often don't work in the City but at, say, Canary Wharf (whose inhabitants include Barclays, Citigroup, HSBC, JPMorgan Chase) or Mayfair (which is where the hedge funds tend to be). It's amusing to note that the first historian ever to mention London, the Roman Tacitus writing in the middle of the first century AD, commented that the place "was much frequented by a number of merchants and trading vessels"—in other words, two thousand years ago it was already all about money.

code staff People, in the UK's regulatory regime for banks, at a senior level who do things involved with how much risk the bank takes on. New rules were brought in so that these people can have their bonuses clawed back if they do risky things that subsequently go wrong. Most of the big banks have a couple of hundred code staff, whose average earnings in 2011 were £1.16 million at RBS, £1.05 million at HSBC, and £2.4 million at Barclays.

commodity In the economic sense, something that is bought and sold as if it was fungible—as if one example of it was essentially indistinguishable from another. Coal is fungible and is a commodity, but books, say, aren't: one ton of coal is like another, but one ton of books isn't. The world's largest commodities exchange is the Chicago Mercantile Exchange, as depicted in the movie *Trading Places*—which is quite a good primer in the way commodities markets work, a lot more accurate than most movies with a financial backdrop. An amazing range of things are traded as commodities, from crude oil and coffee—which are respectively the number one and number two most valuable commodities—to iron, salt, soy beans, pork bellies, and every imaginable mineral, metal, and ore. Cocoa beans, for example, are a commodity; the price of cocoa butter rose by 70 percent in the year to mid-2013 because of bad weather in the Ivory Coast. (Almost exactly the same thing happens in *Trading Places*, except the commodity is frozen orange juice and the location is Florida.) Commodities in general, once the effect of inflation was allowed for and excluding oil, fell in price for about 150 years, until the turn of the twenty-first century; since then they have had an astonishing boom in prices. The main cause of the boom has been the growth of China, whose industrial output increased by 22 percent every year on average in the first decade of this century. Making more stuff means you need more stuff to make it with—hence, a commodity boom.[27]

The quest to find and extract commodities from troubled places is one of the darkest aspects of the contemporary economic system: "blood diamonds" are the best known of these products, but there are many more and many whose stories go untold. Much of the world's computer equipment functions by means of tantalum capacitors, which are made with an ore called coltan, much of which comes from the Congo, where it's extracted from mines run by warlords using slave labor.

From the business point of view, if your product or service is "commodified" or "commoditized," it means people can get it from anywhere and there is no reason why your version of it is unique. When people talk about the news having been commodified, it means you can now get your news from anywhere, so there's no reason to pay for it—which is bad news for newspapers.

competitiveness A quality usually linked to productivity. The more work, and the greater the value of the work, that gets done in a typical hour, the more productive the relevant individual, company, or indeed entire economy will be. Countries can increase their competitiveness by getting more work out of their citizens for less money; this Germany did in the early years of the twenty-first century, going from being "the sick man of Europe" to its economic heart in less than a decade. Politicians like to talk about competitiveness because it sounds less painful than "doing more work for less money with fewer employment rights," even though that in practice is what it tends to mean.

compound interest The single most important thing to know about from the point of view of your own finances. Money people are so aware of its power they don't talk about it any more, because they have internalized its importance; otherwise, they'd be talking about it all the time. My favorite example of the power of compound interest concerns the Native Americans who sold Manhattan to Peter Minuit in 1626 for some beads and trinkets worth about $26. A grievous rip-off, obviously. But if the Native Americans had been in a position to invest the $26 at 8 percent interest—historically a by no means unprecedented rate—and had left the investment to compound annually, it would by now be worth a useful $282 trillion, far more than enough to buy the whole place back. The miraculous power of compound interest to grow money is a wonderful thing, except that it's just as powerful applied to the growing size of debts.

confidence interval A very useful idea from statistics: it attaches a probability to a fact. Most of the science in the UN's report on climate change, for instance, has a confidence interval of 95 percent, i.e., there's a 5 percent, or one-in-twenty, chance that it's wrong. Note that a one-in-twenty chance of being wrong is quite a high chance, when what we're talking about is science or public policy. If every single scientific paper published had a confidence interval of 95 percent, that would mean that one in twenty of them are wrong. In the field of medicine alone, where 872,766 papers were published in 2011, that would give us 43,638 wrong papers in a typical year. That's a lot of wrongness.

consumer surplus A subtle and powerful idea, first stated by Alfred Marshall, describing the effect of competition on prices. This computer, for instance, cost me $1,600 five years ago. In terms of how much use it has been to me, its value is far more than that, at least twenty times greater, I'd say, because of the amount of profitable work it's enabled me to get done: so if I had to pay the full whack for what the computer is worth I would be shelling out much, much more than I did. That difference—between what I would be willing to pay for it and what it actually costs—is my consumer surplus. The creation of lots of different instances of consumer surplus is one of the great strengths of a market economy.

contestability Contestability is the quality of being able to compete or bid for something and is particularly relevant in areas such as government contracts: if there is only one company that can provide a service, then that service is not contestable, and the company can charge what it likes and deliver the service as badly as it likes.

A contestable market is apt to behave much more effectively, from everybody's point of view, than one that isn't contestable.

core capital A supposed measure of a bank's strength, of the amount of money a bank has in reserve to meet its obligations on a very very rainy day. Look at a typical person's balance sheet:

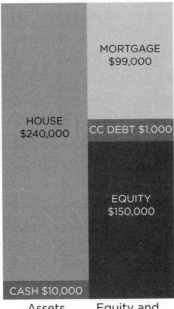

Assets   Equity and Liabilities

Here it's clear where the person's capital is: it is her equity, the part of her net worth that is absolutely and unequivocally hers, in a way that her house isn't, because some of its value is owed to the bank against the value of the mortgage. In banking, things aren't that simple. Banks are allowed to count as their core capital both that simple equity and other stuff such as retained profits and different types of shares and debt that doesn't have to be paid back (or "subordinated debt," as it's known). All of these measures, which under different regulatory regimes permit different types of accounting techniques, have the effect of increasing the bank's core capital number. They are ways of making the bank sound safer than it is. Critics of modern banking prefer a simpler number, the leverage ratio or multiple between the bank's simple equity—the number that stands out clearly in the chart above—and its assets. The banks hate that, because it makes them look less safe. Core capital is one of the central subjects at issue in the Basel III accords on banking; the gnomes of Basel call it Tier One and Tier Two equity.

correlation and cause Confusing these two things is the commonest mistake not just in economics, not just in the social sciences and humanities more generally, but in how most of us think about life most of the time. When we observe two things going together, we seem to have a hardwired tendency to believe that one of them caused the other. But the underlying causal relationship is often more complicated than it seems. One famous example: breast-fed babies in many respects do better than bottle-fed babies. So that's clear-cut: breast-feeding is better. But the fact is that the demographics of breast-feeding and bottle-feeding are different, and so the circumstances of how the babies are raised and fed are more different and more complicated than the plain correlation might make you think. Breast-feeding mothers are richer and better educated than bottle-feeding mothers, and it's hard to get these effects out of the data when you're making a comparison. Breast-fed babies do indeed do better, but the underlying mechanisms aren't all just about how the babies are fed.

There are zillions more examples where that came from. In general, whenever you hear or see anyone claiming a causal link between any phenomena, ask yourself whether it might just be a correlation instead. Tim Harford gives one of the best examples of the confusion between correlation and cause: James Lind, the doctor who in 1747 proved that lime juice prevented scurvy, had initially thought that the best preventative was beer. That was because a ship's beer ran out a few weeks into a sea voyage, around the same time that scurvy symptoms started to manifest. Lind performed an experiment in which scurvied sailors were systematically given different treatments, and voilà, lime juice was the cure. The initial link between beer and scurvy was a correlation and not a cause. This would make a great story for a cute little nonfiction book if the Royal Navy had immediately acted on this information and caused a revolution in scurvy care; in fact, though, it took forty years before the navy made lime juice compulsory on long voyages. (Note that the story of scurvy is a sequel to the story of longitude, as told by Dava Sobel in a book of that name: the ability to determine longitude made it possible for ships to regularly go on much longer voyages, which made scurvy a bigger problem.)

costs Everyone knows what costs are. In economics, though, the word is used as a euphemism for "people," so when a company or government talks about "cutting costs," what it really means is "sacking people." Saving money by moving business to the Internet is one way of cutting costs, because for any consumer process, it's about twenty times more expensive for a company to do something over the phone than over the Internet, simply because one involves people and the other doesn't.

cost-benefit analysis One of the most useful ideas in economics, something it's worth doing in your own life when you face a tricky decision—and also, strange as it seems, when you're not facing any particular decision, and life seems just to be puttering along. The idea is to draw up a calculation of what something—a purchase, a change of job, a house move, any life choice—costs and what it benefits you. This might sound obvious, but the critical factor is to include the costs of both making the choice and of not making it. That's the factor that we often instinctively leave out: the cost of not doing, of going on as we are.

CPI The consumer price index, made up by calculating the price of a representative basket of goods and services, excluding housing costs, which are included in the retail price index (RPI) instead. The UK's Office of National Statistics has a very good description:

> A convenient way of thinking about the CPI is to imagine a very large "shopping basket" full of goods and services on which people typically spend their money: from bread to ready-made meals, from the cost of a cinema seat to the price of a pint at the local pub, from a holiday in Spain to the cost of a bicycle. The content of the basket is fixed for a period of 12 months, however, as the prices of individual products vary, so does the total cost of the basket. The CPI, as a measure of that total cost, only measures price changes. If people spend more because they buy more goods this is not reflected in the index.
>
> The quantities or "weight" of the various items in the basket are chosen to reflect their importance in the typical household budget.[28]

This isn't an exact science, since the kinds of things people buy change over time, and may indeed change as prices change—if, when times are hard, you switch from eating steak to eating chicken, and the price of steak goes up but that of chicken doesn't, then that particular piece of inflation isn't relevant for you. It follows from this that different people experience different rates of inflation: the one-number-fits-all nature of the official figure is to some extent misleading: it's an average, and your mileage may well vary.

"C.R.E.A.M." A song by the Wu-Tang Clan that should be on a required-listening playlist for all who are or want to be in business for themselves. The acronym stands for "Cash Rules Everything Around Me," and it's probably a safe assumption that the song draws on the life experience of its producer and Wu-Tang leader, RZA, who dabbled in drug dealing as a young man.

From an economic point of view, he's right, and more good businesses go broke because of cash flow problems than for any other reason. You can have a great idea, great product, and great future ahead, and still go under because there's not enough money coming in to meet today's bills. As the old saying has it: sales is vanity, profits is sanity, cash is reality. More generally, it's interesting just how much the subject of money, economics, business strategy, and so on features in rap music: I don't think there's ever been a form of music, anywhere in the world, with such a focus on money (and I don't just mean modern Western popular music; I mean all music). That must come from a rap emphasis on "keeping it real": since money is a real, pressing concern for rappers, they rap about it. Perhaps the apotheosis of this attitude is to be found in Jay Z's insistence that he's not a businessman but a business, man. That's true, and there is an amazing book about his business interests, *Empire State of Mind: How Jay-Z Went from Street Corner to Corner Office*, by Zack O'Malley Greenburg: put it like this, his talents as an entrepreneur equal or exceed his talents as a musician. A company called Phat Startup offers business lessons derived from rap music, and has on its website possibly the greatest photograph in the world, of Jay Z straightening Warren Buffet's tie.[29]

credit Another one of those ideas that are too big to sum up in a lexicon, but there are a few points to make. The first is that without credit, the entire economic order doesn't function: it's that basic. And that in turn is why the credit crunch was such a big deal. "The main thing that went wrong, that nobody had seen coming," a banker told me, "was that all the credit in the world would dry up at the same time. That was the thing that was unimaginable." Second, credit is, as the name implies, based on belief, on credence and credibility: it is ultimately a form of trust and of confidence. This in turn means that factors having to do with optimistic attitudes, with what Keynes called "animal spirits," are much more important than you can put into any economic model. There is a built-in element of the irrational, of pure mood, in the functioning of credit and of markets more generally. Third, and finally, one of the most brilliant things the financial services industry ever did was to take the word "debt," which people were brought up to consider a bad thing that you want to avoid, and to rename it as "credit," which sounds like a good thing that you want more of. This is a major example of reversification at work.

credit default swap (CDS) A financial instrument arising from interest rate swaps. The simplest way of looking at a CDS is as a form of insurance. If you are receiving interest from someone to whom you've lent money, you may start to wonder what happens if she starts to have trouble paying you. If you get worried, you might want to insure the interest you're getting, so that in the event of a default by your borrower, you still get your money. That's a credit default swap: you pay someone a fee to take on the risk of default, and in return, in the event of a default, she pays you the money you are owed.

This might sound straightforward, but the picture is complicated by the fact that you can take out a credit default swap against loans you haven't actually made. That's right: you can insure against the risk of a default not of your own loan, but of somebody else's loan. That's less like insurance and more like a form of gambling, since you're basically betting on someone else's debts. Credit default swaps of this sort played a big role in the credit crunch.

currency wars Conflicts that happen when countries adopt "beggar thy neighbor" policies: they make their own currency cheap to bolster their own exports. Since the crisis of 2008 there have been accusations that China in particular has been carrying out a form of currency war—though the renminbi has risen sharply since 2011, and it's not clear the charge still holds. Another country benefiting from an artificially weak currency is Germany, which has reason to be grateful to the weaker countries in the euro zone for keeping the value of the currency down, and hence making German exports more affordable. Having too high a currency can cause severe economic problems, which has been the case in many sectors of the Australian economy: the Australian dollar, its strength boosted by commodity wealth, was so highly valued that it devastated the country's retail sector—it was so easy to buy stuff from abroad using supercharged Australian dollars that local shops found it nearly impossible to compete. The Swiss were so worried about something similar happening to them that in September 2011 the Swiss National Bank set out to buy "unlimited quantities" of foreign currency as a way of setting a minimum exchange rate of 1.2 Swiss francs to the euro.

customer-facing All the bits of a business with which a customer engages. In banking, for instance, lots of the most important infrastructural parts of the business are hidden away out of sight and are not customer-facing.

cyclical and countercyclical A phenomenon that is cyclical moves in the same way as most other things in the economy; a phenomenon that is countercyclical moves in the opposite way. If you spend a lot when you are earning a lot, you are spending cyclically; if you take the opportunity to save money when it is rolling in, you are behaving countercyclically. The need for banks and indeed whole economies to behave countercyclically has been a theme of the Great Recession. If everyone reacts to recession by spending less money, the recession will get worse: Keynes called this the "paradox of thrift." What's needed is for more people to behave countercyclically. In a similar way, banks and governments should in future be encouraged to build up greater reserves during the good times.

Davos Another metonym: it's a place in Switzerland, the setting for Thomas Mann's novel *The Magic Mountain*, but also the place where the World Economic Forum has its annual meeting of 2,500-odd delegates and hacks. The World Economic Forum is run by a Swiss academic called Klaus Schwab, who founded it in 1971 as the less grandiose European Management Forum; its self-published history of its first forty years calls itself "a partner in shaping history." The organization is "committed to improving the state of the world." In practice it is mainly a rich people's club, committed to preserving the existing world order. It is funded by donations from "member companies," which are the usual Dr. Evil wannabes—Goldman, Google, GE, and that's only the Gs. The annual theme is always some magnificent piece of content-free corporate bullshit: 2013 was "dynamic resilience." Note that Davos is also the first name of the pirate Davos Seaworth in *Game of Thrones*, and is nearly the same word as Davros, evil creator of the Daleks, in the BBC series *Doctor Who*.

dead cat bounce An apparent but illusory recovery in a falling market. It's the same kind of bounce a dead cat would give if you chucked it out a window: not a very big one. If you're wondering who on earth would be so sick as to come up with a metaphor like that, greetings, and welcome to the world of money.

deadweight costs The things that are indirect consequences of tax. If you raise tax on business, you raise more money from the businesses that are paying tax; but the increased rates of tax will cause some other firms to go broke and therefore stop paying tax altogether. That is a deadweight cost of the tax rise. A government will notice the tax it receives from the tax rise, but may not pay enough attention to the tax it is no longer receiving from the firms that have gone under. Deadweight costs are difficult to measure because to do so involves an attempt to put a price on this missing economic activity. Advocates of lower taxes argue that governments consistently understate the impact of dead-weight costs.

debt and deficit It's amazing how often you hear the debt and the deficit mixed up when people, even informed-seeming people, are talking about the economy.

Mr. Micawber in *David Copperfield* says it best: "Annual income twenty pounds, annual expenditure nineteen nineteen six, result happiness. Annual income twenty pounds, annual expenditure twenty pounds ought and six, result misery." That's a deficit: when your income is less than your expenditure. In the case of Micaw-ber's example, the deficit is sixpence; in the case of the USA, it was $680 billion in 2013—but the principle is the same. As for the debt, it's nothing more than the sum total of all the deficits accumu-lated over time: total US figure, $17.4 trillion, and counting. Sudden changes in the level of deficit, such as the one immediately after the credit crunch, have the effect of spooking the markets: creditors are worried that they won't get their momey back. A high level of accu-mulated debt, though, is more a question of political choice; stable democracies can operate with high levels of debt for a long time.

debt for equity A kind of deal sometimes used by companies that have hit difficulties and are having trouble repaying their debts. What they can do is swap their debt, i.e., the money they owe, for equity, i.e., for a share of the business. So the lender, instead of get-ting the stream of repayment money it's been expecting, gets to own an underlying piece of the business itself. In the case of a pub-lic company, this usually means the lender swaps bonds in return for shares.

decoupling What happens when two processes that used to be linked start to operate independently. In recent years it has taken on a specific meaning, to do with the separation of the rest of the world economy from the performance of the United States. Because the USA is the biggest economy in the world, and because the US dollar is the world's reserve currency, the US economy and the spending power of the US consumer have since the Second World War in effect been the driving force of the world economy. The question at issue after the credit crunch and during the Great Recession was whether new sources of growth in the world, particularly the developing and emerging world and very specifically China, would be able to keep growing at a sufficiently strong rate to keep the global economy in motion. That's what decoupling came to mean: whether world economic growth could decouple from the fate of the US economy. The answer seems to be "sort of." The world economy has kept growing, not as fast as it did in the glory years before the Great Recession but reasonably: the IMF's figures for 2011 to 2014 were, respectively, 3.9, 3.1, 3.1, 3.8 percent growth, which is neither good nor bad. The IMF data make it clear that most of that growth is coming from the emerging and developing economies.[30] That's decoupling. Australians know all about decoupling, because it's one of many places in the world where it's already a dominant economic reality: there, China is already an economic superpower.

default Missing a deadline to pay back your debts. A default can take many different forms, from a restructuring agreed after negotiation with creditors, in which the time frame for repayments and the interest rates for repayments are mutually agreed; or it can be chaotic, when a government suddenly announces that it cannot meet its obligations. A chaotic default on the part of Greece was on the top of everybody's worry list in 2011, not because Greece is an important economy but because nobody knew how the consequences of default would play out across the rest of the euro area. In general, financial markets are keen to make default sound like the end of life as we know it, though the fact is that countries do default—Argentina in 2001, Iceland in 2008—and life went on.

deflation When money loses value over time, prices gradually go up: that's inflation, and it is a normal fact of economic life. When money gains value over time, prices go down: that's deflation, and it is a freak condition with grave, near-fatal consequences for the operation of any economy. That might sound strange, because wouldn't it be cool if our money was just automatically worth more? The answer is a firm no: if you think about it, money being worth more is another way of saying that other things are worth less, including our labor. Because money gains in value if left in our bank accounts, we spend as little of it as we can. Our debts grow in value, too. The economy slows and then stops. A pall of gloom and stasis settles over the entire economy. Economists and politicians are terrified of this prospect, and terrified of deflation, especially of the idea that the debts they run up will automatically be worth more, rather than being reduced by inflation. (That's one big reason governments quite like inflation, because it reduces the value of their outstanding debts.) The country with the most extended experience of deflation in the modern world is Japan, which has been living through it for more than two decades. Now, Japan is not a disaster, and you could argue that it is culturally more interesting, with more of an emphasis on personal development and individuality, than during its hubristic boom during the seventies and eighties; but the social contract in the developed world is implicitly based on an economic model with rising prosperity built in. A society that doesn't have that has a different version of the contract between its generations. Deflation helps the people of yesterday, inflation the people of tomorrow.

deflator The number you use when working out the value of money minus the effect of inflation. Say you are thinking about some financial decision two years in the future. You know it's going to cost a certain amount of money—say, $10,000. To work out what that amount is worth in today's money, you need to apply a deflator, to take away the effect of inflation. If the inflation rate is 5 percent, then your deflator is 5 percent, compounded over two years: $9,050.

deleveraging One of the many boring-sounding economic words with a scary real-world meaning. It is the process of reducing leverage, i.e., the ratio between what you earn and what you're borrowing. If you pay down your mortgage, you are deleveraging. While deleveraging is OK in any individual case—indeed is often a very good idea—if everybody deleverages at the same time, it means that everybody is concentrating on reducing debt rather than spending money. In a recession or slowdown, this makes economic conditions worse. If governments, businesses, and households all have too much debt, and all set out repaying their debts at the same time, it's an economic disaster. That's why the British prime minister David Cameron had to backtrack on a speech he was planning to make to the Tory party conference in 2011: "The only way out of a debt crisis is to deal with your debts. That means households—all of us—paying off the credit card and store card bills." It was pointed out that this was a genius formula for making the recession worse, so he had, very embarrassingly, to withdraw the lines from his speech. John Maynard Keynes and other economists wrote a public letter in the depths of the Great Depression, saying, "The public interest in present conditions does not point towards private economy; to spend less money than we should like to do is not patriotic." [31]

depression An extended downturn in economic activity. Calling a downturn a depression is a way of raising the rhetorical stakes. There is no generally agreed standard for a depression; some observers think the downturn since 2008 qualifies. The bench-mark is pretty high, though, as established by the Great Depression of the thirties: in the United States, where the decline from peak to trough was steepest, the economy shrank by 33 percent and unem-ployment hit 25 percent. In the Great Recession the US economy shrank by 5.1 percent, peak to trough, and unemployment hit 10 percent. In the UK the GDP decline was 7.1 percent and unemploy-ment hit 8.3 percent. Five years after the start of the crisis, the UK economy was still 3.3 percent smaller than it was before the trouble began. I think Great Recession about covers it.

deregulation The process of ripping up rules, and the main demand of the financial world in the Anglo-American world for about thirty years. The financiers got what they wanted, culmi-nating in measures such as the repeal of the Glass-Steagall Act separating retail and investment banking in the United States, and the "Big Bang" deregulating the City of London in October 1986. The momentum behind deregulation grew to such an extent that in the case of newly invented financial derivatives, the indus-try was able successfully to lobby Congress to pass a law, the Com-modity Futures Modernization Act, which prohibited the making of any laws to regulate the new inventions. In other words, not just deregulation, but an outright ban on any regulation in the future. The idea behind deregulation was that markets could do a better job of regulating themselves than regulations ever could. It has been comprehensively disproved by the events of the credit crunch.

derivatives If you're a farmer worried about the value of next sum-mer's wheat crop, you can sell it ahead of time for a fixed price. So now you have a contract to deliver x amount of wheat by a specific date—and that contract can now be bought and sold. That contract, which derives its value from the underlying goods, is known as a derivative. The derivative contract can be bought and sold many times, whereas the wheat will be delivered only once; people betting on the value of next year's wheat crop may turn that derivative over on a daily basis between now and next summer. That's why the market in derivatives can be many times bigger than the value of the underlying assets. Chicago and London have the world's biggest derivatives markets; in London more than a trillion dollars of the things are traded every day.

destocking Reducing levels of inventory: storing less of the stuff you sell. It can be confusing for economists, because if you're looking at last year's figures and comparing them with this year's, you may not be comparing like with like: last year all the sales were new products, but this year you emptied out your storage warehouse, because you were worried about being left with loads of stuff you couldn't sell. So last year you ordered lots of stuff from the supplier, but this year you didn't order any, because you were just selling off stuff you had in storage. That means orders are down and work at your supplier is down, but you yourself are selling just as much stuff. The resulting economic data will be hard to decode. This happened after the credit crunch and was one of the reasons why the precise situation of the economy—how much trouble we were in—took some time to become clear.

devaluation Reducing the value of a currency. It can be an active process, in which a government actively chooses to reduce the value of its currency, going so far, on occasion, as to do so by fiat: Harold Wilson's Labour government did this on 19 November 1967, reducing the value of the pound against the dollar by 14 percent, from $2.80 to $2.40. "It does not mean that the pound here in Britain, in your pocket or purse or in your bank, has been devalued," Wilson said, in the full knowledge that it wasn't true. (He'd been the youngest ever economics don at Oxford.) The other kind of devaluation

is more passive and happens as a currency weakens because people prefer not to own it: this happened to sterling after the credit
crunch, when the pound lost more than 20 percent of its value
against the dollar and euro. It's curious that Wilson's devaluation
helped destroy his government's reputation for economic competence, whereas a bigger but less overt fall in the value of sterling had
no such effect—which only goes to show that the active process of
explicit devaluation is a lot riskier for governments than the sneak-
ier second sort. Governments often like the idea of devaluation
because it makes a country's exports cheaper and helps manufacturing industry as a result. The effect on ordinary citizens comes in
the form of higher bills for imported goods and energy.

developing and emerging These terms, which are used all the
time in economics to describe the growing economies of the non-
Western world, don't have an agreed definition. There's a faint
sense of embarrassment and foot shuffling about the term "emerging" in particular, because it sounds so patronizing, like those
school prizes for "most improved." (Or the only prize ever won during her school career by the late Princess Diana, an award for the
best-kept hamster.) Developing economies are poorer than emerging ones, but again there is no agreed threshold for the distinction.
Brazil, Russia, India, and China, the famous BRICs, are generally
seen as emerging economies, and so are Mexico, Indonesia, and
Turkey; South Korea is sometimes on these lists, but some other
economists regard it as a fully developed economy. It isn't on the
IMF list of emerging economies, which adds the following to the
countries already mentioned: Argentina, Bulgaria, Chile, Estonia,
Hungary, Latvia, Lithuania, Malaysia, Pakistan, Peru, Philippines,
Poland, Romania, South Africa, Thailand, Ukraine, Venezuela.
Everywhere else is either part of the developed world or is devel-
oping—but note that the term implies that all poor economies are
moving forward, even if they aren't.

dividends What are paid out if you own a share, at agreed intervals, and to a specific amount per share. Dividends reflect the amount of profit the company has earned in the relevant period: the dividend is how that profit is paid to the owners of the company, the shareholders. Although much of the coverage of the stock market focuses on how the price of shares goes up and down, history shows that about half the value of stocks has always come from the dividends they pay.

dove A term often used in regard to inflation: an inflation dove is someone who thinks that the economy needs as much stimulus as it can get and that to raise interest rates would be a disaster. Inflation doves love quantitative easing and any other associated loose monetary policy. The opposite of a dove is a hawk.

downgrade When a ratings agency lowers its rating on the debt issued by a company or country, that is a downgrade. Ratings agencies do that because they think the bond has grown in risk. A downgrade can have important consequences, because some types of investors, such a municipalities and public pension funds, are by law allowed to invest only in specific grades of debt: if a bond is downgraded, that can mean that some investors have no choice but to sell their bonds. That in turn will push the prices down further.

downsize A term that means sacking people. In private life people sometimes use it to mean spending less money, often by moving to a smaller house with a smaller mortgage, or no mortgage at all.

eating their lunch Outdoing or defeating others, often by outcompeting them or stealing their customers.

EBITDA An acronym, used by students of the stock market and business in general, for earnings before interest, tax, depreciation, and amortization. This is the raw measure of how much money a company is earning before it has to pay out these various financial costs. Once they are paid out, the earnings can look very different; but because most of these costs are tweakable, and can refer to events carried over from, or carried over to, other years, it's useful to be able to look past them at the underlying earnings. The picture of a company's finances with and without EBITDA is a bit like looking at someone's earnings before tax, mortgage payments, credit card payments, alimony, and clever accountancy advice.

ECB The European Central Bank, which is the central bank of the euro zone. It's chief task is to set interest rates, and its explicit target is to keep inflation close to but below 2 percent. The bank is located in Frankfurt and is seen by some as being too German in its focus, with the longstanding German emphasis on inflation not being relevant or helpful at a time when what the euro area needs more than anything else is growth. The irony is that this German-feeling institution is currently headed by the Italian Mario Draghi, known as Super Mario for his effect on calming speculation about the future of the euro zone. He did that with no more than three words, saying in July 2012 that he would do "whatever it takes" to save the euro.

Eddie Murphy rule A proposed rule put up by the CFTC to prevent people from using misappropriated government information when trading in commodities markets. It's based on the scam Eddie Murphy and Dan Aykroyd pull in the dénouement of *Trading Places*, so should really be the Murphy-Aykroyd rule.

equities What you invest in when you buy shares in a company. Bear in mind the typical (oversimplified) balance sheet: figure 2. They are called equities because you are buying a piece of the equity. For most of the twentieth century equities were the best asset category to invest in for the long term, though they had a terrible fifteen years or so, until a recent spike in prices whose main cause is probably the effects of quantitative easing.

ESM The European Stability Mechanism, which began operating in October 2012, the euro zone's firewall and bailout fund. It created a fund of up to €780 million to protect euro zone countries that get into trouble and can't repay their debts. Countries in receipt of an ESM bailout will in turn have to promise to sign up to a strict regime of austerity in public spending policy and tax rises. The establishment of the ESM was touch and go, since participating countries had to ratify the treaty in the face of political opposition. In creditor countries this focused on a reluctance to bail out foreigners, whereas in debtor countries it focused on the loss of sovereignty implied in the bailout conditions. There's also an ongoing argument about whether the ESM should be allowed to bail out banks directly, or whether it will have to do it by giving the money to the relevant country first. Governments would prefer the recapitalization to go directly to banks, because that way the debts won't appear on the governments' balance sheets, but this change won't happen until the euro area sets up a supervisory mechanism for all its banks.

ETFs Exchange-traded funds are investment products that combine features of both funds and stocks. Like funds, they are pooled investments, combining a range of assets; like shares, they can be bought and sold directly on stock markets. They offer the advantage of funds in that they provide access to lots of underlying assets through a single wrapper, and yet they are cheaper. Many of them offer access to share indexes such as the FTSE or NASDAQ or DAX, and for people who just want to buy an entire share index, ETFs are a cost-effective way to go. ETFs are increasingly popular with individual investors for exactly that reason. There are equity ETFs, bond ETFs, and commodity ETFs. So, what's not to like? Well, quite a few ETFs are more complicated than they first seem. Instead of just buying the components of an index—a piece of each of the 100 companies in the FTSE100, for instance—some ETFs replicate the movement of these indexes by means of complex techniques involving derivatives. This is fine in fair weather, but these products have not been tested by severe market difficulties, and it seems distinctly possible that some of the ETFs may act strangely if the underlying derivatives hit trouble. People who think they are using an ETF to own, say, gold, may find out that instead they own a complex set of derivatives betting on the future price of gold; and receive unpleasant surprises accordingly.

Eurodollars US dollars invested in banks outside the USA—confusingly, not just in Europe. Their existence reflects the fact that the dollar is effectively a world currency. Nobody knows how big the global Eurodollar market is, but since most international financial transactions are booked in dollars, it is the world's biggest financial market by far.

every economist's favorite joke It concerns the prevalence in economics of certain assumptions, about perfect information, efficient markets, rational consumers, and so on. The joke runs as follows: A physicist, a chemist, and an economist are stranded on an island with nothing to eat. A can of soup washes ashore. The physicist says, "Let's smash the can open with a rock." The chemist says, "Let's build a fire and heat the can until it explodes." The economist says, "First, let's assume a can opener."

It may not be strictly relevant here, but while we're on the subject of a profession's favorite joke, I feel the need to pass on every soccer writer's favorite joke, as told to me at least a dozen times back when I used to spend my Saturdays writing soccer match reports. The story dates back to the days when George Best was the hard-partying most famous footballer in England. A waiter comes into a hotel suite in the morning to find Best asleep on the bed with his arms around two naked women (in more elaborate versions of the story, the current and previous year's Miss World). At the foot of the bed a number of magnums of champagne have been emptied and are upended in ice buckets. Best has been to a casino and the bed is also liberally strewn with £50 notes. The waiter shakes his head mournfully. "George, George," he says. "Where did it all go wrong?"

exchange rates The rates at which one currency is exchanged for another. The crucial fact about them is that because they are measured against each other, they can't all move in the same direction: if the dollar goes up, something else is going down, and vice versa.

extend and pretend One of the things lenders do when they have lent money to someone and don't think they're going to get it all back. They extend the repayment term of the loan, and pretend that the full value of the loan is intact; it's a pretense because the fact of the extension means that the initial value of the loan will now not be fully recovered. This is something banks in particular are prone to doing when they don't want to admit to just how many of their loans have gone bad.

externalities A powerful idea, one of the most helpful widgets in the economic toolbox. Externalities concern costs that are borne not by the person responsible for them but by others around them. The classic example features a factory that manufactures, say, fertilizer and has a highly profitable business doing so, but that in the process pumps out pollutants into a local river. The pollutants have a significant impact on water quality and damage the lives and incomes of residents downstream. In a totally free-market economy, the factory can say, "So what? Not our problem." That is a classic, textbook externality: the real costs of the fertilizer manufacture include the effect of pollution, but the factory is free to ignore these costs. That is, it is free to do so, unless the society around forces it, through legislation, to attend to those costs. The problem of externalities poses a serious challenge to a wholly free-market system, since any business with externalities will tend to try to pass them off onto other people whenever it can. Many of the most visible externalities concern the environment, as in the example I've given, but there are also more subtle impacts from all sorts of other activities. If the lottery encouraged people to engage in irrational thinking about money and saving, and therefore tended to make people unduly passive about their own circumstances, that would be an externality. Very high levels of pay in the financial sector have an impact on inequality and therefore on the quality of life of the community more generally—that's another one.

failing upwards A common occurence in corporate life: someone is given a job, screws it up, and is promoted to another, bigger job just as the first thing collapses; then the process repeats. I bet you can think of your own examples.

fat-finger mistakes Errors that occur when a trader presses the wrong number on a keyboard and accidentally buys the wrong number of something. Presumably there are sometimes fat-finger mistakes when somebody buys or sells too little of something, but you never hear about those, because they have no impact: what you hear about is when somebody buys or sells way, way too much of something. A Lehman Brothers trader based in London wiped £30 billion off the FTSE in 2001 by executing sell orders that were 100 times too big; the same year, a UBS trader in Tokyo sold 610,000 shares in an advertising company for 16 yen when the price should have been 420,000 yen; in 2005 a trader at Mizuho, Japan's second-biggest bank, accidentally sold 600,000 shares in a company that had only 14,000 shares to sell; in April 2012, a clerk fell asleep on his keyboard with part of his face—I'm guessing the nose, or maybe a cheek—on the 2 key and accidentally turned a pensioner's transfer of €62.40 into one of €222,222,222.22 (that's £191 million). The supervisor failed to notice the mistake, which was caught later by the bank's systems. There is no moral to these stories, other than that people make mistakes and systems need to be designed to minimize and contain the consequences of those mistakes.[32]

Federal Reserve The central bank of the USA. It does what other central banks do: runs monetary policy, supervises the operation of the financial system, and acts as the lender of last resort. It's called the Federal Reserve System because it operates through twelve regional branches, each of which supervises the banks in its own area. As the Fed's own website explains,

> Many of the services provided by this network to depository institutions and the government are similar to services provided by banks and thrift institutions to business customers and individuals. Reserve Banks hold the cash reserves of depository institutions and make loans to them. They move currency and coin into and out of circulation, and collect and process millions of checks each day. They provide checking accounts for the Treasury, issue and redeem government securities, and act in other ways as fiscal agent for the U.S. government. They supervise and examine member banks for safety and soundness. The Reserve Banks also participate in the activity that is the primary responsibility of the Federal Reserve System, the setting of monetary policy.[33]

The whole idea of a central bank has been controversial in US history, with antifederal critics correctly arguing that it would have immense and to some extent undemocratic power—which, it turns out, is exactly why a central bank proved necessary, since without it the financial system kept suffering from unmanageably severe crises. The Fed is in general opaque and secretive about its own processes; while it was for years assumed to have an inflation target, it was only in January 2012 that the governor of the Fed, Ben Bernanke, made the target explicit at 2 percent.

fiat money The kind of money that is easy to get your head around is money that has something real behind it, some physical thing that you can exchange for your cash. Once upon a time your banknotes had behind them the weight, literally, of gold: you could in theory turn up at a bank and exchange your cash for a specific quantity of the precious metal. This practice was linked to the way paper money had been invented in Europe: customers with gold would hand it over to a goldsmith/banker to look after it, and receive a receipt in return; because these receipts were by definition secured by the value of gold, they began to be used as currency in their own right. (That might sound apocryphal, but the story comes from the Bank of England's own website.)[34] The invention of paper money was an obvious development from there. British banknotes still promise to "pay the bearer on demand" a specific amount, but this is no longer backed by anything other than the authority of the state, which has decided to create the money of its own accord: and that is what fiat money means. It is money that is essentially willed into being by the power of the state. There is something slightly freaky about the thought, I find.

fiscal and monetary I reckon I had got to my late forties and had heard these two terms used several times a day for my entire life—say, a few thousand times each—before I bothered to find out what they mean. "Fiscal" means to do with tax and spending, and is controlled by the government; "monetary" means to do with interest rates, and is controlled by the central bank.

5.6 In the UK, the number you multiply by the number of days you work in a week to get your annual allocation of paid holiday leave.

So if you work 5 days a week, you get 28 days holiday: 5 x 5.6 = 28. That's the maximum: if you work 6 days a week, the top statutory whack remains 28 days. That's five weeks and 5 days holiday, by law. This is the most generous statutory holiday entitlement in the world, though there is no requirement that an employer lets you take bank holidays off; an employer can include bank holidays as part of your holiday entitlement, which would leave you with 20 days, which is four weeks. In continental Europe employees have fewer statutory days off, but employers tend to add bank holidays on top, so they often end up with more holiday in total.[35] The USA, amazingly to non-Americans, has no statutory vacation entitlement. That, right there, is the single biggest argument for trade unions, since it is thanks to unions that ordinary citizens in other countries got these rights.

This means that in an ordinary year, a British person in full-time employment works 233 days and has holidays plus weekends for a total of 132 days off. So in a working year you spend 63.8 percent of your days at work and 36.2 percent of your days elsewhere. Over a typical lifetime, assuming you work an eight-hour day from 20 until 65, and live the standard UK life expectancy of 80.75 years, you spend 11.86 percent of your time at work, or if you want to express it as a percentage of your waking hours, 23.71 percent. This means that in a normal life span, more than three-quarters of your adult waking hours are spent not working.

Forbes cost of living extremely well index (CLEWI) An amazing thing I came across while researching the question of just what it is that very very rich people do with their money. As _Forbes_ says, the CLEWI is to the very rich what the CPI is to "ordinary people." There are forty items on it, and they are hilarious, though perhaps you shouldn't show them to your left-wing aunt if she's suffering from high blood pressure: Russian sable fur coats from Bloomingdale's, shirts from Turnbull and Asser, Gucci loafers, handmade John Lobb shoes, a year at Groton boarding school, a yacht, a horse, a pool, a Learjet, a Roller, a case of Dom Perignon, forty-five minutes at a psychiatrist's on the Upper East Side (!), an hour's estate planning with a lawyer, and, amusingly/annoyingly, a year at Harvard.[36] In 2012, the CLEWI went up 2.6 percent but the CPI went up only 1.4 percent. That means the gap is narrowing! Oh wait, no it doesn't. The net worth of the 400 richest people in America went up by 11 percent, from $1.53 trillion to $1.7 trillion.

forward guidance A policy in which central banks say in advance what they are going to do, as a way of introducing greater levels of confidence into the market. This might not sound like a big deal, but central banks, perhaps because they're acutely aware how many things aren't under their control, highly prize the few things that are—so the act of binding themselves in advance to a particular course of action upsets them. However, the unprecedented recent years of crazy-low interest rates and kooky new policies such as QE have made the markets very anxious about what happens when there's a change in direction; this in turn has led to a demand for something resembling forward guidance. In effect, the markets are asking for a bit of notice before the banks turn off the money hose. So both the Federal Reserve and the Bank of England have started to adopt a policy of forward guidance, and have both immediately run into the main problem with it. This is that markets know a central bank will in the event of difficulties always do what it feels needs to be done, and this fact will always trump whatever guidance has been given in advance. Forward guidance therefore ends up being a bit like that thing where children make their parents promise to do something, and the parents promise that they will, and then add, "unless we change our minds, forget, or can't be bothered."

Frankfurt Often used as an metonym for several different things: the European Central Bank, which is based there; the German view of economic issues ("Frankfurt thinks that . . ."); and the more general economic interest of the euro area, especially as opposed to the interests of the City of London. Frankfurt in this last sense is bitterly envious of the City's preeminent position in the world of global finance. It dearly wants some of the City's action, and is trying to target the City through European-wide measures on subjects such as bonuses. Frankfurt is quite likely to have another go at curbing London when a more unified banking system is brought in in the euro zone. One of the ironies is that inside Britain, the antibonus rules are one of the most popular things the euro authorities have ever done. Frankfurt's big problem is that London is a much more attractive and interesting place to live, especially for the demographic who work in finance: as a former mayor of London, Ken Livingstone, put it, "Young men want to go out on the pull and do a lot of cocaine, and they can't really do that easily in Frankfurt."

fraud A perennial fact in the world of finance and money. As finance has got more virtual and computerized, and as the sums involved have got bigger and can be moved more easily, frauds have got bigger too: it's noticeable that the biggest fraud trials in the history of the both the United States and the UK, those of Bernard Madoff and Kweku Abodoli, have happened in the last five years. In all the talk about the need to punish bankers, it seems to have gone largely unremarked that the Fraud Act of 2006 has a section dealing with "fraud by failing to reveal information." That seems to me to cover the PPI scandal, in which banks sold policies that they knew would be of no use to their customers—but nothing has happened about that.

free trade The system in which countries trade with each other without tariffs and taxes. At the moment free trade is more of an aspiration, or a direction of travel, than a full-blown system, and at the global level there are many restrictions on free trade; the body that regulates and supervises the status quo is the World Trade Organization. There is free trade within NAFTA, comprising the USA, Canada, and Mexico, and free trade within the European Union, and there are also bilateral agreements between countries and groups of countries. There has never been a war between two countries that trade freely with each other.

Friedman, Milton (1912–2006) One of the most influential economists of the twentieth century—in some people's judgment *the* most influential—not least because his policies were central to the governments of Ronald Reagan and Margaret Thatcher, and led to the neoliberal turn in economic policy that is still dominant today. Friedman studied the Great Depression, and didn't so much contradict the Keynesian view as expand on it, by coming to see the crisis as a problem with the money supply, or the amount of money available to circulate in the economy. That question became central to his thinking. He was also hugely influential, through his central position at the University of Chicago, in the expansion of economic thinking to other areas of life, especially through his emphasis on the idea of rational expectations: that people's actions, when parsed correctly, can almost always be found to have an economically rational foundation. Let it be noted that there is a big difference between the range and sweep of Friedman's work across a broad range of academic disciplines and a huge number of books and articles, on the one hand; and, on the other, the fairly simple, even crude, policies into which these ideas were translated by governments. His subtle and broad-ranging mind produced ideas whose practical manifestations boiled down to cutting taxes on the better-off and to raising interest rates to cut inflation. He is often seen as the polar opposite of Keynes.

fundamentals In investing, fundamentals are the underlying realities of a business, in terms of sales, costs, and profits. Investors who specialize in fundamentals—Warren Buffett would be the great example—pore over annual reports and balance sheets looking at these numbers. That might sound like common sense, of a slightly boring sort, but many investors do nothing of the kind and instead look at trends and momentum and themes and try to second-guess the way the market will move. Keynes gave a famous description of what this kind of nonfundamentals investor does: he is looking at a photo of six girls and trying to pick, not which girl he thinks is the prettiest, and not which he thinks most people will think is the prettiest, but which most people will think most people will think is the prettiest. "It is not a case of choosing those [faces] that, to the best of one's judgment, are really the prettiest, nor even those that average opinion genuinely thinks the prettiest. We have reached the third degree where we devote our intelligences to anticipating what average opinion expects the average opinion to be."[37] In other words, the nonfundamentals investor isn't trying to work out what companies he should invest in, or what company most investors will think they should invest in, but which company most investors will think most investors will want to invest in. Having made and then lost a packet investing like that, Keynes came to deem it simpler, safer, and better to stick to fundamentals. He made fortunes as a fundamentals investor for himself, his college, and the investment funds he ran.

fungible An important idea in economics, easier to grasp than to define clearly. (I mentioned to the cultural commentator Bryan Appleyard that I was trying to define "fungible," and he immediately texted me back, "Can be turned into a fung.") Something is fungible if it can be substituted, in part or in whole, by an equivalent amount of the same thing. Money is fungible, indeed that's one of its main characteristics—you can swap a $100 note for a hundred

$1 bills, or ten $10 notes, or whatever, and it is all the same thing. Commodities are fungible—oil, coffee, gold. It follows that anything fungible is much more easily traded than something that isn't. Fungible things are the basis of all currencies: in medieval Japan, for instance, the currency was based on a specific quantity of rice, the koku, which in principle was enough rice to feed somebody for a year. (That's about 150 kilos of rice.)

G7, G8, G20 These really blur into each other when you hear about them in the news, I find. The distinctions are as follows:

The G7 is for finance ministers and central bank governors only. It meets annually. The website says it is "an informal forum of countries representing around half of global economic output," consisting of the United States, the UK, France, Germany, Italy, Canada, and Japan. The countries on the list represent 66 percent of the world's accumulated wealth.[38]

The G8 is for the heads of governments of the rich industrial countries; it consists of the same countries as the G7, plus Russia. It's an annual meeting with a series of minimeetings to prepare and set the agenda. The group was created after the oil price shock of 1973, and Russia was added as a member in 1997. The EU is represented but doesn't chair or host meetings. The membership is increasingly anachronistic, since according to the IMF the list of rich countries by size of economy now goes as follows:

1. EU (I know it's odd to list both the collective EU and also individual countries, but that's what they do)
2. USA
3. China
4. Japan
5. Germany

6. France
7. UK
8. Brazil
9. Russia
10. Italy
11. India
12. Canada

The G20 is again for finance ministers and central bankers. The organization focuses on the operation of the financial system. It contains the usual suspects from that IMF list above, plus South Africa, Mexico, Argentina, South Korea, Saudi Arabia, Australia, Indonesia, and Turkey. Here is the organization's account of its own membership criteria: "There are no formal criteria for G20 membership and the composition of the group has remained unchanged since it was established. In view of the objectives of the G20, it was considered important that countries and regions of systemic significance for the international financial system be included. Aspects such as geographical balance and population representation also played a major part." Translated into English, that means, "We had to include the Saudis because they've got all the bloody oil, OK?"

GDP Gross domestic product is the measure of all the goods and services produced inside a country. Imagine for a moment that you come across an unexpected ten dollars. After making a mental note not to spend it all at once, you go out and spend it all at once, on, say, two pairs of woolly socks. The person from the sock shop then takes your tenner and spends it on wine, and the wine merchant spends it on tickets to see *Beneath the Valley of the Ultra-Vixens*, and the owner of the cinema spends it on chocolate, and the sweet-shop owner spends it on a bus ticket, and the owner of the bus company deposits it in the bank. That initial ten bucks has been spent six times, and has generated sixty dollars of economic activity. In a sense, no one is any better-off; and yet, that movement of money makes everyone better-off. To put it another way, that first tenner has contributed sixty dollars to US GDP. Seen in this way, GDP can be thought of as a measure not so much of size—how much money we have, how much money the economy contains—as velocity. It measures the movement of money through and around the economy; it measures activity. If you had taken the same ten bucks when it was first given to you and simply paid it into your bank account, well, the net position could be argued to be the same—except that the only contribution to GDP is that initial gift of ten dollars.

All this means that GDP is both indispensable as a measure of what's happening in a country and a very rough-and-ready tool. Many good things don't contribute to GDP and many bad things do. The famous-to-economists example is divorce: when people get divorced they end up paying lots of lawyers' fees. All this adds nothing to anybody's happiness except that of the lawyers, but it adds plenty to GDP. Your house has just burned down, and you've lost everything? That's too bad; on the other hand, it's great for GDP, because you're going to have to rebuild it and rebuy all your stuff. (Note that this doesn't include assets that already exist, such as houses: buying a house doesn't add to GDP, but spending money on renovating one does.)

That's not the end of the problems with GDP. The figures are approximate, and change over time, as more data come in; they keep being revised not just for months but for years. At a time like the current moment, when incomes are staying flat, taxes are rising, benefits are being cut, and inflation is eroding incomes, many people are having a steadily lower standard of living—in fact, the steepest contraction in standard of living for decades. That fact doesn't show up at all in GDP figures. To get a rounded picture of a society's condition, you need to use other criteria as well as GDP; though it is still, in a rough-guess way, the most important and revealing number about a society's economic state.

GDP per capita The total GDP of a country divided by the number of people in the country. It is a measure of how rich the country's citizens are on average—though it is a very very rough measure of that, since a country's wealth is often very unevenly distributed. Also, a country's population could be rising sharply so that its GDP in total is going up even as each individual citizen is becoming poorer. The list of countries in order of total GDP and GDP per capita is interestingly different. Data are from the IMF for 2012, adjusted for purchasing power parity (which is why it's different from the G8 list above):

GDP per capita	GDP total
1. Qatar	1. EU
2. Luxembourg	2. USA
3. Singapore	3. China
4. Norway	4. Japan
5. Brunei	5. Germany
6. Hong Kong	6. France
7. United States	7. UK
8. United Arab Emirates	8. Brazil
9. Switzerland	9. Russia
10. Canada	10. Italy
11. Australia	11. India
12. Austria	12. Canada

Speaking purely for myself, quite a few places high on the left-hand list are places I have no desire to live, which probably reflects the fact that the per capita GDP figures are skewed towards small countries that either are rich in resources or are tax havens.

Gini coefficient A numeric technique for measuring a society's inequality. It's used to measure income inequality in particular. A Gini coefficient of 0 would mean perfect equality, in which everyone had the same income; a Gini coefficient of 1 would be perfect inequality, in which one person had all the money and everybody else had nothing. Here are the top ten least-equal countries in the world, as measured by the CIA, with the most unequal at the top:[39]

1. Lesotho
2. South Africa
3. Botswana
4. Sierra Leone
5. Central African Republic
6. Namibia
7. Haiti
8. Colombia
9. Honduras
10. Guatemala

And here are the top ten most equal, with the most equal at the bottom:

10. Finland
9. Austria
8. Slovakia
7. Luxembourg
6. Norway
5. Denmark
4. Hungary
3. Montenegro
2. Slovenia
1. Sweden

In this list the UK comes in at number 60 out of 136—remember, a lower Gini is better—and the USA at number 41. It's important to note, though, that the UK number used here is from 2008, and since then the UK Gini number has gone downwards, i.e., it's improved, because the impact of the Great Recession has made the country more equal. This in turn points to one of the problems of measuring inequality: an unemployed person getting a job can increase statistical inequality, whereas an employed person being fired can increase it. This means it's a fairly rough mathematical tool; still, at least for comparing societies with each other, and a society's broad direction of travel, it's a useful one.

Note that although people sometimes write Gini as GINI, as if it was an acronym—I must admit I thought it was an acronym, standing for something like General Income Noncorrelation Index—he was actually a dude, the Italian economist Corrado Gini, who published the coefficient in a 1912 paper. Embarrassingly, Gini turned into an ardent fascist, author of "The Scientific Basis of Fascism."[40]

Glass-Steagall The generally used name for the law passed in the United States in 1933 that separated commercial or retail banking (which deals with the kind of banking activity that takes deposits) from investment banking (which invests in securities and makes bets on behalf of itself and its customers). The relevant parts of the law were repealed, after decades of lobbying from the banks, in 1999. People often speak of Glass-Steagall as a magic formula for making banks safe, but it's worth emphasizing that the distinction between the two kinds of banking had been steadily eroded to the point where it was barely functioning. Also, many banks that did not breach the line between retail and investment banking went broke, and had to be bailed out; Lehman Brothers, which almost brought down the global financial system, had no customer deposits. Still, the United States had very rocky banks before Glass-Steagall was brought in, and has had very rocky banks since Glass-Steagall was repealed, so maybe it's right to draw the obvious conclusion—that the period when Glass-Stegall was in force was safer for banks.

GDP world The total GDP of the world—so that would be all the economic activity on Earth—is $71,830 billion, or $71.83 trillion. This is according to the CIA, so it must be true.[41]

Note that the number adjusted for purchasing power parity is $83,120 billion. Planetary GDP per capita is $12,700, the unemployment rate is 8 percent, the employment balance is 35.3 percent work in agriculture, 22.7 percent in industry, and 42 percent in everything else, or, in economist-speak, "services." The world's total burden of debt, government and personal and corporate all added together, is 313 percent, or $223.3 trillion. That means our planet has the equivalent of a mortgage three times its income.

GFC A term that seems to be used mainly in Australia, but is so useful that it ought to have caught on more widely: it means Global Financial Crisis. The English-language Chinese newspapers call it the Western Financial Crisis, which is a bit cheeky of them.

gold The metal has been mined since the days of King Croesus in Lydia ca. 550 BC—hence, "rich as Croesus." It has been used as a currency and source of value ever after, despite or because of the fact that it has almost no practical use or value in itself. The exception, amusingly, is in the most modern industry of all, technology: for the first time in history, we actually have a practical use for gold. It's been estimated that about 12 percent of the world's gold is in use in electronics. (The other place where it has a practical use is in Vietnam, where all property purchases are made in gold.) Gold does not tarnish, is portable but satisfyingly heavy, looks attractive, is fungible or easily interchangable, and is very hard to mine—that's a virtue, for a currency, because it means there's no easy way for someone to find loads of it and make the value decline. All the gold in the world would fit in a cube roughly twenty meters on each side. Those reasons add together to make gold historically the most popular underpinning for coinage and thence for paper money and modern currencies. Gold hasn't played this role globally since 1971, when President Nixon ended the Bretton Woods system, in which the US dollar was underpinned by gold reserves and linked to foreign currencies through fixed exchange rates. The value of gold sharply declined after that, losing two-thirds of its value, but in the noughties, as global uncertainties rose, gold had an extraordinary ten years, surging in price from $271 an ounce in 2001 to a peak of more than $1,800 in 2011. The explanation for that is that "gold is where money goes when it's scared." That makes no sense at all, really, because gold has no actual innate value, but for about a decade it did seem to be true—though it again lost a quarter of its value around the end of 2013, and as of February 2014 was trading at $1,250.

My personal favorite fact about gold is that because it takes extraordinarily strong forces to make it, all the gold in the universe comes from the inside of exploding supernovas or, according to a new theory, from inside colliding neutron stars. Either way—awesome.

gold bugs Investors obsessed by gold. They often think that gold is the only legitimate source of value for a currency, as well as the only truly safe investment. In the world of money, the general view of gold bugs is that they are nuts.

gold standard A historical link between the value of currencies and the government's store of gold. It had a long run as an idea. Although the link between paper currency and gold was abandoned almost everywhere, the US dollar had its value underpinned by gold reserves until 1971; since most currencies were in turn pegged to the US dollar, gold kept its role at the center of the global economic system until that point.

governance A term used in the world of money as a blanket euphemism for everything concerning competence and corruption. "There are concerns about governance" means, "They are thieves and/or idiots." For anyone interested in the full ramifications of this question, I recommend a look at the work of Transparency International, which publishes an annual list of countries in descending order of perceived corruption.[42] The UK comes in at 14 and the United States at 19: the Scandinavians and New Zealanders stand at the top.

Graham, Ben (1894–1976) An important figure in the history of investing, who wrote what many people regard as the single best book of practical investment advice, *The Intelligent Investor*. He made a big fortune for himself by following his own advice. The partnership in which he did that was in Warren Buffet's judgment the first hedge fund. (There is a not very interesting argument about who created the first hedge fund—though as I write that, it occurs to me that there is a not very interesting argument about pretty much everything, when it comes to the question of who did it first. Maybe we should just ban arguments about who did something first. Warren Buffett, though, worked for Graham and has said that Graham's hedge fund was the first he knows of, on the basis that it paid a percentage of profits and used "long-short" investment techniques, i.e., betting both on things going up and on things going down. I say elsewhere that Alfred Winslow Jones created the first hedge fund, but wanted to note that Buffett thought the credit should go to his mentor.)

The most important piece of Graham's strategy was always to look for a "margin of safety" in investment. He took investment seriously, which might sound banal, given that people had been investing for hundreds of years before his first book, *Security Analysis*, came out in 1934; but Graham applied a methodical and quantitative approach to investing that was new and, in its day, shockingly scientific. In fact, any amateur investors inclined to take a punt on the basis of their intuitions—their observation that Target was busy this morning, their liking for shiny things made by Apple, their feeling that drug companies must be a good bet because we're all getting older or their sense that Martha Stewart Living Omnimedia is worth a go because of something somebody said in the gym—all these investors will find Graham shocking to this day. To all of them, Graham would have said that they aren't investors at all but speculators. An investor acts not on intuition but on rational analysis and number crunching, with the goal of finding businesses that will protect the money you've invested and pay you a reliable return. If you aren't doing the analysis and finding businesses that fit those two criteria, you're speculating—in other words, gambling.

Graham had a number of quantitative techniques for establishing the safety of the money he was investing, and all of them rely not at all on sentiment and hunch but entirely on looking at the company's books and seeing the level of debt, earnings, and value of any current assets. As he said himself, "If you were to distill the secret of sound investment into three words, we venture the motto, MARGIN OF SAFETY."[43] The ideal investment for Graham had little or no debt, and a built-in margin in the form of assets that were worth more than the figure for which the company was trading in the markets. So the "intrinsic value" of the company—the worth of all the bits added together—was higher than its price. This meant that if everything went wrong and the company collapsed, and had to be sold off as separate components like a chopped-up stolen car, the investor would still turn a profit.

An investor who applied this technique precisely and consistently would be guaranteed not to lose money. That's always assuming she was making investments on the basis of accurate information, which unfortunately isn't an assumption that we can safely make. The corporate scandals and disasters of recent years have made it clear that you can't give blanket across-the-board trust to any company data, even where you'd have thought it was most reliable, in the case of high-visibility, large-capitalization public companies. One of the things I've been doing since I began taking an interest in the world of money is ask people involved in that world what they do with their own money. My question in essence is whether they do the things we civilians are advised to do, in respect of pensions and equity investments and the like. I reckon I've asked forty or so finance professionals this, and I haven't yet met a single one who follows the advice given to civilians. Their reasons for not doing so are always twofold, and always the same: they say (a) the fees charged are too high, and (b) you can't really tell what's going on inside these companies. Graham was well aware of this problem, though I still think he'd have been shocked by the fact that it is still with us, and on such a large scale. He was the dominant intellectual influence on Warren Buffett, who studied under him at Columbia University and then went to work for him.

Greater Fool theory A manifestly daft idea that occasionally lets some people make money before then costing a lot more people a lot more money. It is the opposite of investing in fundamentals. In Greater Fool theory, an investor buys something—shares, a house—knowing that the price is unjustifiably high, but not caring, because he is sure that the price of the thing is going up. He lets it go up for a bit, then sells it to the next idiot: the Greater Fool. The idea is that it doesn't matter what the underlying realities are, just as long as there's a Greater Fool down the line. This is a reckless strategy, for the obvious reason that at some point the price is going to stop going up; but it is very difficult thing to resist the momentum of a rising market, especially when everyone around you is coining it. Isaac Newton, who has a claim to be the most intelligent person ever to have lived, and who knew a lot about the operation of money thanks to his day job as master of the King's Mint, himself fell victim to the Greater Fool theory. When the South Sea bubble came along, Newton could see it was based on nothing and was certain to collapse; it was certain to collapse; it was certain to . . . oh, the hell with it, since everyone else was making to much money, he piled in too. Then the bubble collapsed, and he lost all his money. The moral of the story is (a) that it's hard even for very bright people to hold their nerve during a bubble and (b) that the temptations of Greater Fool theory are strong, and should be resisted.

Grexit The hypothetical exit of Greece from the euro zone.

growth An increase in GDP. The great thing about growth is that it allows governments to meet rising expectations in all areas while also keeping taxes stable. No, low, or negative growth means it can't do those things, and will have difficulties meeting its promises both to its own citizens and to the people who have lent it money.

haircut A term from the world of investment bonds. It means that the people who have lent money to a company or government—the bondholders—aren't going to get all their money back. A haircut is usually part of a restructuring of debt, in which the agreed timetable for paying back money is also changed. I've noticed that people in the world of money quite like the casually macho feel of "haircut"—"I'm not saying there won't be a haircut, but they'll lose like a hundred million, tops." It took me some time to understand the metaphor behind haircut, but I get it now: it's not like going to a fancy salon to have your hair done: it's a standard, one-size-fits all army-type haircut. The idea is that everyone loses the same amount of hair/money.

hawk A term often used in regard to inflation. An inflation hawk is someone who is sharply on the lookout for signs of inflation, and is at any moment likely to announce that interest rates should be raised to keep inflation down. Quantitative easing gives inflation hawks the conniptions. The opposite of a hawk is a dove.

Hayek, Friedrich (1899–1992) An Austrian-born philosopher and economist who was one of the driving forces behind the rise of neoliberal economics in Britain and America. His book *The Road to Serfdom*, first published during the Second World War, had a strong impact: it argued that state planning and intervention in the economy had over time an inevitably negative effect on individual liberties. Central planning, in Hayek's view, led inexorably towards totalitarianism. Hayek was an interesting thinker whose works are still readable today, and are more subtle and inflected than one might think from the cartoon version that was adopted by the political right. I sometimes think that Hayek was taken up by the right not because his ideas influenced their thinking (which is what people tend to say—Margaret Thatcher claimed to have read him while still at school) but because he provided a rationale for things they wanted to do anyway: cut spending and shrink the state. He was an important economist too, and won the Nobel Prize in 1974; he was particularly interested in the question of how people make choices.

high-frequency trading This practice is, to use a technical term, some seriously scary shit. Its origins lie in the fact that a big part of what financial institutions do is try to make money in ways that are guaranteed to succeed. Not probable, or likely, but guaranteed. This is an old theme in the history of money, roughly equivalent to the search for the philosopher's stone that would turn base metals into gold: the quest for a technique to make money that is without risk. In pursuit of that goal, some companies have turned to light-speed trading: a mixture of computer equipment and proprietary mathematical techniques, used to buy and sell equities not just within minutes, or within seconds, or within fractions of seconds, but within microseconds. It seems that in many cases these banks are also executing orders for clients, and therefore have information about the flow of orders that are passing through the market.

Their algorithms sniff out these trades, buy some shares, and sell them microseconds later for a tiny but guaranteed profit; repeated with sufficient frequency and sufficient volume, this makes them a lot of money. More than half of all the equity trading in the United States is high-frequency trading: that means most of the market is buying and selling not by people but by computer programs.

To succeed, these techniques depend on speed. To get that speed, traders build ever bigger computers, ever closer to the exchanges where the trades are executed; they compete for ever more direct cable routes between trading locations. The route between the commodities exchange in Chicago and the stock exchange in Wall Street offers an example: firms using proprietary cable have managed to shave the time for an order to go back and forth between the two cities from a laggardly 14.4 milliseconds using bog standard cable to a profitable 8.5 milliseconds using proprietary techniques involving microwaves. That means making money in the gap between 0.014 and 0.008 seconds. There's also a race to lay more direct cable between New York and London, all in pursuit of the same guaranteed profit.

The alarming thing about high-frequency trading is that nobody really understands it. The mathematical techniques involved are secret. History suggests that there are risks in the fact that many of the tricks involved are likely to do the same thing in the same way, and therefore be prone to dramatically exaggerating movements in the markets—remember, equity markets now mainly consist of this kind of trading. It was computer-based portfolio insurance—computer programs all doing the same thing at the same time—that caused the Wall Street crash of October 1987. It seems to have been high-frequency trading that caused the "flash crash" of 6 May 2011, in which the US stock market fell by more than 10 percent and lost $1 trillion of value in less than twenty minutes. But the causes of the flash crash are still not really understood. That, right there, is really alarming.[44]

HNWI High net worth individual, a reference to a rich person as defined by the financial services industry. The definition is fixed: it means he or she has more than a million dollars in financial assets—meaning assets other than their "residences, collectables, consumer durables and consumables." Globally, there are 11 million people in that category, with a total worth of $42 trillion. This way of defining a rich person is of use to people in the money business, who are on the lookout for individuals to advise—hence the emphasis on financial assets. You can have a house worth $10 million but not be an HNWI. An UNHWI is an ultra-high net worth individual, meaning more than $30 million in financial assets. According to the World Wealth Report, the USA has 3.44 million HNWI.[45]

holes in the balance sheet A strange metaphor, evoking the annoying ripped bit where your big toe accidentally went through the top sheet, whereas what it actually means is that some of the stuff listed on a bank's books as its assets are worth less than the balance sheet says they are. Balance sheets are very uninformative about what assets actually are, and just say things like "customer loans." Loans to do what, though? Buy houses? Start businesses? Make into mounds of cash that are then used as comfortable soft furnishings? What? If some of these assets aren't worth what they're supposed to be worth, the bank lending the money has a hole in its balance sheet. At the moment the European Central Bank is carrying out an "asset quality review" to go around the European banks and study the quality of their assets, on the lookout for exactly these kinds of holes. The smart money says they are going to find lots of them, and the real question is what they'll do next.

hollowing out An important phenomenon in the modern world. A private equity guy once told me how it's done: "You get some capital together and buy a company in Germany that makes machine parts. Then you close the factory and move the manufacturing to China, where the quality control maybe isn't as good but it costs a tenth as much to make, and because you still own the brand and control the distribution network, none of your customers will notice." That is hollowing out: the process by which jobs disappear from an economy while external appearances remain largely the same. Whole sectors of the economy have been hollowed out by the Internet and by outsourcing abroad. There's a very good description of it in Jaron Lanier's book *Who Owns the Future?*:

> At the height of its power, the photography company Kodak employed more than 140,000 people and was worth $28 billion. They even invented the first digital camera. But today Kodak is bankrupt, and the new face of digital photography has become Instagram. When Instagram was sold to Facebook for a billion dollars in 2012, it employed only thirteen people. Where did all those jobs disappear to? And what happened to the wealth that all those middle-class jobs created? [46]

One of the places where hollowing out can be seen most clearly is in the English countryside. I was in a pretty corner of Sussex last summer, outside a village photogenic enough to be the backdrop of a TV murder mystery, passing through a landscape that looked as if it had been unchanged for two hundred years—all while the friend with me, who lives there full-time, explained that the image of stability and continuity was entirely illusory. The larger houses were lived in by hedge funders who spend three nights a week in London, the smaller houses by City workers who commute, and the fields that once provided the livelihood for hundreds of people, once the raison d'être of the village, now employed one person full-time, and were owned and rented out by a hedge fund manager. The picture was more or less the same; the underlying reality was wholly different. That's hollowing out.

hot money Money that moves around the world in search of profit, irrespective of all other considerations. Last week, commodities; this week, London property; next week, Nigerian banks. The sudden movement of hot money has been a crucial factor in every national economic crisis of the last twenty-odd years—the Mexican and Asian and Russian meltdowns of the nineties, the Icelandic and Spanish and Irish crises of the noughties, and so on. As the world economy has gradually opened up and deregulated and grown more interconnected, hot money has become an increasingly prominent feature of its operations. It's an important item of faith in mainstream economics that the completely free movement of capital benefits everybody, and the system is certainly designed to act on that faith: international movements of capital have grown from about 60 percent of GDP to more than 450 percent in the last twenty years. The trouble is that while the downsides of the rapid movement of hot money are clear when a crisis hits, nobody has been able to prove a clear benefit to the ordinary citizen of this free flow across borders of multiple trillions of dollars. It's also the case that the country whose economy has grown more rapidly and more sustainedly and has transformed more lives than any other, China, doesn't permit the free flow of capital across its borders.

hot waitress index One of several fanciful techniques for predicting the direction of the economy. Some of them are genuine attempts at working out which way things are going by looking at wider social trends: one of them is the idea that skirts get shorter during boom times, presumably because people feel frisky. Some of them are so obvious they hardly need stating: the better the economy in an area is doing, the harder it is to find a taxi, or the more cranes you see when you look out the window. Well, duh. The hot waitress index is a joking variation on that: it suggests that the better an economy is doing, good-looking women get better and better work—what the girls in Lena Dunham's *Girls* refer to as "pretty girl jobs," as gallery receptionists and suchlike. When times are harder, the girls who would otherwise get pretty girl jobs instead end up working as waitresses. So the worse the economy is doing, the hotter the waitresses.

hype cycle A term coined by the research firm Gartner to describe the process in which a new invention or technology is hugely hyped when it arrives; then found not to live up to the hype; then, when the hype has quieted down and you're no longer hearing so much about it, the thing gradually starts getting better and begins to do the things it was supposed to do when it was first hyped. The general rule is that things start getting genuinely useful some time after you stop hearing about them.[47]

hyperinflation The terrifying phenomenon when inflation gets out of control. The most famous example was Germany after the First World War: In 1914, the German mark had stood at 4.2 to the dollar; by the start of 1922, it was 190 to the dollar; by the end of the year, it was 7,600. By November 1923, a dollar was worth 630 billion marks, a loaf of bread cost 140 billion marks, and Germany was disintegrating under the strain. The result was the destruction of German society as it was then constituted, which led directly to the rise of the Nazis—a history that needs to be borne in mind whenever it seems the Germans are being a bit uptight about holding the line against inflation in the euro zone.

IMF The International Monetary Fund. This is the organization, created by the Bretton Woods agreement, that takes money from member countries and disburses it to countries in need of a cash injection, always with strict conditions attached. The IMF insists on sharp crackdowns on public spending, removing price controls, privatizing state-owned businesses, and liberalizing trade. To countries on the receiving end of this process, it sometimes seems as if the IMF imposes an off-the-shelf kit of solutions regardless of local history and difficulty and circumstance. The first country ever to receive one of these IMF bailouts was the UK, in 1976, when it was given a loan of £2.3 billion. The IMF also has a supervisory role overlooking the world financial system, and issues reports on the health of countries' economies. If it's going to make an unfavorable report, countries go into overdrive to lobby the IMF to dilute any criticisms—British officials are especially well known for that. One way of looking at the IMF is to see it as the global financial bad cop, whereas the World Bank is the cuddly hippies handing out loans for development projects.

immigration A hotly contested issue in politics, but not so much in economics. The birthrate in the developed world, especially Europe, is too low. The next generation of taxpayers, who will pay the bills for all the health and pension costs incurred by people now coming up to retirement age, aren't being born in sufficient numbers. The "replacement rate," i.e., the rate of childbirths needed to sustain a population at its current level, is 2.1 per woman. (It's higher in the developing world because more children die.) The birthrate in the EU is 1.59, a dramatically lower rate than that in the United States, where the number is 1.89. That's a big shortfall. Since the next generation of taxpayers are not being born, they will have to be imported: that is why the Western world needs high and sustained levels of immigration. We could have lower immigration, but that would mean ending the welfare state in its current form.[48]

Politicians have a duty to explain this reality, which is not going to go away. The problem in countries with high levels of immigration is that the benefits of the immigration come in the medium and long term, but the problems it brings come in the short term. A small town that suddenly has a population of multiple thousands of immigrants and no corresponding increase in funding to the relevant services can find that it has real difficulties with access to schools, health care, and housing. Government at the national level is far too slow to respond to the immediate needs of communities affected by immigration in this way. The long-term benefits of immigration are general; the short-term costs are local. It should not be beyond the competence of governments to address that discrepancy.

inflation The process by which things gain in price over time. To put it differently, it is the process by which money loses value over time. Inflation is a much studied and much argued-over subject in economics, but, amusingly for noneconomists, there is no settled consensus around the question of what causes it. (In the Middle Ages and early modern period, when there was no understanding of inflation as a process, people came up with all kinds of wild speculation about rising prices, blaming profiteers, the king's evil counselors, witchcraft, the Jews.) There is, however, consensus that a degree of inflation is a good thing, because it gives some wiggle room to adjust growth by means of interest rates: if inflation is nonexistent and interest rates have already been cut, then the government has no obvious way of stimulating growth. For this reason, the inflation target in the USA and the UK is 2 percent and in the euro area the target is "close to but below 2 percent," the idea being that this confers stability in prices without the risk of deflation. Higher inflation than that is problematic for reasons that are clear from history and were accurately predicted by John Maynard Keynes, in his critical account of the Versailles treaty:

> By a continuing process of inflation, Governments can confiscate, secretly and unobserved, an important part of the wealth of their citizens. By this method they not only confiscate, but they confiscate *arbitrarily*; and, while the process impoverishes many, it actually enriches some. The sight

of this arbitrary rearrangement of riches strikes not only at security, but at confidence in the equity of the existing distribution of wealth. Those to whom the system brings windfalls, beyond their deserts and even beyond their expectations or desires, become "profiteers," who are the object of the hatred of the bourgeoisie, whom the inflationism has impoverished, not less than of the proletariat. As the inflation proceeds and the real value of the currency fluctuates wildly from month to month, all permanent relations between debtors and creditors, which form the ultimate foundation of capitalism, become so utterly disordered as to be almost meaningless; and the process of wealth-getting degenerates into a gamble and a lottery.

Lenin was certainly right. There is no subtler, no surer means of overturning the existing basis of Society than to debauch the currency. The process engages all the hidden forces of economic law on the side of destruction, and does it in a manner which not one man in a million is able to diagnose.[49]

That was exactly the process that destroyed Weimar democracy and helped Hitler grab power. Governments have to pretend to hate inflation because it eats into the wealth of its citizens, but at the moment many indebted governments would secretly like the rate to be higher, because it would diminish the real value of the amounts they owe—remember, inflation makes money worth less, including the cash value of debts. For some time now, cynical observers have thought that the likeliest outcome of the Western world's debt problems would be a rise in the rate of inflation.

infrastructure Transport, power, telecoms, water supplies, sewers, and all that good stuff: the basic physical structure of a nation. It is one of the areas that the USA has underinvested in during recent decades.

insolvent The term means your liabilities are greater than your assets, and/or you don't have enough cash to meet your immediate debts. It is illegal to trade while insolvent.

insurance A great idea—but it is distressing how often, in its real-life manifestations, it turns out to be a scam dependent on the customer's not having read the small print. My learning moment in respect of this involved a burst pipe that I thought was insured; it turned out that the water damage was insured but the broken pipe wasn't, so more than 80 percent of the cost was uncovered. So now I read the small print. Once you start doing that you become more cynical about insurance. I was recently looking at mobile phone insurance that claims to cover loss or theft. The small print says that the insurance does not cover situations in which the phone is "left unattended" or "left in a public place," and in relation to theft the usual wording goes something like this: "Theft from the person is not covered unless force or threat of violence is used. Theft whilst in any form of public transport or public place is not covered unless force or threatened force is used." In other words, if you lose it or have it stolen in any of the normal understandings of those terms—i.e., you go out with your phone, and come home without it, and don't know what happened in the interim—you're screwed.

It would be wonderful to live in a world where we don't have to read the small print. Instead we live in this world. Read the small print.

interest rates If I had to pick one term that summed up my reason for wanting to write this book, it would be "interest rates." I must have heard interest rates mentioned in the news thousands of times before I found out why they were so important. When the financially literate talk about interest rates, they're bringing to bear a whole set of linked ideas about inflation, unemployment, the cost of borrowing, the exchange rate, the political impact of rising mortgages, the conditions of trade for business, the price of exports, the balance of payments, and the growth or contraction of the economy—all packed into two words, "interest rates." Blink, and all the ideas packed into these two words have gone zooming past. To people who don't speak finance, the language can seem impenetrable and the interlocking ideas too complex to be grasped or unpacked at the necessary speed.

The reason interest rates matter so much is that the interest rate is the cost of money at any given moment. It's also the rate at which it is possible to invest risk-free, because you can buy a government bond at the prevalent interest rate, and it's guaranteed to pay you back. This means that when interest rates go up,

1. life is harder for businesses, because money is more expensive, and
2. people will tend not to invest in companies, preferring to invest in risk-free bonds, and
3. the stock market will fall for that reason, so
4. confidence in general will fall. In addition,
5. people with mortgages will find it harder to make their repayments, and those who are coming off fixed-rate deals may suddenly see a dramatic increase in their monthly repayments.
6. That means mortgage defaults will rise, so
7. there will be downward pressure on house prices, and
8. some people will be in negative equity, which will stop them from spending money,
9. the currency will rise, because higher guaranteed rates of investment will attract money into buying the country's debt, so
10. life will become harder for manufacturing businesses, because their exports will be more expensive. Also,
11. inflation will fall—remember, inflation means that money is

worth less, whereas a rise in interest rates means that money is more expensive.

There's more, too, but these eleven things provide a starting point for all the things that are completely taken for granted by people who speak money when they hear "interest rates."

interest rate swaps Financial techniques in which two parties do what it says on the tin: they swap interest rates. The most common example is when A has a floating interest rate and B has a fixed rate, and they both, for their differing reasons, would prefer to be on the other kind of deal. So they enter into a contract where A pays B's interest rate, and B pays A's. Much of this action is between sophisticated market players who are betting on their judgment about the movement in rates; some of it is a form of hedging, of complex calculations designed to set off against each other and minimize risks about the movement of interest rates. Unfortunately some of these swaps were mis-sold by banks, with the effect of severely damaging small businesses that didn't know what they were getting into and thought they were reducing their risks. Instead they were locking themselves into unfavorable deals that were ruinously expensive to undo. The UK interest rate swap scandal has attracted less attention and opprobrium than the PPI scandal, perhaps because the victims tended to be small businesses rather than individuals, but in its essential detail—banks knowingly selling customers an unsuitable product—it was the same.

inventory The amount of stuff a business has in stock. It's an entire branch of management and logistics—not the most riveting to outsiders, and management of inventory is a classic example of something that the customer notices only when it goes wrong. Cisco, the Internet hardware company, at one point earlier this century was the most valuable company in the world, until—oops!—it found it had miscalculated the value of its inventory by so much that it had to write off $2.25 billion.

investment bank A bank or part of a bank that deals in securities, i.e., shares and bonds and all other sorts of investment tools. A retail bank or commercial bank is a bank or part of a bank that takes deposits and deals with the ordinary bit of banking we all know and need: take our deposits when we have spare cash, lend us money for our mortgages or businesses or whatever when we need it. The model in which a bank does both of these things is called universal banking, which the banks like because it is profitable, though I haven't seen a single even halfway convincing argument that universal banks convey any benefit at all to the general public.

Jáchymov I bet you've indirectly referred to this place in the Czech Republic at some point in the last week; if you're interested in money you will certainly have used it at some point in the last day, maybe even in the last hour. How so? Can you guess? Give up? Well, the Bohemian town of Jáchymov is known in German as Joachimsthal—does that help? It was the site of a famous silver mine, a town that grew tenfold in population between 1516 to 1526 as it became the center of a boom based on the manufacture of a silver coin known as Joachimsthaler. It in time became known as thaler, or taler. The coins were a standard size and form of currency throughout much of Europe for four hundred years, and it's from this ubiquity that we get the word "dollar"—so every time a dollar is mentioned, someone is unknowingly citing this otherwise obscure spot in rural Bohemia.

Japan The country is often held up as a horror story, a tale of unremitting gloom and an illustration of just how badly an economy can go wrong if its underlying difficulties are not addressed. In the case of Japan, a gigantic bubble in property and other assets that built up through the eighties popped in the midnineties, and two decades later, the economy has still not recovered. A big part of this is the existence of zombie banks: banks that can't lend money and therefore can't help the economy, because they are sitting on huge amounts of worthless loans. If the banks fess up to the real value of their assets, they will have to admit that many of them aren't worth anything like their supposed value on the bank's books; they prefer to not admit anything and sit there staring at computer screens, saying, "Computer says no," every time someone tries to borrow money. So the entire economy has ground to a halt and deflation has set in, which in turn means that money gains value over time, which in turn is another reason not to spend it, which makes all the other problems worse. Thanks to deflation, the value of the currency keeps going up, which is terrible news for Japan's many manufacturing businesses. Meanwhile the government's debts mount higher and higher, since this economic slowdown reduces the tax take and forces it to borrow money to meet its obligations. The new government of Shinzo Abe is trying to tackle this problem by printing money and introducing inflation; it's a huge and very risky experiment, and it's too early to say whether or not it's going to work.

So, all this is a disaster. Except it isn't really a disaster, and life goes on, with most Japanese people continuing to have a standard of living far higher than it was in the easily rememberable past. This matters for the rest of the developed world, because with slowing growth and an aging population, the Japanese model could well be our future. Part of the strangeness of Japan is that its population is aging and shrinking; if there are fewer people, all other things being equal, GDP will drop, even if everyone is just as well off. That too is a possible glimpse of our future.

I have tried out on Japanese people the theory that with the economy flat, people, especially younger people, spend more energy and emotion on other areas of life than work, and that Japanese culture is more varied and individualistic as a result, more focused on private and internal sources of value; they tend to say, maybe.

J. P. Morgan (1837–1913) An extraordinary figure in the history of American finance, a banker of unimaginable wealth and power who saved the American economy with loans not once but twice, in the "panic of 1893" and again in the "panic of 1907." It's curious how readily we forget that bank panics and crashes have been a regular feature of American life: the lesson that banks can't be trusted to regulate their own affairs and stay solvent in the process is one that, you'd have thought, would have been very thoroughly learned by now. Morgan's financial concerns were so all-encompassing that when his bank was broken up by the Glass-Steagall Act of 1933, it turned into three different institutions, all of them very big: the bank J. P. Morgan and Co., the investment house Morgan Stanley, and the overseas investment bank Morgan Grenfell in London.

jubilee A word with a number of meanings, but in his book *Debt: The First 5,000 Years,* the anthropologist David Graeber advocates a global jubilee in the specific sense of a cancellation of all outstanding debt in the developing world.

Keynes, John Maynard (1883–1946) One of the greatest minds ever to dedicate himself to the study of money—I put it like that because although many very clever people have spent most of their lives thinking about money, it's noticeable that there haven't been many geniuses attracted to the field, minds of the order of Mozart or Einstein or Shakespeare. What stands out about Keynes is the range and depth of his thinking: profound insight into the mathematical underpinnings of economics and probability; theoretical work into economic modeling that has arguably never been matched, in what is one of the field's two most important books, *The General Theory* *of Employment, Interest and Money*; journalistic and political interventions of unparalleled trenchancy and insight, in works such as *The Economic Consequences of the Peace* and *The Economic Consequences of Mr. Churchill*; important hands-on political-economic work, including the design of the postwar economic order at the Bretton Woods agreement; and extraordinary success as an investor on both his own behalf and that of the funds he ran. Because his name turned into an adjective, he is often seen as a simple advocate of more government spending in any and all weathers, though there's a lot more to his ideas than that; it seems to be the fate of economic thinkers that they are co-opted for service on one side or another of overfamiliar political dividing lines. He said many superbly vivid things about money and economics, though it has to be admitted that his most important book, *The General Theory*, is often opaque and overcompressed.

kleptocracy A system of government characterized by theft, particularly theft by the richest and most powerful people in a society. It poses an especially big problem in the developing world, but is not confined to it. The world's top ten kleptocratic heads of state, according to the global anticorruption organization Transparency International, were (as of 2004) these:

1. Indonesia, Suharto (amount stolen, $15 billion–$35 billion)
2. Philippines, Marcos ($5 billion–$10 billion)
3. Congo, Mobutu ($5 billion)
4. Nigeria, Abacha ($2 billion–$5 billion)
5. Yugoslavia, Milošević ($1 billion)
6. Haiti, Duvalier ($300 million–$800 million)
7. Peru, Fujimori ($600 million)
8. Ukraine, Lazarenko ($114 million–$200 million)
9. Nicaragua, Aléman ($100 million)
10. Philippines, Estrada ($78 million–$80 million)

These are just the heads of state: many countries are kleptocratic in that their entire ruling class runs on theft. Also, in some countries the kleptocracy runs on the basis of legal expropriation rather than outright theft—in Russia, say. Every one of these men (all men) was a president and there are no monarchs on the list, which doesn't mean that no monarchs are kleptocrats, just that their thefts tend to be legal. The British queen's personal net worth of $500 million was accumulated in large part thanks to the exemption from income tax negotiated by King George VI in 1937. Without that, the high rate of tax after the war would have wiped out most or all of the Windsors' wealth. (This is just the queen's personal fortune, to be distinguished from the stuff that belongs to the monarchy as an institution: the Crown's estate is worth another $10 billion, Buckingham Palace $5 billion more, and the art that belongs to the nation but that the royal family treats as their property is worth maybe another $1 billion.) That wealth was not stolen in the same way that Mobutu stole his, but it was expropriated from the collective wealth through the nonpayment of tax—which is closer to a kleptocratic arrangement than to a democratic one. If we accept this line of arguing, then the number 8 spot on the list belongs to "UK, Windsor, $500 million." Just saying.[50]

Kondratiev cycle Named after Nikolai Kondratiev (1892–1938), this cycle is a long slow wavelike pattern in economics, in which a period of expansion is followed by a period of stagnation and then of collapse and recession, over a period of forty to sixty years. The industrial revolution and the arrival and impact of the railways are examples of phenomena that to some look like Kondratiev cycles. There's no real proof of the existence of these waves, and most economists don't believe in them, but they have their fans. The theory cost Kondratiev his life: his idea implied that capitalism would go through these cycles but continue, whereas official communist ideology was that capitalism would inevitably destroy itself. He was sent to the Gulag and executed by firing squad in 1938.

Laffer curve The most influential idea ever to have first arrived in the world on a cocktail napkin. Arthur Laffer (1940–) is an American economist who explained this idea to two officials in the Nixon and Ford administration in 1974. The idea was in essence that government would raise more money in tax by cutting tax rates. Laffer drew a curve that plotted tax rates against the income raised from tax. He made the point that at 0 percent tax, the government raises no money, but at 100 percent tax, again, the government raises no money, because nobody will do any work if the government confiscates all the proceeds. So the tax rate that raises the most money isn't automatically right at the top end of the scale; governments will often raise tax revenue by cutting rates of tax. As you can probably imagine, this idea is very, very popular with rich people. Reagan's administration was the first to put this theory into practice. The two officials to whom Laffer pitched the idea were Donald Rumsfeld and Dick Cheney, so it is literally the case that the same people who cooked up the second Iraq war also brought us tax cuts for the rich. To quote the napkin itself, "The consequences are obvious!"[51]

La ricchezza è una ragione A remark by an eighteenth-century Italian economist, the abbé Galiani, first brought to my attention by the writer James Buchan. "La ricchezza è una ragione tra due persone": richness is a relationship between two people. This seems to me one of the truest things ever said about money. Galiani's maxim says that richness, the idea of having plenty of money, is not an inherent state, nor is it an absolute one. Richness is about the amount of money you have compared with the people you see around you. It's about where you are in relation to others and where they are in relation to you; whether you can have the things that you see other people have. When I followed up an initial query about Galiani, Buchan wrote back that "economists are not much interested in the idea or the man." He's right, and it's surprising, because microeconomic research into how people think about money is proving that Galiani's ideas are correct. It is a consistent finding in this field that people are happier when they are richer than their neighbors even if this means they are less rich in absolute terms: people would rather earn $60,000 in a place where average earnings are $40,000 than earn $80,000 where the average is $100,000. That's because *la ricchezza è una ragione tra due persone.*

Law, John (1671–1729) An amazing figure, a swashbuckling and piratical mixture of economist and adventurer, who killed a man in a duel, was sentenced to hanging for murder, escaped and fled to the continent, became a theorist of the virtues of paper money, was made controller general of finances in Paris to help finance Louis XIV's wars, had good ideas about abolishing monopolies and private tax collection, but caused a huge speculative bubble in the Mississippi Company and almost bankrupted France. Funnily enough, the theoretical underpinnings of Law's ideas about money and the creation of national wealth are now seen as largely valid. There is a fascinating account of Law and his ideas in James Buchan's *Frozen Desire.*

leading indicators Signs of something that's about to happen, ahead of its happening. Lots of cranes on the skyline, for example, are an indicator of economic activity, because they are a sign that building is taking place—but the decisions that led to the building would have been taken some time ago, so they aren't a leading indicator, but instead are what's known as a trailing indicator. Business hiring can be a leading indicator, because it shows businesses anticipating increased demand. Business confidence is usually a leading indicator.

lender of last resort One of the most important roles played by central banks: when confidence is short and there is a credit crunch, just as there was in 2009, and nobody is lending to anybody else, the central bank steps in and lends money to keep the system running.

leverage The term, as I mentioned in Part I, has a number of different meanings in finance and is used differently in different contexts. The one highest on the political agenda at the moment is the kind of leverage used in banking.

In banking "leverage" is used in a particular sense. Consider a standard balance sheet, with assets on one side and liabilities plus equity on the other. Here "leverage" means the multiple of assets over equity: the amount by which what you have lent exceeds what you straightforwardly own. It is expressed as a ratio or as a percentage: a bank with an equity ratio of 20 has an equity level of 5 percent. The big banks have alarmingly low equity ratios, and critics of their current condition are focusing on this as a vital issue for bank safety. An important recent book by Anat Admati and Martin Hellwig, *The Bankers' New Clothes: What's Wrong with Banking and What to Do about It*, argues for much higher levels of bank equity as the simplest, quickest, most practical, and safest way of reducing bank risks to the rest of the economy. Deutsche Bank, for instance, the biggest bank in Europe, in July 2013 had assets of more than €2 trillion but an equity ratio of only 1.63 percent. Not long afterwards the bank announced that it was going to shrink its balance sheet, and hence improve its equity position, by a fifth. Let's hope that's enough. There are lots of more complex ways of calculating bank capital, but Admati and Hellwig are convincing in their argument that this simplest of them is also the best. The Basel III rules on banks are seeking a global leverage level of 3 percent, which to many observers, including this one, doesn't seem high enough.

lex monetae The legal principle by which a country chooses the denomination of its own debts and liabilities. This can come into play in a big way if a country leaves the euro. In that eventuality the country would be certain to switch the denomination of its liabilities to the new currency—say, in the event of Greece, switching from the euro to the new drachma. The principle of *lex monetae* states that creditors who owned Greek debt would have no choice but to accept payment in new drachma—so the words *lex monetae* are really just a polite Latin way of saying, "Suck it, creditors." The complicating factor, though, is that there are very many legal contracts denominated in euro but set out in other jurisdictions, and it isn't clear whether the courts will accept the principle of *lex monetae*. Will a German court, supervising a German contract between a German company and a Greek counterparty, a contract unambiguously stating that payment is in euro, accept payment in new drachma? This is one of the problems with the creation of a currency area that has no exit mechanism, i.e., the euro zone, and it has the potential to be a biggie.

Libor The London Interbank Offer Rate is or was the single most important number in international financial markets, used as a reference point throughout the global financial system. Libor is the range of interbank lending rates, set after consultation between the British Bankers Association and more than three hundred participating banks. During the daily process, each bank is asked the rate at which it could borrow money from other banks, "unsecured," in other words backed only by its own creditworthiness rather than by specific collateral. The banks are asked, in effect, what would your credit be like today, if you had to ask? During the credit crunch, the *if* aspect of Libor became overpoweringly apparent, since the salient fact about the interbank market was that banks were refusing to lend money to each other. That, in essence, was what the credit crunch was—banks being too scared to lend to each other. In the very dry words of Mervyn King, the then governor of the Bank of England, Libor became "in many ways the rate at which banks do not lend to each other." Euribor, the euro version of Libor, is at the moment even worse, since in very many cases these banks would be more likely to voluntarily turn themselves into lap-dancing clubs rather than make unsecured loans to each other. The rates are largely fictional—and not realist fiction.

It seems bizarre that something so central to the global markets—$360 trillion of deals are pinned to the Libor rate—should have such a strong element of invention or guesswork. The potential for abuse is obvious. Since lots of money can be made betting on movements in these rates, and since the banks help to set the rates, surely it would be very easy to, you know, make a big bet on their movement, and then give the rate a little nudge. . . . The entire banking industry said that it was shocked, shocked at the thought that anyone could consider this kind of behavior a possibility. After the credit crunch, when investigators started taking an energetic interest in Libor, it turned out that this was exactly what had been happening, not just at one or two banks but across an entire swath of the industry. "This dwarfs by orders of magnitude any financial scam in the history of the markets," said a finance professor at MIT. Mervyn King maintained that the bankers involved were guilty of criminal fraud. From this perspective, the important fact about Libor is that while the rate is controlled by the British Bankers Association, it is widely used, indeed is omnipresent, within the US financial system. So manipulation of Libor is a crime not just in the finance-friendly City of London but also in the eyes of US law enforcement. That has profoundly changed the mood music, and the resources devoted to investigating wrongdoing. If Libor had been of relevance only within the UK, the same actions could have taken place in the same institutions, and my suspicion is that we wouldn't have heard a word about it.

The full scorecard from the Libor scandal isn't yet in plain sight: we're somewhere in the middle of the story, and there will be more news, more revelations, and more settlements to come. In June 2012, Barclays paid £59.5 million in fines to the Financial Services Authority (FSA), $160 million to the US Department of Justice (DoJ), and $200 million to the US Commodities Futures Trading Commission (CFTC), making a nice round total of about £290 million. (It's worth pausing for a moment to register the full magnitude of that: from one single bank, more than a quarter of a billion quid in fines.) Its chairman, Marcus Agius, and chief executive, Bob Diamond, both resigned. In December the Swiss bank UBS agreed to pay $1.2 billion to the DoJ and the CFTC, £160 million to the FSA, and 59 million in Swiss francs to the regulators back in the old country. Total, £970 million, from a bank that had already lost £1.4 billion thanks to Kweku Abodoli and another £500 million in fines to the US authorities for helping rich Americans dodge their taxes. In February 2014, RBS was next up. It paid $325 million to the CFTC, $150 million to the DoJ, and £87.5 million to the FSA, total about £390 million.

Deutsche Bank, Citigroup, Credit Suisse, and JPMorgan Chase, four of the biggest banks in the world, are under investigation, along with many of their peers, and the bodies pursuing them include not just the DoJ, CTFC, and FSA but also a variety of US state-level attorneys general. There may be even worse news ahead for the banks, because these settlements represent only the criminal and statutory fines leveled against them. Libor reaches so deeply into the financial system that the fact of its manipulation opens not a can but an entire universe of legal worms. If people out there can prove that they lost money because of manipulation of Libor, the scandal is going to get dramatically more expensive. The bad news, as the cases wend through the US legal system, could keep coming for years.

life expectancy The source of extraordinary progress in the developed world: we're all living longer. A utilitarian, who defines the best outcome as the one that maximizes the happiness of the greatest number of people, would say that nothing can matter more than more people living longer in good health. Following on from that, you could argue not only that it's the most important thing to have changed in our society but, at the philosophical level, that it isn't possible for anything to be more important. While many of the most striking economic statistics come from the developing world, where there is most room for improvement and progress, progress in relation to life expectancy is an exception; societies that were already, by global standards, rich have undergone a remarkable extension in life expectancy in recent decades. Two years have been added to US life expectancy in the last decade, taking it from 76.8 years at birth to 78.7. Since the population is in other respects less healthy—measurably fatter and more sedentary and more prone to the associated diseases—this has to rank as a triumph of medicine. We have better diagnosis, better medicine, and better access to medicine; and, perhaps equally important, we smoke less. The rate of deaths from heart disease has dropped by more than 40 percent.

There are some real oddities in the statistics. Deaths from "unintended injuries" have gone up by more than 10 percent, even though motor vehicle–related deaths, the most important type of accidental death, have fallen by more than a third—what's that about?

This is great news all around, but there is a caveat, in that the increase in life expectancy trashes the assumption that states have made about the cost of looking after their aging populations. Pension and health care projections are, not to put too fine a point on it, wrong, in ways that governments are going to find it extremely difficult and unpopular to address.[52]

limited liability The invention whereby the existence of a company sets a limit on how much money investors can lose. When the company loses all its money, it goes broke; before limited liability, the investors in the company would then be personally liable for any outstanding debts, and could end up bankrupt. The invention of limited liability was central to the creation of the joint stock company, which is the basis of modern capitalism: the company is a legal entity, like a person, in which shareholders have shares and exercise control in proportion to the number of shares they own. You can have a company without having limited liability; in the United States, a joint stock company in its modern sense is just that. In the UK, this structure is called unlimited liability. It obviously makes the shareholders a lot more careful, since they are on the hook for all losses, not just the losses up to the point where the company goes broke. One of the quick fixes sometimes suggested for the excessive risks in modern banking is to make the banks unlimited liability partnerships. That wouldn't work for retail banking, where there is a strong social interest in keeping banks lending, but it might be a viable structure for investment banks, and would certainly make their risks more in line with their rewards. The British bank C. Hoare and Co. is unusual in being an unlimited liability bank, wholly owned by one family.

London Whale The nickname of Bruno Iksil, the trader at J. P. Morgan's London branch who was paid $7.32 million in 2010 and $6.76 million in 2011, and then in 2012 lost $6.2 billion betting on credit default swaps. The first response of Jamie Dimon, chairman and CEO of J. P. Morgan, was to describe the affair as "a tempest in a teacup," until the scale of the losses became apparent. The thing that's interesting about his nickname is that "whale" is a term from gambling: a whale is a punter who gets free hospitality from casinos because he (usually a he) bets such huge sums. According to the amazing Senate subcommittee report into the affair, by the time the bets went wrong, Iksil and his colleagues were out on the limb for $157 billion[53]—this nearly four years after the collapse of

Lehman Brothers, when the lessons about excessive risk taking were supposed to have been learned.

long and short To be long on something is to think that it's going to go up in value, and to have invested accordingly. If I'm long on Apple, it means I own the shares and am holding them expecting them to rise in value. To be short on something is the opposite—and shorting is a lot more controversial, because you are betting that the value of something will go down. The most common way of shorting is by borrowing a security from someone else and selling it, in the hope that the price will drop, so that when the agreed moment arrives to give it back, you can buy it for less than you paid, sell it back to the person who lent it to you, and pocket the proceeds. Since the data on these kinds of deals are publicly available, the fact of shorting the share will be known to the market. This means that by shorting the share you are helping to create a negative vibe around it, and thereby doing your bit to drive the price down. This will make the people who own that particular share hate you, because you are, in effect, trying to make them lose money.

Madoff, Bernard "Bernie" The perpetrator of the biggest financial fraud in history, defrauding his clients to the tune of $18 billion. He ran a series of investment funds that offered returns whose consistency, never failing to offer double-digit returns, should have been extremely suspect—in fact it was this very consistency that raised the suspicions about Madoff. When Madoff's frauds were exposed in 2008, it turned out that he had been running a classic Ponzi scheme, in which the new money being paid into the funds is given directly to older customers, to make it look as if the investments are successful. After his arrest Madoff said that the Ponzi scheme had been running since 1991 and that he had never made any real investments with his clients' money. He pled guilty to eleven felonies in March 2009 and was sentenced to 150 years in jail.

Manias, Panics, and Crashes An amusing book by the economist Charles Kindleberger, who as I said in Part I is something of an intellectual hero of mine. As the title suggests, it's an account of manias, panics, and crashes in history, and proves incontrovertibly that these are facts of life that just won't go away. The great lesson of Kindleberger's book is to be wary of certainty. The history of manias, panics, and crashes is largely the story of people who were certain: nothing makes it more likely that you will get something completely wrong than the certainty that you have got something completely right.

margin call When you buy something on margin—usually a derivative—you are putting down only a piece of the full price of an asset, to cover the amount that is thought to be at risk. Say you're buying $100,000 of wheat futures, with a contract date a year away. You're certain not to want all that wheat, and you and the person selling to you are well aware of the fact: what you're doing is holding on to the contract for a bit and then selling it on. The price will go up and down in the meantime but will do so within a fairly narrow band. So what you do is buy the wheat on margin, for $10,000, to cover the amount the wheat might go down before you sell it. You buy the wheat for $100,000 but hand over only $10,000 in cash. (This is a form of leverage: with $100,000 of capital, instead of buying one lot of $100,000 wheat for cash up front, you can buy $1,000,000 on margin.) Unfortunately after a month, the wheat price has dropped by $5,000 so to cut your losses, you sell it for $95,000. You lost $5,000 of the amount you put down on the margin, and chalk it up to experience.

What, though, if the price of wheat drops by more than the margin you have put up? Say it falls by $15,000. Then the person who sold you the wheat rings you up and says, sorry old boy, margin call, we need some more money to cover that wheat you've bought. You stump up another $10,000 to cover the new margin. That's fine if you have the money—but if you don't, and especially if you have bought lots of similar contracts and have lots of margin calls arriving simultaneously, then suddenly you're in real trouble. If you had gone the full monty and used your $100,000 to buy $1,000,000 of wheat on margin, you'd have just used the power of margin to lose all your money, and another $50,000 on top.

In finance, a margin call can also be triggered by doubts about an institution's creditworthiness. In the collapse of Lehman Brothers, one of the short-term triggers was other banks deciding Lehman needed to put up more collateral—in effect to raise more money against the possibility of a margin call.

margin, high and low Margin in this sense is the amount of profit a business owner makes by selling something. An Italian restaurant owner once told me that more than anything else in the world, he loves pasta. I asked him why, expecting an answer along the lines of Marcella Hazan's remark that nothing had contributed more to the sum of human happiness than humble-seeming pasta. He said, "Because of the margin." With some of his simpler pastas, his ingredient costs were as low as $1 a serving and he could charge as much as $12. The normal margin in the restaurant business is 200 percent on the cost of food, so he was well ahead; with his other dishes, with pricier ingredients, the margin was sometimes less than 100 percent.

Some businesses have high margins: in the first quarter of 2012, Apple hit a level of gross margin of 47.4 percent. That level of margin is astounding, but it also has a built-in problem, which is that it cannot last. If your margin is that big, somebody is going to come after your business. That's because they can undercut your prices by a significant factor and still make a lot of money. In Apple's world, the company that's come along and done that is Google, via the Android ecosystem on mobile phones—which is why, less than a year after recording that record margin and having the most profit-

able company quarter in the history of capitalism, earning $13 bil-
lion in profits on $46 billion in sales, the share price had fallen by
40 percent. Apple's margins were just too good; they were a standing invitation for people to come after their business.

Companies with much smaller margins are much harder to compete with. Wal-Mart, the biggest company in the world by sales, has
operating margins that are often as low as 3 percent. That might
sound unattractive from the investors' point of view, but the thing
about margins that low is that it's incredibly difficult to compete
with them. They're exerting remorseless downward pressure on
every aspect of their business, from purchasing to the supply chain
to stocking to their retail spaces to pay, to everything else. Good
luck going head-to-head with that. One of the reasons the stock
market likes the look of Amazon's business, even though at the
moment it makes hardly any profit, is that it sees Amazon not as
a glamorous Apple-like technology firm but as a future version of
Wal-Mart, a giant with margins so low nobody else can compete.

market capitalization The total value of all a company's shares: it
is what it would cost you if you bought the whole of the company
from its current owners at the current market price. If a company
has a million shares, and the shares cost $10 each, the market cap
is $10 million.

Marx, Karl (1818–1883) The most powerful critic capitalism has
ever had, and very well worth reading, even or especially if you don't
agree with all his conclusions. One of the most impressive things
about Marx is his attempt to start with first principles and build
from there: he looks at what commodities are, where value comes
from, and then gets to work on his intellectual edifice. If you haven't
read Marx, you're likely to underestimate what a lively writer he
was: a good place to start to get a feel of it is with *The Eighteenth
Brumaire of Louis Napoleon,* his near-contemporaneous account of

the 1851 coup in which Napoleon's nephew seized power. (The title refers to the month Brumaire, which in the French Republican calendar overlapped October and November.)[54]

When people study Karl Marx, they sometimes forget how harsh the capitalist order looked in the nineteenth century. Infant mortality is one way of thinking about that. Only three of Marx's seven children survived to adulthood. This was a tragic fact, but not an unusual one. Infant mortality in Victorian Britain was at the rate of 150 deaths per 1,000 births. A difficult number to contemplate. UK infant mortality today is 4.85. That's an improvement by 3,092 percent—and, by the way, many countries have done better than Britain and have lower rates, since the UK ranks only thirty-second in the world. The US comes fifty-fifth, with a rate of 6.17. The global infant mortality rate is 35 per thousand, less than a quarter of what the British rate was in Marx's day.

material well-being A blanket term for measuring how well-off people are in the round, not just in terms of how much money they have. It's used in opposition to a narrow emphasis on GDP and tries to emphasize factors such as health, life expectancy, equality, education, and opportunity. If the future of the world is to involve lower GDP growth, which certainly seems likely in the developed world at least, then other factors contributing to material well-being will become more important. We could have flat or low GDP growth but be living longer, be better educated, feel happier, and have less inequality—which would be a win. The attempt to find hard, non-touchy-feely ways of measuring material well-being is a focus of interest in some areas of economics at the moment. One popular measure, produced by the UN, is the Human Development Index or HDI, which crunches together life expectancy, years spent in education, and GDP per capita, to come up with a single hard number. There are four categories, ranging from "very high human development" to "low human development." These are the top twelve countries:

1. Norway
2. Australia
3. USA
4. Netherlands
5. Germany
6. New Zealand
7. Ireland
8. Sweden
9. Switzerland
10. Japan
11. Canada
12. South Korea

The bottom ten, counting down to number 168, are all in sub-Saharan Africa:

159. Burundi
160. Guinea
161. Central African Republic
162. Eritrea
163. Mali
164. Burkina Faso
165. Chad
166. Mozambique
167. Democratic Republic of Congo
168. Niger

McJobs Low-pay, low-status, low-security, low-prospects jobs of the sort done by workers in McDonald's—hence the name.

mean and median The mean is the average: for any group, you add whatever it is you're measuring together, divide it by the number of people in the group, and that's the mean. The median is the person in the middle, with 50 percent above and 50 percent below. When the mean goes up and the median stays still, that is a sign of rising inequality. Imagine a football team whose star player gets a $1,000,000 pay raise. The team's average pay will go up, but the median—the bloke in the middle—will be paid the same. That's proof that inequality in the team has risen. In the Anglo-American world, the mean and the median have diverged sharply in the last few decades, as inequality has measurably increased. Only the people at the top are better-off; everyone else is finding life harder. In the United States there has been no increase in the median wage in the last three decades, even as average earnings have gone up sharply. That's because most of the increase in pay is concentrated right at the top of the income distribution, with half of all the increase in income since 1980 going to the richest 1 percent of the population.

These facts weren't prominent on the political radar screen before the economic crisis, but the hard times through which most people are now living have made them increasingly aware of the gap between how most of them live and how the rich do. It's one thing to be told that the rich are getting a bigger slice of the cake while the whole cake is growing and your own slice of the cake is also getting bigger. It's another thing when the cake is shrinking, but the rich person's slice is continuing to grow.

mercantilism The discredited economic doctrine that dominated economic and foreign policy in Europe for hundreds of years: the idea that countries' economic interests are competing and not cooperative, and that countries should export their way to riches, at the expense of their neighbors. It implies the development of captive overseas markets, often in the form of colonies, and also of protective tariffs and taxes.

Merkel's numbers A piece of data much quoted by Angela Merkel, the German chancellor: 7/25/50. Europe has 7 percent of the world's population, 25 percent of its GDP, and 50 percent of its social spending.

microeconomics and macroeconomics The biggest distinction in the field of economics: it's not an ideological divide; it's just a categorical separation between the different kinds of work that economists do. Macroeconomics was born in the aftermath of the Great Depression, and is the attempt to understand economies on large scales, everything from taxes to trade, fiscal and monetary policy, balance of payments, and all that stuff. It is remarkable how little agreement there is on large areas of macroeconomics: it sometimes seems as if the field is subject to the same rule that William Goldman lays out about Hollywood: "Nobody knows anything." (On a platform with some economists, I once joked that it was the only field of human inquiry that you could sum up in a single word, "wrong." It got a laugh, but the macroeconomists ignored me in the bar afterwards.) Microeconomics is the study of people's motivation and behavior by means of economic principles. It tends to focus on small things, sometimes small things with big consequences. One study, for instance, looked at the important question of free jam, and how many samples a retailer should offer if he wants the customer to try jam and then buy some afterwards. The study found that if you offer too many types of free jam, the customer goes into a tailspin, suffers from too much choice, and doesn't buy any: the optimum number of samples was six.[55] Another microeconomic study that I liked concerned the rates charged by transsexual prostitutes in the middle of their sexual transformation, who in some countries charge less than straightforwardly female prostitutes and in other countries charge more. The conclusion reached was that they charge more in Catholic countries. At least, that's what I think it said, but I can't find the reference anywhere so now I'm wondering if I imagined it. Anyway, that's the distinction: macro = wrong, micro = jam/transexuals.

middle class The term has a different affect in the United States and the UK. In the United States it is used as a positive term to embrace people who aren't rich and who work hard and are aspirational. US politicians will openly praise the middle class and pitch for their votes: President Obama, for instance, spoke about "a grand bargain for middle-class jobs." As the political commentator Ana Marie Cox pointed out, "Americans like to think of themselves as middle class." [56] In the UK, "middle class" is used as a mainly negative descriptor, implying complacency and insularity: in an argument, if one person calls another person middle class, they think they have won. "Working class," on the other hand, can never be used as a negative descriptor.

Millennium Development Goals A set of global targets announced by the UN in 2000, setting eight targets to be achieved by 2015, from a starting point of 1990. The targets were (among other things) to halve infant and maternal mortality, to halve the number of people who live in absolute poverty, and to double the percentage of children getting at least a primary education. A full report on the MDGs, including an account of how much progress has been made towards them, is available on the UN's website. [57]

misery index A country's inflation plus unemployment rate. The idea is that by adding them together you get a good sense of how miserable people feel in a country at a given moment. The higher, the worse. At the moment the United States' is 8.2, which is pretty low by global standards—well below the OECD rich-country average of 11.0. Can you guess the most miserable moment in modern US history? June 1980, when the index peaked at 21.98 percent. Some economists have proposed refinements to the misery index, in the form of the growth misery index (which takes account of GDP growth) and the super misery index (which incorporates growth and also the deficit). The most miserable country in the world, on the basis of these measures, is Zimbabwe.[58]

moat Something protecting a business from competitors, especially from new entrants to the business seeking to compete on price. Looking at a business, investors often ask, "Where's the moat?"—i.e., what's to stop someone else from coming and doing the same thing?

momentum An entertaining phenomenon in the world of money, because it shouldn't exist. The theory of efficient markets says that "prices have no memory" and that there is no pattern behind the way they move other than that of a change in realities—greater or lesser demand for the thing, or new information about it, or new perceptions about its prospects. This is a profoundly entrenched item of faith in the modern edifice of economic theory. Unfortunately, it's not true, and it is a proven fact that prices have momentum: if a price went down or up yesterday, it is more likely than not to go down or up today as well. Many funds exist to exploit this effect, and on any given day a large part of the market is made up of "momentum trading."

monetarism When he was putting together the multivolume supplement to the *Oxford English Dictionary*, the lexicographer in charge, Robert Burchfield, had the final responsibility of deciding which words went into the dictionary and which didn't. Since the whole point of that great masterpiece is that it is a historical dictionary of every word in use, the bar for inclusion is set pretty low: if you're a word, all you need is a couple of genuine citations, and you're in. When he was signing off on the letter *M* for the second volume of additions to the dictionary, two words were right on the margin for inclusion. One was "middlessence," a fairly horrible new word, following on from T. S. Eliot's inspired coinage of "juvescence," by an imaginative leap from "senescence," in his poem "Gerontion." The other new word, equivalently rare and marginal, was "monetarism." Both words narrowly made the cut. This reflects the fact that in the late sixties and thereabouts, monetarism was an obscure, marginal, discredited idea from the distant fringes of economics. By 1979, it had become the guiding principle of UK economic policy, under the leadership of Margaret Thatcher, the most determined monetarist ever to have charge of a developed economy.

The principles of monetarism grew out of the study of economic history, via the work of Milton Friedman. Monetarism's central focus was on the amount of money in the economy. The idea, simply put, is that the way to control an economy is to control the amount of money moving around inside it. In the 1970s and early 1980s, Britain was suffering from high inflation, which monetarists see as a "disease of money." Monetarist policy dictated a reduction in the amount of money in circulation, and sought to achieve that end by making money more expensive—in other words, by raising interest rates. This policy worked in the medium term, though at the cost of hugely increased unemployment, and consequently increased social division. By the late 1980s, monetarism had gone back out of fashion, where it remains to this day, largely because it is a theory that makes predictions about the ways things should work, and these theories were contradicted by events such as the decoupling of inflation from the money supply in the early noughties. In monetarism, these two phenomena are linked; in reality, they proved not to be, because the early years of this century saw the money supply go up but inflation stay down. The money supply turned out to be a model rather than a permanent truth: in this case, it went wrong by failing to allow for the impact of growth in China.

Monetarism is generally seen as the ideological opposite of Keynesianism.

monetize A word that has played a central role in the information and Internet revolution. When you monetize something, you make money out of it. If you are making and selling an actual physical thing, this process is fairly obvious: people either buy it or they don't. You monetize your product or you go broke. In the Internet world, companies often seek growth first: "Grow big fast" is the axiom. Much of the time, the strategy for monetizing the product comes later. This is a sensationally good way of going broke, and it is far, far less common to successfully monetize an idea than to run out of cash before you do. Google is an extremely rare example of successful monetization, in that it grew hugely fast and then worked out a way of making money on the hoof. Google did it by copying the company Overture, which had figured out how to make money by selling ads attached to searches; it is still the case that of Google's huge range of products, from Gmail to YouTube to Google+ to Calendar to Maps to Voice, only one, search advertising, actually makes money. Whenever someone asking you for money says, "We'll work out a way to monetize it later," it is a good idea to run away.

This use of the term "monetize," endemic in the world of startups and the Internet, is so recent it isn't yet in the *OED*.

money supply The amount of money in an economy at any given moment; because monetarism believes that this is the central issue in the functioning of the economy, the definition, analysis, and measuring of the money supply is central to it. At the start of the Great Depression, for instance, one of the major problems facing the world economy was that currencies were tied to the gold standard, so that when more money in circulation was needed, it was literally the case that there wasn't enough money in the world. The question of money supply is complicated, though, because the amount of money sitting in bank accounts or in government bonds or moving through transactions in any given day can all be measured in different ways, and argued over accordingly; so to nonmonetarists, arguments over the money supply sometimes shade into a faintly comic form of theology.

monopoly and monopsony Two forms of what economists call market failure, in which the normal mechanisms of supply and demand don't work, because there is a structural problem with the functioning of the market. In the case of monopoly, the market failure is that there is only one supplier of a particular good or service. There is only one place you can shop. So the supplier can charge anything it likes, and the service it provides can be as bad as it likes (and yes, British Telecom, it is indeed you of whom I'm thinking). A monopsony (a word I have to admit I rather love), on the other hand, is an economic system in which there are many sellers but only one buyer.

At the moment monopoly power is growing on both sides of the Atlantic. We know that for sure because of the Herfindahl-Hirschman index, a rather groovy way of putting a numerical value on the concentration of monopoly power.

moral hazard A term most people had never heard before the financial crisis of 2008, but it was used so often during the crisis that we all got sick of it. There is moral hazard when there is an economic structure that does not penalize, and at worst actively encourages, reckless behavior. Bailing out the banks, for instance, creates a classic form of moral hazard, because it exempts those banks from the consequences of their mistakes. Perhaps the most spectacular example during the credit crunch was the bailout/nationalization of AIG, the company that had insured most of the world's credit default swaps, and as a result was on the brink of going broke. Banks had taken out insurance with AIG, and there was a case to be made for punishing them for being so stupid. Instead AIG got its bailout, which mainly involved direct transfers of cash to the

banks that were its counterparties. The banks suffered no consequences for their mistakes, and so had no incentives to avoid such
mistakes in the future—a textbook example of moral hazard. It was
worry about moral hazard that made the Bank of England slow to
act when the first signs of the credit crunch appeared with the collapse of the bank Northern Rock in autumn 2007. The term is close
to being an example of reversification, but perhaps it's more like a
simple obfuscation: what we're really talking about is the bad guys
getting away with it.

mortgage The word literally means "dead pledge," and if it were
called that maybe more people would think twice about getting one.
It is a classic example of a financial entity that would scare people
off if they thought more clearly about what it is: a highly leveraged
form of long-term borrowing with regular demands for cash payment against an illiquid asset that is known to be even more illiquid
in difficult times.

Mr. Market Markets are frequently spoken of as if they have thoughts
and feelings and intentions, and this puzzles outsiders: I've often
been asked what on earth it means when commentators say, "The
market thinks that . . ." The answer is that markets aggregate a whole
range of widely divergent views and end up in effect expressing a single aggregate opinion. This process is discussed fascinatingly and at
length in James Surowiecki's brilliant book *The Wisdom of Crowds*.
It's often an aid to clarity to regard the market as an individual,
expressing an individual view: "The market hates sterling today,"
for instance, even though many of the people taking part in that
market in fact think the exact opposite. It is crucial to remember
that this individual, dubbed Mr. Market by Ben Graham in his book
The Intelligent Investor in 1949, is bipolar. His moods are all over the
place, and he has a particular tendency to veer between irrational
optimism and equally irrational despair. As Graham put it,

Imagine that in some private business you own a small share that cost you $1,000. One of your partners, named Mr. Market, is very obliging indeed. Every day he tells you what he thinks your interest is worth and furthermore offers either to buy you out or to sell you an additional interest on that basis. Sometimes his idea of value appears plausible and justified by business developments and prospects as you know them. Often, on the other hand, Mr. Market lets his enthusiasm or his fears run away with him, and the value he proposes seems to you a little short of silly.

If you are a prudent investor or a sensible businessman, will you let Mr. Market's daily communication determine your view of the value of a $1,000 interest in the enterprise? Only in case you agree with him, or in case you want to trade with him. You may be happy to sell out to him when he quotes you a ridiculously high price, and equally happy to buy from him when his price is low. But the rest of the time you will be wiser to form your own ideas of the value of your holdings, based on full reports from the company about its operations and financial position.[59]

The reality of Mr. Market's up-and-down moods doesn't square at all well with the theory of efficient markets.

multiplier An idea that until the Great Recession was completely out of fashion in economics. Asking an economist about the multiplier would have been like asking an astrophysicist about her star sign. That's changed, mainly because of the need to think through the consequences of cuts in government spending. The multiplier is the amount by which a chunk of government spending benefits the whole economy, by being spent and respent. So $100 in somebody's pay packet is spent on booze, toothpaste, cinema tickets, and children's shoes; and then the owners of the bar, pharmacy, cinema,

and shoe shop go ahead and spend the money in their turn, and so
on and on. All these transactions contribute to GDP. The number
of times the initial $100 is spent is the multiplier. It follows that the
multiplier is a very important number when it comes to calculating
the impact of government spending, and especially of cuts in government spending, because if the multiplier is more than 1, say is
1.5, it follows that by cutting $10 billion from spending you're mak-
ing the economy shrink by $15 billion—exactly what you don't want.
(Unless you're an ideologue who thinks that shrinking the size
of the state is more important than growing the economy; that's
something quite a few advocates of austerity do privately think, but
won't say in public.) There was a big kerfuffle in economics when
the IMF, which has for decades been the global bad cop when it
comes to government spending, announced in the October 2012
edition of its *World Economic Outlook* that governments around the
world had been basing their calculations on austerity packages on
the basis of a multiplier of 0.6. That would mean that for every $10
billion cut, the real impact on the economy would be a contraction
of $6 billion. The IMF looked at historical data and concluded that
the real multiplier for austerity cuts was much higher, in the range
of 0.9 to 1.7. That would mean that the same $10 billion cut was in
fact doing up to $17 billion of damage. This would do a lot to explain
the news that austerity was proving much more harmful to economies than anyone in power had expected. The fact that it was the
IMF announcing this, though, was a big part of the shock, since the
IMF is the organization whose off-the-shelf package of measures
for troubled economies always includes a huge dose of austerity.

nationalization The taking into state ownership of private assets
or industries. It used to be the central pillar of the Labour Party's
economic policy, in the form of clause 4f of the party constitution,
calling for common ownership of the means of production, distribution, and exchange, until Tony Blair led the charge to abol-

ish it in 1994. Nationalization had gone entirely out of favor in most of the developed world until governments found they had to nationalize banks in order to save the financial system in 2008. A partial list of nationalizations since 2008 would include AIG and General Motors in the United States; two of the UK's four biggest banks, Lloyds-HBOS and RBS; the Belgian bank Dexia, much of the Spanish banking system; and so on.

neoliberal economics The dominant economic school in the Anglo-American world since about 1980. It is the intellectual force behind deregulation, free trade, privatization, lower taxes, and lower levels of state involvement in the economy. In neoliberal economics, it doesn't matter if the rich get much richer, as long as the poor grow better-off too; this implies that rising levels of inequality must be accepted as the price for growing general prosperity. The Great Recession, which has shown the rich continuing to grow richer while everyone else struggles, is either a severe challenge to the neoliberal model or a refutation of it.

Nobel Prize in economics It isn't really a Nobel Prize; it's actually the Sveriges Riksbank Prize in Economic Sciences in Memory of Alfred Nobel, founded in 1968. There are those who think that the prize is more trouble than it's worth, and confers excess legitimacy on the fashionable economic models of the moment. The prize provides a lot of comfort for people who think that the entire field of economics is mostly bullshit. The 2013 prize was an absolute classic in this respect. It was awarded both to the person who created the theory of efficient markets, Eugene Fama, and the man who has mounted the most sustained empirical critique of the theory, Robert Schiller. It's like awarding a prize both to Galileo, for saying that Earth isn't the center of the universe, and to Pope Paul V, for saying that it is. Nassim Nicholas Taleb, a particularly trenchant critic of the prize, has argued that investors who lost money in the credit crunch should sue the prize for giving credibility to mistaken mathematical theories of how things should be priced. "I want to make the Nobel accountable. . . . Citizens should sue if they lost their job or business owing to the breakdown in the financial system."[60] This is a bit like Richard Dawkins's idea that astrologers should be sued for fraud, in that it's unlikely to happen but fun to think about.

no-recourse loans Loans in which the person who has borrowed the money can stop paying the loan, forfeit the asset against which the loan was made, and walk away. The textbook example involves mortgages that go wrong: the borrower, realizing that the math has gone against him or her, decides to stop paying the mortgage and to give up the house. This is something that you would do only if the loan was for a large part of the value of the house—or even, in many cases, when the mortgage was actually for more than the house is worth. (That's called negative equity: when the mortgage is for more than the property.) No-recourse loans have been denounced as a ridiculous cosseting of feckless borrowers, but one of the ironies of the Great Recession is that no-recourse loans helped the US economy in an unexpected way: by forcing banks to admit to bad property debts, they've helped bank balance sheets to stay honest and have helped avoid the Japanese and European curse of zombie banks. That in turn has helped keep the US economy moving—not moving rapidly, agreed, but better than the economies of its developed-world peers.

OECD The Organization for Economic Cooperation and Development is a Paris-based economic organization whose origins were in the postwar Marshall Plan. It has thirty-four member countries, all of them democracies with market-oriented economies, and its mission is to promote trade and economic progress. It would be going too far to say that the OECD has a lefty flavor, but its agenda is more progressive than that of many other economic institutions, and it is a reliable source of interesting research, quite a lot of it consisting of things that governments don't necessarily want to hear. An example was the recent study of how current levels of literacy and numeracy compared with those of previous generations, which showed that in some countries, the United States and the UK among them, people in their sixties had higher skills than people in their early twenties—which is hard to read as evidence of progress.[61]

one-off charges Items that appear in a set of accounts that should be there only once, and are there because of a specific set of circumstances. You'll sometimes hear that "Dr. Evil Incorporated made a loss of $100 million last year, but underlying profits were $500 million before one-off charges connected with last year's unsuccessful attempt to take over the world." There is a faint whiff of suspicion about one-off charges, especially when they are connected with obvious mistakes: although the specific error might be a one-off, the tendency to make boo-boos may well be more permanent, and more expensive.

onions Onions, particularly their price, provide an example of the kind of thing I'd never thought about until I began taking an interest in the subject of money and reading the financial pages. Here is my favorite money-related onion fact: onions are so important in India that the government has twice fallen, in 1980 and 1998, because of surges in their price.[62]

opportunity costs A very useful idea to take from economics is the cost of choosing one thing as opposed to another thing, in terms of what you're giving up. The opportunity cost of booking your holiday earlier is the chance of booking a cheaper holiday at the last minute, or being able to take up a last-minute invitation to somewhere else: that's what you're choosing to forgo. My dad used to call opportunity costs "Chinese profits" and "Chinese losses": I always assumed that this was slang in general use, but I can't find any references to it on the Internet, so maybe they were terms he'd made up for himself. (He worked for a bank in Hong Kong, which maybe explains it.) A Chinese profit was a profit you made by not doing something else: if you thought about selling one share to buy another, but didn't, and then the second share went down, that was a Chinese profit—you'd profited compared with what would have happened. If you made the same choice, but the share you didn't buy went up, that was a Chinese loss—you'd lost compared with what would have happened. That is a vivid practical way of thinking about opportunity costs.

options A type of financial derivative that gives the holder the right, but not the obligation, to buy or sell something at a specific price on a specific date. Apple shares today are $420. Say you think that Apple's share price is going up. You buy the right to buy Apple shares for $500 in six months' time. If Apple shares have risen to $550, then when the time comes you buy them for $500 and sell them for $550 and have made an immediate profit; if the share price is less than $500, you don't exercise your option and instead just walk away, and all you've lost is the cost of the option. The same process works in reverse: you can buy an option to sell the share when it's falling. If you thought the share price was falling, you could buy the right to sell it for $350 in six months' time. If the share price has fallen to $300, you can buy it for $300, then sell it for $350 and make an immediate profit; if it's above $350, again, you just walk away. In an ideal world, options would be used only to minimize and spread and manage risk; in practice they are used to magnify the size of bets. When combined with the ability to borrow money, and to buy on margin, they provide an effective way of taking on a lot of risk.

A futures contract is the same as an option, but there is an obligation to buy or sell the security at the agreed time. It follows that futures are riskier than options, and therefore cheaper.

OTC Short for over the counter, which in turn means sold directly from one party in a transaction to another, rather than bought through an exchange. The difference is that when securities are bought through an exchange, the exchange knows how many of them there are in circulation, and what they're worth. If securities are bought directly over the counter, there's no central registry, so nobody knows the value of what's out there. This was a big issue during the financial crisis, as the existence of trillions of dollars in OTC derivatives meant that the financial world was playing a gigantic game of simultaneous pass-the-parcel, with nobody knowing who was ultimately on the hook for huge losses.

output The amount of stuff produced in a given period of time by a given individual, company, or nation. If your output goes up, the entity involved becomes richer; if it declines, it gets poorer.

overhead All the things you need to pay for that don't directly contribute to whatever it is you're selling. Labor is not an overhead and neither are materials, because they directly contribute to your thing, but your other costs are. In the restaurant business, for example, you have staff, the cost of ingredients, and then everything else is overhead—electricity, rent, taxes, licenses, professional charges, insurance.

PLOG A persistent large output gap, in which an economy performs below the level it could be producing at for a sustained period. Some economists think that Britain is in the grip of a PLOG.

P2P A term all the vogue in certain circles at the moment: it means peer to peer, and in the context of finance refers to lending, usually in the form of microcredit or small loans. A number of companies are offering this service as a way of providing, on the one hand, access to credit for people who are finding it difficult to obtain it through conventional channels and, on the other, a way of earning a decent rate of interest on money while also doing something socially useful. The growth of P2P is an extension of the ideas of the Nobel Peace Prize–winning Bangladeshi economist Muhammad Yunus, who came up with the idea of microcredit, or small loans to people too poor to have access to conventional bank credit. P2P is controversial because the rates of interest can be high and also because it is a way of profiting from the poor—even if it is a creative, flexible, useful, and much-appreciated way of profiting from the poor. It is an example of capitalism at its most flexible and creative, rather than any kind of challenge to the capitalist order.

At the same time, P2P lending and microcredit also begin to raise the question, what exactly are banks for? It has long been an irony of economics that in a purely efficient market, banks would not exist. Lenders with excess capital would directly seek out borrowers who need the capital, and both would benefit from the transaction, rather than the current model in which banks borrow money at say 0.25 percent and lend it at 5 percent and pocket the difference. Big companies already cut banks out of the process of borrowing, by raising money through issuing their own bonds. P2P offers a glimpse of a world in which this process has been democratized: people have realized how the system works and are beginning to cut banks out of the picture.

paradis fiscal The wonderful French term for tax haven—I love the idea that a tax-free location is a form of paradise, in which people spend all their time cavorting on yachts.

petrodollar Money made by selling oil; these transactions are denominated in US dollars because the USA made a deal with Saudi Arabia, after the collapse of the Bretton Woods agreement in 1971, as a way of maintaining demand for the US dollar as the de facto global reserve currency.

positional goods Things whose value is determined not by how useful they are in themselves but by the fact that other people can't have them. The term was coined by Fred Hirsch in his 1976 book *Social Limits to Growth*. Positional goods are tools for signaling status, and the fact that the owner of the positional good is doing better than the people around her. The idea is that as economies grow, more things become more available and more affordable to more people; but some things don't, because their supply is fixed. A painting by a fashionable painter, or a house in a posh address, is a positional good; only the richest people can afford it.

PPI An acronym for payment protection insurance. There was nothing inherently sinister about the product being sold in PPI. The products in question were supposed to provide insurance for customers who owed payments that they for one reason or another were no longer in a position to make. The two classic examples would be mortgage payments or credit card payments, and the two classic reasons for needing insurance would be falling ill or losing your job. If you took out PPI, you would, in the case of sickness or redundancy, have your mortgage and/or credit card debt taken care of by the insurance you had so prudently bought in advance.

The problem was that many of the people who bought the policies would not, in the real-life instances for which they were buying the policies, be able to use them. Two categories of people who were not eligible to make claims against PPI were the self-employed and anyone with a preexisting medical condition. They couldn't use the insurance, but they were, in their (our) hundreds of thousands, sold it anyway. They weren't told the basic facts about the insurance they were buying, facts that were not merely marginally relevant or potentially relevant but that directly contradicted the raison d'être of the policies. The banks sold them to customers in the knowledge that they were not and would never be of any use to them. In many cases, customers bought products that had PPI tacked on, without being told that they were being charged a premium for insurance that for many of them was useless. That's what's costing the banks all that money now: refunding the money paid, plus interest that was added on top, plus 8 percent interest, which could have been made if the money wasted on PPI had been put to some legitimate use. The average payout by the banks is in the region of £2,750.

The simplest way of stating the magnitude of the PPI scandal is to point to the size of the amounts that the banks are going to have to pay out to settle it. The first mentions of PPI as a potential liability for the banks had the then astonishing, then unprecedented amount of £1 billion mentioned as a possible upper limit to the damage. When the crucial court case against the claims was lost by the banks in April 2011, the FSA knew it was going to be expensive: its estimate of the cost to the industry was £3 billion. But that turned out to be a huge underestimate. To get a sense of how far the benchmarks for PPI have shifted, in the last quarter of 2012 one bank alone, Lloyds, had to increase its provision for settling PPI claims by £1.5 billion. Then, in February 2014, it had to make another £1.8 billion of provision. These are amazing sums: instead of £1 billion as an all-time maximum penalty for the entire industry, we have now arrived at a point where one bank in one three-month period has to spend £1.8 billion, not to cover its total liability, but just to cover the extra liability it has acquired in that three months. In fact, Lloyds' total provision for PPI has now hit £10 billion, more than the full cost of the London Olympics, just from that one bank. Across the industry, the latest estimates for the total cost of the PPI scandal have kept going up, and then up again, and then up a bit more, and are now at £1.5 billion for HSBC, £2.2 billion for RBS, and £2.6 billion for Barclays. Across the industry, the most recent guesstimate for the total cost is £16 billion.

price/earnings ratio If the stock market pages had to be cleaned up and reduced to one single number, the only piece of information that you were allowed to know about any given company at any one moment, the number to use would be the price/earnings ratio, or P/E ratio. The P/E ratio is the real cost of a share: the price itself is largely irrelevant; what matters is how expensive the share is in terms of what the company is actually earning. A single share of Apple costs $420 today, and a share of Amazon costs $301, so that means Apple is more expensive, right? Wrong. If you look at the companies' respective earnings, a share of Apple costs just over 11 times what the company earned last year, whereas a share of Amazon is valued at 3,500 times earnings. In other words, Amazon is 300 times more expensive than Apple. That might seem nuts, but the price is based on the idea that in the future, Amazon will earn huge amounts of money, so you buy the share now in order to get in early for the huge takeoff that is going to come. Apple on the other hand is more of a known quantity, so you are getting what you pay for. It's very difficult to know what the realistic P/E ratio is for any stock: as Burton Malkiel put it in his efficient-market theory investment classic, *A Random Walk Down Wall Street*, "God Almighty does not know the proper price-earnings-multiple for a common stock."[63] Historically, companies with low P/E ratios—what are known as "value stocks"—have tended to outperform those with high P/Es, in part because a high P/E implies high expectations that are easily disappointed.

private company A company that isn't quoted on the stock market and whose ownership is still in private hands—in practice, usually those of a single family. The biggest private company in the world is Cargill, the US food-booze-ciggies-fertilizer-corn syrup conglomerate, followed by Koch Industries, followed by Mars; big international private companies include Ikea and Lego. Why stay private, when floating on the stock market brings you a massive chunk of cash? The reason is that while going public brings a huge amount of money right at the moment of IPO, it also brings the need to appease investors, obey reporting requirements, keep sucking up to markets, and pay out profit in dividends rather than reinvesting them to grow the business.

privatization The opposite of nationalization: it means taking assets owned by the state and selling them to companies or individuals. It was a central feature of Margaret Thatcher's economic policy from 1979 and continued under subsequent governments; it also caught on elsewhere in the world and is now a standard part of the IMF tool kit when it imposes conditions on indebted countries in return for loans. "Privatization" is a fascinatingly modern word, whose first documented usage in the contemporary sense was in 1970. Privatization was such a dangerous and potentially explosive idea that no mention of it was made in Mrs. Thatcher's 1979 election manifesto.

producer capture The process in which the people who work at something end up taking it over and running it for their own benefit, rather than for the benefit of their clients and customers. When schools are run for the convenience and benefit of teachers rather than pupils, and hospitals are run for the convenience and benefit of their employees rather than of patients, that's producer capture.

productivity The amount of goods produced in a specific amount of time: it measures how much you get out for how much you put in. It is perhaps the single most important number in economics, because it does more than anything else to determine whether a person, a company, or a country is getting richer. Indeed, at the national level, being richer and being more productive are close to being the same thing. It is no accident that *The Wealth of Nations* begins with a long consideration of economic productivity, through the example of a hypothetical pin factory. That said, productivity can be difficult to measure, especially in areas such as health care, where it's very hard to compare like with like over time and with different treatment regimes.

progressive taxation A system in which the rich pay more tax than the poor. It is one of the ten main demands of the *Communist Manifesto*, so it's amusing that progressive taxation is accepted as a basic axiom of the political order pretty much everywhere in the developed world, as is the tenth demand, that for universal education and an end to child labor. (Side note: the angriest, most dangerous British radicals in the nineteenth century were the Chartists. Of their once controversial six demands, five are now entirely standard democratic practice; the one exception is for annual elections to Parliament.) Having said that, a progressive income tax can still end up with the poor paying a greater proportion of their income in tax overall, because they pay a much higher proportion in indirect taxes such as sales tax. Progressive taxation can have some paradoxical effects, because the rich end up paying such a large share of the overall income tax that they end up with more power—that is, when they do actually pay it.

Joseph Stiglitz, writing in the *New York Times*, argues,

> What should shock and outrage us is that as the top 1 percent has grown extremely rich, the effective tax rates they pay have markedly decreased. Our tax system is much less progressive than it was for much of the 20th century. The top marginal income tax rate peaked at 94 percent during World War II and remained at 70 percent through the 1960s and 1970s; it is now 39.6 percent. Tax fairness has gotten much worse in the 30 years since the Reagan "revolution" of the 1980s.
>
> Citizens for Tax Justice, an organization that advocates for a more progressive tax system, has estimated that, when federal, state and local taxes are taken into account, the top

1 percent paid only slightly more than 20 percent of all American taxes in 2010—about the same as the share of income they took home, an outcome that is not progressive at all.

With such low effective tax rates—and, importantly, the low tax rate of 20 percent on income from capital gains—it's not a huge surprise that the share of income going to the top 1 percent has doubled since 1979, and that the share going to the top 0.1 percent has almost tripled, according to the economists Thomas Piketty and Emmanuel Saez. Recall that the wealthiest 1 percent of Americans own about 40 percent of the nation's wealth, and the picture becomes even more disturbing.[64]

prop trading In proprietary trading, banks bet their own money for their own benefit, as opposed to making such trading only on behalf of their clients. It is supposed to be banned by the forthcoming Volcker rule.

quantitative easing (QE) An "unconventional" technique used by governments and central banks when interest rates are too low to go down any further, but the need for economic stimulus still exists. QE involves a government buying back its own bonds using money that doesn't actually exist. It's like borrowing money from somebody and then paying her back with a piece of paper on which you've written the word "Money"—and then, magically, it turns out that the piece of paper with "Money" on it is actually real money. Another way of describing quantitative easing would be if, when you look up your bank balance online, you had the further ability to add to it just by typing numbers on your keyboard. Ordinary clients can't do this, obviously, but governments can; then they use this newly created magic money to buy back their own debt. That's what quantitative easing is.

The idea is that since interest rates are so low, it's in no one's interest to sit on this newly created money. If you are one of the bondholders who has sold your government debt back to the government, you will now go and spend your new cash on something that yields a higher rate of return. You'll buy shares with it, or invest it in your business, or something—anything—else. In the UK, the government has spent magic money on QE to the tune of £375 billion, an amount equal to 23.8 percent of GDP. The numbers for American QE are even bigger: $2.3 trillion in magic money, though because the US economy is so big—$16.6 trillion—QE is smaller in proportion, at a mere 13.9 percent of GDP.

We don't really know whether QE has worked; the consensus among economists is that it has, but no one knows to quite what extent, and it's also the case that nobody knows what's going to happen once QE stops. In fact the "unwinding" of QE is on many people's list as the possible trigger for the next market meltdown. Will money pour from riskier activities back into people's bank accounts/mattresses, with catastrophic consequences for every business and individual in the world who needs credit? That's one of the reasons for concern about the effects and consequences of QE over the medium term—if a medicine is guaranteed to make you very sick when you stop taking it, and you know that one day you'll have to stop taking it, then maybe you shouldn't start taking it in the first place. More generally, QE taps into the fear that governments' printing of money always leads to dangerous levels of inflation, and that inflation, like a peat bog fire, is all the more dangerous when it's cooking up underground.

The simplest, and maybe most helpful, way to think of QE is as the creation of magic money elves. The elves wave their wands and recite their incantations and then emerge from the magic money cave burdened with crocks of newly minted gold. Remember, though, that in almost every mythology featuring elves and fairies, the magic beings are morally ambivalent: they give you what you want, but there's always a price to pay, and it's always a price that you aren't expecting. Lots of economists think that's exactly the case with QE.

ratings agencies The bodies that assess the creditworthiness of companies and governments, and award grades to the debt, from triple-A downwards. The three biggest of the ratings agencies are Moody's, Standard and Poor's, and Fitch.

The agencies are immensely important to global financial markets, because the ratings they award don't merely determine perceptions of risk; they often have a statutory force, since many institutions are forbidden by law from investing in any debt that has too low a rating. Debts above this threshold are "investment-grade"; debts below it are "junk bonds." Mistakes in the assessments and mathematical models used by the ratings agencies played a central part in the credit crunch. There's a dark comedy to the way the ratings agencies are still taken seriously by the markets, given that their performance so far this century has been the very definition, the epitome, of an epic fail.

rational expectations (or rational choice) A central assumption in the discipline of economics: the idea is that most of us most of the time behave in ways that are rationally consistent with our understanding of our own self-interest. This is a useful assumption to make when building economic models; the fact that it's manifestly not true leads to all sorts of entertaining intellectual contortions when the assumers try to apply their template to the real world. That many of the thinkers involved are supersmart makes it all the funnier. For a flavor of the field, I recommend a look at the Nobel Prize citation for the Chicago economist Gary Becker: "A basic idea in Becker's analysis is that a household can be regarded as a 'small factory' which produces what he calls basic goods, such as meals, a residence, entertainment, etc., using time and input of ordinary market goods, 'semi-manufactures,' which the household purchases on the market."

Here's a tip for young parents: if, after a series of broken nights, you get into an argument about the allocation of household chores and parenting duties, I recommend trying to win the dispute by citing Becker's Nobel-winning "A Theory of the Allocation of Time."[65] This sentence will give you a flavor: "Nevertheless, the elasticity of demand for number of children does seem somewhat smaller than the quantity elasticities found for many goods." When it comes to rationing, it makes sense that "women, the poor, children, the unemployed etc., would be more willing to spend their time in a queue or otherwise ferreting out rationed goods than would high-earning males." Your partner is certain to defer to your clear Chicago reasoning and may well follow up with an apology.

The best justification and explanation of rational choice theory that I've read, which is also the best account I know of the use of models in economics, comes in a thriller, *The Fatal Equilibrium*, whose authors, writing under the pseudonym Marshall Jevons, were two economists, William Breit and Kenneth Elzinga. Their hero solves crimes by using economic principles, and in the course of doing so gives this brilliant peroration on what models are:

> Economists can't use laboratories in their research—people would argue and cajole and possibly lie if you experiment with, say, their income and assets over time. So being barred from experimenting with real participants in a laboratory, we develop theories that are evaluated, not by their realism, but by their usefulness. "Usefulness" of course means theories that are tolerably good predictors of outcomes or have implications that are borne out in practice. It's true that economists have theories with assumptions that are unrealistic. When [an economist] assumes that people are highly rational maximizers of utility, that doesn't mean he is stating a view of human nature that he believes is realistic. He is doing what has to be done to make the subject matter of his discipline empirically manageable. Utility maximazation is one of the most powerful

generalizations we have. Its usefulness has been borne out over and over again. All you can ask of an economist is high logical standards and corroborating empirical evidence. But the theory will be a generalization, ignoring many of the real world's details. . . . Physicists assume perfect vacuums. They assume frictionless plains. We don't complain to them—hey, that's unrealistic, do we? Of course not. Economists assume utility maximization and test theories from that base.[66]

RBS The Royal Bank of Scotland was at one point, measured by the scale of its assets, the biggest company in the world. It got that way mainly by growing through acquisitions, the last of which, the purchase of ABN Amro in October 2007, was a disaster that helped destroy the bank. By April 2008, RBS was going back to the markets to raise more capital; on 13 October 2008, RBS had to be taken over by the government, otherwise it would have collapsed, and there would have been a bona fide national emergency. The bank lost £24 billion that year, the biggest loss in British history. The man in charge of RBS, Fred Goodwin, was stripped of the knighthood that he had won for "services to banking." The UK government still owns 82 percent of RBS, and at the time of writing is sitting on a loss of about £15 billion.

real and nominal The terms designate numbers either with (real) or without (nominal) the effect of inflation. Because of inflation, all charts that reflect prices will, over time, head upward: strip out the effect of inflation, and the charts can look very different. Take the example of the most profitable US movies ever made. On the left is how the chart looks if you consider the sums of money in real terms, and on the right is the chart in nominal money (the figure in parentheses is the placing on the real-money chart):

Most Profitable (real)	Most Profitable (nominal)
1. *Gone with the Wind*	1. *Avatar* (14)
2. *Star Wars*	2. *Titanic* (5)
3. *The Sound of Music*	3. *Marvel's The Avengers* (27)
4. *E.T.: The Extra-Terrestrial*	4. *The Dark Knight* (29)
5. *Titanic*	5. *Star Wars: Episode I* (17)
6. *The Ten Commandments*	6. *Star Wars* (2)
7. *Jaws*	7. *The Dark Knight Rises* (63)
8. *Doctor Zhivago*	8. *Shrek 2* (32)
9. *The Exorcist*	9. *E.T.: The Extra-Terrestrial* (4)
10. *Snow White and the Seven Dwarfs*	10. *Pirates of the Caribbean: Dead Man's Chest* (94)

Note how movies have gotten worse: on the nominal, and therefore more recent, list, seven of the films are franchises, one is based on a theme park ride, and the top two are by James Cameron.[67]

recession A general decline in economic activity across an economy. It means everyone is doing and spending less. The general measurement of this, sometimes called a "technical recession," is when GDP declines for six months (two quarters in a row). You can have an economy doing pretty well but with a sharp decline in one specific sector—construction, say—which causes a technical recession that doesn't actually reflect the broader trends. The reverse is also true: you can have a generally declining economy being artificially kept out of technical recession by one or two booming sectors.

reducing payroll A term meaning "sacking people."

redundancy A word meaning "sacking people."

reform Something of a weasel word. In its modern economic usage it never, ever, not once, means "hiring more people and giving your current workforce more generous pay and conditions." Instead it usually means "sacking people" and making the ones who are in work do more for less. Sometimes it means "opening up sectors of an economy to more competition"—but this is more often talked about than achieved.

regulatory Everything to do with government-made rules. "Regulatory risk" is the risk of the government's coming along and changing the rules. This is particularly the case in areas of high public visibility, especially concerning sectors of the economy that were formerly in public ownership, such as utilities companies and the railways.

rent A word whose meaning in economics is more specific and maybe more interesting than its use in normal life. In daily life we all know what rent means: it's the money we owe our landlord. In economics, the definition is a little different: it involves all the activities in which somebody makes extra money without doing or making anything, simply by virtue of his control over something that other people need. Rent is the extra money that somebody makes compared with what he would make if there were genuine competition. Economists dislike rent, because it's economically inefficient and unproductive. Much of the profitable activity in the banking and financial sector is a form of rent. This is true for big companies engaged in takeovers and mergers and share offerings and other large-scale financial engineering, which have to deal with the big investment banks; it's also true for the rest of us, who have nowhere else to go except the banks when it comes to taking our deposits, lending us money for mortgages, and so on.

In the opinion of some observers, one of the reasons why the current growing gap between the rich and the poor is especially dangerous is that it is being accompanied by a growth in "rent seeking" behavior. A typical feature of such behavior is the attempt to take a bigger piece of the existing pie, rather than to make the pie bigger. A useful definition of rent seeking was given by Matthew Taylor of the RSA: "using market position to make money without adding value." When the rich lobby for tax breaks at a time of no economic growth, they are indulging in rent seeking. All corruption is a form of rent seeking.

repo A repurchase agreement, in which A sells B something, while simultaneously promising to buy it back at a specified future date. It's a bit like selling something to a pawnshop. Why would a financial institution want to do a thing like that? Sometimes, it's for pretty much the same reasons people go to pawnshops—because they need the cash immediately, in order to balance their books; sometimes it's as a part of much more complicated strategies to do with the mix of risks and assets on their books; and sometimes it's a bit more shady than that, as when Lehman Brothers, just before the bank collapsed, used a repo to hide $50 billion of dodgy assets from the Feds.

reserve currency A currency held in large quantities by foreign governments and companies: at the moment, the global reserve currency is the US dollar. (In the first quarter of 2013, the dollar made up 62.2 percent of foreign exchange reserves, the euro 23.7 percent). That means in effect that the dollar is the earth's currency: for instance, almost all commodity transactions are priced in dollars, including the most important one of all, oil. Being able to print as much of the global reserve currency as it wants is a huge economic advantage for the USA.

resource curse A bitter thing. It refers to the tragic fact that the discovery of natural resources in a poor or developing country often turns into a disaster. The resource—oil, gold, minerals, whatever—becomes the source of conflict over ownership, from petty local violence to outright civil war; control of it and access to it leads to corruption, as foreign actors pour in attempting to profit from the resource; and the gushing fountain of cash produced by the resource prevents any balanced development of the economy, as the whole country becomes dependent on the profits arising from one specific thing. Perhaps the most vivid example of the resource curse in the modern world is the Congo, which is in resource (especially mineral resource) terms one of the richest countries in the world, and where 5.4 million people have died in conflict since 1998.

restructuring Buying time to pay back a loan by changing the terms of how much, when, and how long a borrower has to pay back the debt. A restructuring almost always involves the lender's accepting that he will get less money than he had hoped. In many cases it is a discreet form of default. Note that it is almost impossible for an ordinary person to restructure a loan; it's something only governments and companies can do. The reason for that is the age-old rule that if you borrow ten grand and can't pay it back, you have a problem, but if you borrow a hundred million and can't pay it back, then the lender has a problem. So the bigger loan is much more likely to get restructured than the small one.

rich lists Such lists are good fun, but they shouldn't be taken too seriously. A journalist at the *Financial Times* once told me, "We'd love to do one and we often talk about it, but the problem is you just can't stand it up." That's a journalist's way of saying that the facts and numbers are impossible to verify. The three best-known rich lists are compiled by the *Sunday Times* in the UK and by *Forbes* and *Bloomberg* in the United States and globally. There's an entertaining difference between the kind of money that wants to hide from rich lists (mainly, old and inherited) and the kind that wants to feature prominently (mainly, new and entrepreneurial). The Saudi prince Alwaleed Bin Talal went so far as to sue *Forbes* for, he claimed, deliberately understating the extent of his wealth.[68]

It's interesting that the richest monarch in the world, who in 2011 (the last time *Forbes* did a rich-monarch list) was King Bhumbibol of Thailand at $30 billion, is hovering only at around the number 10 mark in the broader global rich list. In that list Carlos Slim, Warren Buffett, and Bill Gates tend to jockey for the 1, 2, and 3 slots, with Amancio Ortega of Zara coming up on the rails.

rights issue An occurence when a company issues new shares in its equity. Companies do this in order to raise capital, but rights issues tend to be unpopular with existing owners of the company's equity, because they dilute the equity already in circulation. If a company has 10,000 shares worth $10 each in circulation, and issues another 1,000 shares to raise some more money, the value of the existing shares is accordingly diluted. If the share price doesn't move— which it shouldn't—both new and old shares will now be worth $9.09 each, and the company will have raised an additional $9,009.

The exception to this general principle that rights issues are unpopular comes when much of a company is privately held, often by the people who launched the company and their early backers. Say you found a firm and still (with your buddies) own 100 percent of it. If you have a rights issue for 10 percent of the company, and the shares raise $100,000, then it follows that the other 90 percent is worth $900,000—so you have magically created a market price for the rest of the shares. This kind of rights issue will make you popular with your fellow equity owners. During a bubble, companies in the hot sector of the economy—in recent decades, these haved tended to be tech firms—often have rights issues that imply astoundingly high valuations for the rest of the company. When the bubble pops, most of these valuations look silly. Before that happens, though, these sorts of rights issue are used by banks—who control the rights issue process—as a way of rewarding favored clients, in a one-hand-washes-the-other scam: you do a lot of business with the bank, and it rewards you with early access to the rights issues of promising young companies.

rightsize A verb meaning "to sack people." It is arguably the worst of the various euphemisms for sacking people, because whereas other terms for firing people might involve an element of regret, this one just says that it was "right." Imagine how it feels to be told that to be the right size, your employer needs to get rid of you.

risk A term that has almost the opposite meaning in economics from the one it has in normal life. When we use the word "risk" in normal conversation, we mean risk—the chance that something bad will happen. But economists use it in a much more precise way: they use it to describe the mathematical likelihood of a specific outcome. If you roll a die, the chance that it will land on a specific number is in this sense a risk. Figuring out the way these kinds of risks work is one of our great achievements as a species. Once upon a time we were at the mercy of incomprehensible forces, but now to a large extent we can control and manage all sorts of risk, by assigning accurate numeric values for the probability of given outcomes.

When economists talk about risks, this is what they mean: outcomes that they can precisely control with the use of probabilities. These are central to modern economics, and to the models that economists build. The idea is that participants in a market know the range of possible future outcomes, assign probabilities to them, and then act on them. Mathematical models of this economic sort of risk are central to modern finance. Many of them are things of great beauty and complexity, but it is an unfortunate fact, made clear by the credit crunch, that a lot of them are also wrong. That was because the people making the models had confused risk, where you can assign precise values to probabilities, with uncertainty, which is very different: uncertainty can't be modeled and consists of the kinds of events that are very unlikely but nonetheless happen all the time. The seductive power of the idea that we can manage risk, and assign numbers to it, led very clever people to make the mistake that we can also control uncertainty—a different thing altogether. So risk has been reversified, to mean a range of outcomes about which we're mathematically confident.

There's another frequent confusion that enters the picture with the economic discussion of risk. The term is sometimes used to mean variability, i.e., the amount a price has moved up and down. This leads to mix-ups, and none other than Warren Buffett has pointed out how daft it is that a company can be much cheaper to buy, because its stock price has fallen—which means that it is less risky, since you're risking less money when you buy it—and yet by some economic measures it would be considered a greater risk, because the statistical variability of its price has risen.

risk-on, risk-off The name of a phenomenon that first showed up during the credit crunch, and has now become a feature of the way markets work. Consider the fact that it's not possible for all currencies to go down at the same time, because they're denominated against each other: if the pound falls, it's falling relative to other currencies, which means that they are going up. It used to be thought that something similar was true for the various kinds of economic assets. If people fancy property more than shares, property prices go up and shares go down; ditto bonds rather than commodities, or any of the other things that people can buy. What happened during the credit crunch, though, was the very action described on that poster advising people, "Now Panic and Freak Out." Investors panicked and freaked out about all assets—so the price of everything fell, all at once, even the prices of things that are in an economic sense opposite to each other. People who are skeptical of the value of stocks often buy government bonds, and people who think the whole system is on the brink of collapse often buy gold: but during the crisis, the price of all these things, even gold, fell together. In other words, the market wasn't making its usual collective assessment of the odds, so much as it was simply running away screaming. When confidence started creeping back into the system, it looked as if everything was going up at the same time; then people grew anxious again, and everything fell; then confidence gradually returned, and things crawled upwards; and so on. This new model, in which investors and markets seem to either like or dislike everything simultaneously, is called "risk-on, risk-off." The idea is that investors are feeling either willing to take risks because they're sufficiently confident about prospects for markets in general, in which case it's risk-on, and prices go up; or they're nervous, and it's risk-off, and prices fall. They're either piling in everywhere, or they're stuffing the money under their mattresses and curling up in the fetal position. This phenomenon has become so pronounced that there's now an index, the HSBC Roro index, that tracks it.

risk weighting A process used by large financial institutions to work out how much capital they need to hold in order to balance their lending. They figure it out by calculating how risky their various assets are and assigning values accordingly. Imagine that you have lent $10,000 to each of three people: your reliable business partner, your fairly reliable neighbor, and your disreputable uncle. You calculate that you have a 90 percent chance of getting money back from your partner, 75 percent from your neighbor, and 50 percent from your uncle: so now the risk-weighted value of the assets as they appear on your books would be $9,000, $7,500, and $5,000. Note that these are probabilities, and could all turn out much worse than that, in which case you might well go broke. Banks use a super-complicated version of this risk weighting to calculate their own levels of safety; it is notoriously the case that different banks can emerge with wildly different levels of risk weighting, and therefore of safety, from the same kinds of asset. One of the targets of people who want to change banking rules is to move away from complex risk weighting and use simpler and cruder measures of how much margin of error a bank has if its assets go bad. The banks hate those cruder, simpler measures. The trouble with the current system using risk weightings, though, is that its complexity makes it unworkable. Give three analysts a look at three sets of bank books, and they will all come up with different risk weightings and different numbers for the various kinds of capital the bank is supposed to hold. This degree of complexity helps make the whole financial system unsafe.

RPI The retail price index is largely the same as the consumer price index, or CPI, with the vital difference that it includes housing costs, i.e., the price of people's mortgages. That complicates the picture greatly, because when inflation is high and a government is trying to get it under control, the first and main thing it does is raise interest rates. But doing that makes the cost of mortgages go up. What that means for the RPI is that the measure a government is taking to bring down inflation also helps make the RPI go up: so in times of inflation and higher interest rates the RPI chases its own tail. For that reason, the CPI usually gives a clearer picture of the underlying state of inflation, while the RPI—because housing costs are after all a fact of life, which people are having to pay— gives a more accurate picture of what is actually happening to the cost of living.

Saint-Pierre and Miquelon The answer to the question "Where in North America do they use the euro?" These two islands just off Newfoundland are "overseas collectivities" belonging to France. The population consists of about 7,000 French and French Canadians. Their economy is mainly based on fishing. As well as using the euro, it's also the only place in North America ever to have used the guillotine (in 1889). If you write a novel about that I guarantee it will win loads of literary prizes.

savings and investments I must admit that despite having heard them mentioned together a zillion times, I've always been a bit blurry about the distinction between savings and investments. Is it one of those deals where the two terms are actually the same, as in "stocks and shares"? Answer: no, they're different. Savings are money that you've put somewhere safe, where you know you can get it all back if you need it: money in a jam jar or a bank account or stuffed under the mattress. Investments are things that you have bought with your money that you hope will yield a return in the future, but your money is at risk in the meantime.

Side note: governments hate savers. They don't admit it, but in practice they do. They'd rather the money was in circulation, helping the economy and, not coincidentally, their own prospects of reelection. Government rhetoric is consistenly pro-saver; government policy is consistently anti-saver.

Schumpeter, Joseph (1883–1950) A free-market economic theorist and the only prominent economist ever to have been a minister of finance, in his native Austria in 1919. He was especially interested in innovation, not at the time a central field of study in economics. Schumpeter came up with the term "creative destruction" to describe the way capitalism works. It's an idea that is easier to swallow when it's happening in a field other than the one in which you yourself work. One of the problems with capitalism in its modern form is the speed and thoroughness with which creative destruction is at work in some fields—entertainment being one of them, journalism another—and not at all in others, such as banking, where large entrenched actors have so much power that they are able to prevent change.

securities Any financial instruments that you can buy and sell. It's useful as an umbrella term because it includes stocks, bonds, derivatives, and anything else.

sequestration A term with a completely different meaning in its specialized financial usage. In the rest of life, a sequestration takes place as a result of a court case: the court sequesters, or in effect confiscates, some portion of somebody's assets, usually in respect of nonpayment of a debt, or because the assets were illegally gained. In the US government context, though, sequestration has a specialized meaning, deriving from a 1985 law that ordered mandatory spending cuts—a "sequestration"—if the government exceeded a predetermined level of deficit. The current crisis in US government financing is related to but not directly descended from that: it concerns a law passed in 2011, the Budget Control Act, which ordered across-the-board cuts in government spending unless a cross-party Joint Select Committee on Deficit Reduction could agree on a program to reduce the deficit. It didn't manage to do that, so the sequester program of across-the-board cuts came into effect on 30 September 2013, with consequences that are still playing out.

services An annoying word in economics, because it's so broad in its meaning. Economies are divided into agriculture, industry, and services: in other words, services are pretty much everything. In Britain services are 78.3 percent of GDP. When people talk about the need for "rebalancing" Western economies, this is one of the main numbers they're talking about. Note that while the UK number might sound freakishly high, it's behind both the USA (79.7 percent) and France (world leader at 79.8), and even the manufacturing-oriented Germans have an economy that is 71.1 percent services. That's because in the modern world most of what we do doesn't consist of making physical stuff out of physical stuff—which is the definition of industry.[69]

7 percent Often cited as a kind of magic number in the world of interest repayments. When a government has to pay 7 percent in order to borrow money, it is perceived as being on the point of default. Why? I'm not sure: I've asked various money people, and they merely scratch their heads and say, "I don't know, that's just the way it is." I think it might be that once a government is paying over 7 percent to borrow money it is starting to chase its tail, by borrowing money just to pay back money it's already borrowed; once it gets to that point, it starts to look more attractive just to default on the outstanding debt. But the next time you hear someone on the radio saying a government is at risk because it is having to pay 7 percent to borrow money, bear in mind there's nothing magic about that number.

72 A useful number because you can use it to calculate how long it takes for the power of compound interest to double your money. For any given rate of interest, just divide it into 72, and that's how long it takes: 6 percent, say, will double your money in twelve years; 12 percent will double it in six; 36 percent will double it in two. Cool? Cool. Note that the same calculation can be used the other way around, to work out how quickly inflation will halve the value of a sum of money. Less cool? Less cool.

shadow banks One of the newest things in this lexicon: the phrase "shadow banking" didn't even exist before August 2007. Shadow banking, or the shadow banking system, is plenty of people's candidate for the next big thing to blow up in the global financial system. You could also say it was the last big thing to blow up in the global financial system, since it played a large role in the credit crunch too. Here is Ben Bernanke's definition of the shadow banking system: "Shadow banking, as usually defined, comprises a diverse set of institutions and markets that, collectively, carry out traditional banking functions—but do so outside, or in ways only loosely linked to, the traditional system of regulated depository institutions. Examples of important components of the shadow banking system include securitization vehicles, asset-backed commercial paper (ABCP) conduits, money market mutual funds, markets for repurchase agreements (repos), investment banks, and mortgage companies."[70] The thing about all these institutions is that because they don't take customer deposits in the way that normal banks do, they're much more lightly regulated. The system is interlocking, at many points deliberately opaque, and almost impossible to understand in granular detail, even to the best-briefed financial insiders. In addition, one of the main problems with the shadow system is that it isn't even clear how big it is. With the benefit of hindsight, the US Federal Reserve now estimates that at the time of the credit crunch, the shadow banking system weighed in at about $20 trillion, the regular banking system at around $11 trillion. Unfortunately nobody was drawing any attention to this fact at the time. But these numbers are difficult to tease out and make precise. The best, in the sense of most institutionally trustworthy, estimate I've seen of the current size of the system is that given by the Bank of England's Financial Stability Board in late 2012. That put the total size of the shadow system at $67 trillion. Not a reassuring figure: that's about the same size as the total GDP of planet Earth. Some of the people who get points for being publicly worried about the financial system in the run-up to the credit crunch now have shadow banking at the top of their list of concerns.

shadow value Described as "the dumbest idea in the world" by one of the men who not long ago was seen as its most formidable exponent, Jack Welch, former CEO of GE (which used to be General

Electric, until the law of shareholder value forced the company into other lines of business). It is the belief that—to quote an influential 1970 article expounding it by Milton Friedman—"In a free-enterprise, private-property system, a corporate executive is an employee of the owners of the business," in other words of the shareholders.[71] The employees' sole responsibility is to make as much money for the employers, the shareholders, as possible. The idea is to make money irrespective of all considerations of social responsibility and wider context. In the theory of shareholder value, the corporation is a legal fiction, getting in the way of the responsibility to make money for the owners. The theory of shareholder value has failed even on its own terms, because since it became popular in the late sixties the rate of return on assets and on invested capital has fallen by 75 percent. A countervailing idea of corporations is that they have a life and a character of their own and that the best of them make money by serving customers; customers should come first, rather than shareholders; this idea has gained force as companies that have followed it, such as Apple and Amazon, have had success.

sigma The measure of what's called standard deviation. It tells you how unlikely something is. In a bell curve—that's the normal distribution of data on a graph—one standard deviation from the middle covers just over two-thirds of all the data. For something to be a one-sigma event means that it happens about a third of the time. You should never be surprised by a one-sigma event.

Two sigma covers 95 percent of the data. A two-sigma event is something outside that range of probability; in other words, something that happens 5 percent of the time. That's a one-in-twenty event. From experience, I'd say this is the probability that a social event you're not looking forward to will be canceled on the day. This is the level of accuracy used in things like opinion polls. Two sigma is a threshold often used in science—for instance by the International Panel on Climate Change, which says that the probability that global warming is man-made is 95 percent.

Three sigma is 99.9 percent of the time. We're talking about things that happen only one in a thousand times. If there's a 1,000-to-1 chance of its happening on any given day, then this thing happens about once every three years. Pretty rare. It's about the odds that you will be hospitalized with appendicitis this year—that would be a three-sigma event.

Four sigma is starting to get seriously unlikely. That's 99.993 percent unlikely, meaning 1 in 15,788. It's about the chance that you will die in a fall this year. With five sigma, we're going way past the edges of the humanly probable: it's 1 in 1.74 million. In terms of the chance that an event will happen on a given day, a five-sigma event is supposed to happen one day in every 13,932 years. Six sigma is even bigger; it's one day in every 4,039,906 years, and seven sigma is one day in every 3,105,395,365 years. In recent years, the mathematical models used by banks repeatedly calculated events as being at these levels of probability, despite the fact that the events kept happening. The obvious lesson was that the models were wrong, but the banks went on using them anyway. The overreliance on these models is one of the things that helped cause the credit crunch.

On a personal note, I find it quite helpful to think about these levels of probability in daily life: if the thing you're worrying about is a one-sigma event, it's probably worth a bit of thought. If it's a two-sigma event, you can banish it from your mind until you have some other reason for thinking that it's more likely than that. Anything higher than two sigma, forget about it.

SMEs Small and medium enterprises. In Europe there is a formal definition of the terms: "micro" means up to 10 employees, "small" up to 50, "medium" up to 250. They are of particular importance at the moment, since historically it's SMEs that lead the charge when an economy is emerging from recession.

Smith, Adam (1723–1790) The founder of modern economics as a field of thought, and author of one of the most important books ever written, *The Wealth of Nations* (or to give it its full title, *An Inquiry into the Nature and Causes of the Wealth of Nations*). Everybody should read Smith, because he is such a good writer, still freshly readable to this day, and also because this fundamental text in economics is based on common sense; this in turn gives readers the permission to use their own common sense in thinking about economic questions. It's also worth reading *The Wealth of Nations* to see that Smith is much less doctrinally simple-minded than some of the people who claim him for a narrow modern version of neoliberal capitalist economics. He famously said, "It is not from the benevolence of the butcher, the brewer, or the baker, that we expect our dinner, but from their regard to their own interest. We address ourselves, not to their humanity but to their self-love, and never talk to them of our own necessities but of their advantages."[72] That's the clearest statement ever made of the idea that economics is based on markets, which are in turn based on self-interest. Smith had something of a novelist about him, of the novelist's ability to describe a society to itself, and it was this aspect of his work that gave it such power: he made modern life, the tangled web of relationships and producers and consumers and livelihoods and forces, comprehensible to the people who were tangled in its mesh. He came up with a way of looking at the whole of modern society as a single mechanism.

socialism The system where the ownership of natural resources, property, and the means of production is held collectively.

socialism for the rich The expression is supposed to be a joke, but in the aftermath of the credit crunch it looked a lot like the reality of the financial system, because the fact was that when banks were making huge profits, they paid themselves huge bonuses, but when they were facing collapse, taxpayers had no choice but to step in and bail them out to keep the financial system functioning. The gains were private, but the losses were socialized: and that's socialism for the rich.

sovereign In an economic context the term means to do with nations—I don't know why the word "sovereign" is so popular, but it's a quick fix to replace it with "national." A sovereign wealth fund is a national body of pooled investments; such funds are huge players in the global financial markets, because of their sheer size combined with their ability to act with a single purpose. (The importance of sovereign wealth is a recent phenomenon: the term "sovereign wealth fund" was invented only in 2005.) Sovereign debt means the nation's public debt, as opposed to all the other different kinds of debt owed by the citizens and corporations of a country.

spread The gap between two prices. The term has a number of economic uses, but the main one concerns the divergence between two prices, one used as point of reference and the other as a point of concern. For instance, in looking at the euro zone, German government debt is often used as a point of reference, the idea being that it is the safest in the euro area: when the price of a country's debt moves in relation to German debt, the spread is said to be moving: if the spread is widening, that's a sign that the other country is being seen as at increased risk of default. If the spread is narrowing or tightening, that reflects the increased perception of safety. The financial papers publish a daily list of spreads between government debt and the bund (i.e., German government debt) and T-bonds (Treasury bonds, or US government debt). At the time of writing, for instance, Austrian debt is at +0.4 percent above the bund, i.e., almost identical, whereas Greek debt is at +7.55 percent, i.e., alarmingly higher. In looking for that data, I came across an article from 2008, before the euro crisis, expressing alarm and amazement at the fact that the spread between bunds and Greek debt had hit the unprecedented peak of 1.65 percent . . . which now reads like something from the days of unicycles, spats, and waxed mustaches.[73]

stagflation An occurence when an economy combines stagnant economic growth and high inflation. A classic example came in the USA in the seventies, when GDP was flat or shrinking but inflation was in the high teens. One of the reasons why stagflation is such a danger is that the usual way out of sluggish growth is to lower interest rates and make it cheaper to borrow money; but high inflation implies that interest rates are already too low. On the other hand, the fix for high inflation is to raise interest rates; but that would be certain to depress economic growth even further. The result is that stagflation breeds further stagflation. In the UK and the United States, the policy that broke stagflation was dramatically higher interest rates, which led to a crash in inflation and an eventual reboot of both economies—though not without a high cost in the form of unemployment. Many observers worry that the current government policies of crazy-cheap money and quantitative easing are storing up potential stagflation a few years down the road.

stars, cows, and dogs Model for the way products work. When a new product launches, it will usually be expensive for the company that makes it, but the hope is for it to grow fast, so that it makes more money than it costs: that's a star. Then the market matures and slows down and the cost of the product falls, but if it's a good market, it will continue to generate lots of money: that's a cow (i.e., a cash cow—that's a good thing). Then, as the market cools or fashion changes, the product will still be low in cost, but will also be increasingly low in profit: that's a dog.

stocks and shares Terms for the same thing: the equity of a company. Once upon a time stocks had the specific meaning of all the equity lumped together, i.e., the total stock of the company, whereas a share was just that, a share in the total equity stock. In practice when people say "stocks and shares," they mean equity.

student loans Another candidate for the next big thing to blow up in the US, and perhaps the global, economy. Student loans were the only kind of lending to increase during the Great Recession, and have overtaken credit card debt and car and home loans to become the biggest source of personal debt apart from mortgages. The numbers are big: 37 million borrowers owing about $1 trillion, of which $846 billion is owed to the government and $150 billion is owed to private companies. Most of the debt is owed by people who went to college thinking that they would end up with a degree that improved their earning prospects; unless the economy picks up, that may well turn out to be a mistaken assumption. In that case a lot of those loans will go bad.[74]

I once had the following conversation with an economist:

Me: "A university degree is worth about £250,000 in extra earnings across a lifetime, on average, right?"

Economist: "Yes."

Me: "The government takes about a third of that in taxes. Roughly."

Economist: "Roughly."

Me: "So the government profits by about £80,000 grand for everyone who goes to university. So university should be free because it's an incredibly good investment for the state."

Economist [very crossly]: "No, that's completely wrong."

But he then wandered off before he could explain why it was wrong, so I still don't know.

supply and demand In the opinion of most economists, the single most important principle of economics. The fluctuating relationship between demand and supply explains how prices vary and is the underpinning to the functioning of markets; for that matter, it's an important principle in nature itself. Here's the original diagram from Alfred Marshall, plotting the relationship between supply and demand, which won't help at all:

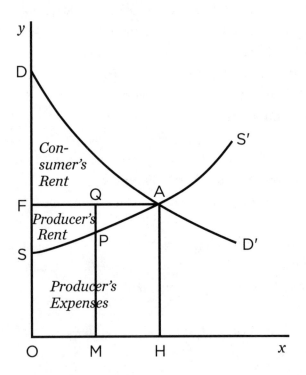

But the basic principle is common sense: if more people want something, the thing becomes scarcer and its price goes up. When fewer people want it, it's easier to get hold of and the price drops.

supply-side Refering to the bits of the economy that produce goods and services. Policies that target the supply side make it easier to make things and make money, and this very often involves a lowering of taxes. For this reason, "supply-side" is code for "rich people"; thus "supply-side economics" in practice means "rich-people economics," because the policies involved—lowering taxes and cutting regulation—are always popular with the rich. One of the ideas behind supply-side economics is the "trickle-down effect," in which the rich get tax breaks and spend money on services provided by people with less money, who then spend money on services provided by people with even less money, and so on, as the money "trickles down" through the economy and everyone benefits. If that was going to work, you'd think that it would have kicked in by now.

surplus theory of value Karl Marx's answer to the question of where value comes from in the first place. The conclusion Marx reaches is to do with workers' labor. He argues that competition pressures will always force down the cost of labor, so that workers are employed for the minimum price: they're always paid just enough to keep themselves going, and no more. The employer then sells the commodity not for what it cost to make it but for the best price he can get—a price that in turn is subject to competition pressures, and therefore will always tend over time to go down. In the meanwhile, however, there is a gap between the price for which the laborer sells his labor, and the price the employer gets when he sells the commodity made by the laborer. That price difference is the money that accumulates to the employer. Marx calls it surplus value. This surplus value is in Marx's judgment the entire basis of capitalism: all value in capitalism is the surplus value created by labor. That's what makes up the cost of any one thing: as Marx puts it, "Price is the money-name of labour objectified in a commodity." In examining that question, he creates a model that allows us to see into the structure of the world, and see the labor hidden in the things all around us. He makes labor legible in objects and relationships.

This, the theory of surplus value, for Marx also explains why capitalism has an inherent tendency towards crisis. As I've said, the employer, just like the employee, has competition pressures, and the price of the things he's selling will always tend to be forced down by new entrants to the market. His way of getting around this will usually be to employ machines to make the workers more productive. He'll try to get more out of them by employing fewer of them to make more stuff. But there's a trap there, because what he's doing, by employing less labor, is creating less value—since the only source of value is the surplus value created by labor. So in trying to increase the efficiency of production, he's actually destroying value, often by making too many goods at not enough profit, which leads to a surplus of competing goods, which leads to a crash in the market, which leads to massive destruction of capital, which in turn leads to the start of another cycle. It's an elegant aspect of Marx's thinking that the surplus theory of value leads directly and explicitly to the prediction that capitalism will always have cycles of crisis, of boom and bust.

There are obvious difficulties with Marx's arguments. One of them is that the analysis can't be proved or disproved, not least because it is partly a contest over definitions. Another is that in quite a few ways it seems intuitively false. Labor manifestly has different value, depending on differing levels of skill in the employee. An example might be an apple pie made by me, since I'm a pretty mediocre baker—cooks and bakers are different tribes, and I'm much more of a cook—and anyone who makes a really good apple pie. The pies would have different values. This problem of skill is impossible to argue away; people's labor just does have different value in different contexts, for reasons that are not easily explained away.

Having said that, I'd now like to say the opposite, which is that this idea of labor being hidden in things, and the value of things arising from the labor concealed inside them, is a much more powerful explanatory tool in the world of the digital than you might think. Take Facebook for instance. Part of its success comes from the fact that people feel that they and their children are safe spending time there, that it is a place you go to interact with other people but is not fundamentally risky or sleazy in the way that new technologies are often perceived to be. But the perception that Facebook is hygienic is sustained by tens of thousands of hours of badly paid labor on the part of people in the developing world who work for companies hired to scan for offensive images and who are, according to the one Moroccan man who went on the record to complain about it, paid a dollar an hour for doing so. That's a perfect example of surplus value: huge amounts of poorly paid menial work creating the hygienic image of a company that at the time of writing has a market capitalization of $146 billion.

Marx's idea of surplus value, his model, asks us to see the labor encoded in the things and transactions all around us. When you start looking for this mechanism at work in the contemporary world, you see it everywhere, often in the form of surplus value being created by you, the customer or client of a company. Any kind of deliberately engineered waiting in line is using your labor to accumulate surplus value to a company. Every time you interact with a phone menu or interactive voicemail service, you're donating surplus value.

Swedish model Just to warn you, if you're looking for the other, noneconomic sort of Swedish model, you've come to the wrong place. In economics it's not a precise term but is used to refer to two things: first, the high-tax, high-welfare, high-security social model that Sweden established in the second half of the twentieth century. Second, less well known and maybe more interesting, is the pattern of industrial ownership, in which large family-owned companies invest for the very long term, with complex and over-lapping patterns of ownership and relationship between big, stable companies—the opposite of the Anglo-Saxon model in which everyone looks at the stock market price and the quarterly profits figures ahead of everything else. This Swedish industrial model is sometimes admired abroad for its long-termism and stability, sometimes deplored for its crony capitalism, depending on how it is perceived as performing relative to its foreign alternatives.

synergy Mainly bullshit, but when it does mean anything, it means merging two companies and taking the opportunity to sack people. For instance, if two companies that make similar products merge, they will have similar warehouse and delivery operations: so one of the two sets of employees will lose their jobs. The idea is that this will cut costs and increase profits, though that tends not to happen, and it is a proven fact that most mergers end by costing money. They take one company with a turnover of $1,000,000 and profits of $100,000 and add it to another company with the same numbers, in the hopes that they will end up with a new company with turnovers of $2,000,000 and profits of—thanks to synergy—$250,000. Instead they create a new company with turnover of $1,750,000 and profits of $160,000. This is called "destroying value." When two companies merge, the first thing that analysts look at when evaluating the deal is how many jobs have been lost: the higher the number, the better. That's synergy.

synthetic A financial instrument that mimics something, without having any of the components of the actual thing. Say you want to create a fund that tracks the value of gold. The simple way to do that would be to buy lots of gold, then issue shares that match the total value of your holdings. But you could also put together a basket of financial instruments that track the price of gold, so that the price of your fund moved in exactly the same way gold does—in which case, your fund would be synthetic. A huge number of financial instruments of all types are synthetic, and synthetic funds played a big role in the kinds of speculation that fueled the credit crunch, a process brilliantly described in Michael Lewis's book *The Big Short*.

T-bonds US Treasury debt, historically regarded as the safest in the world, because the United States is the word's biggest economy, because the US dollar is the global reserve currency, and because the country can print its own money. Thanks to Republican actions in Congress, that status is now in question, and T-bonds lost their AAA super-secure status during arguments about the US government debt ceiling in 2011. The shorter-duration form of Treasury debt, which matures in one, three, or six months, is known as the T-bill, whereas T-notes mature in a range from two to ten years.

technocrat Invented by H. G. Wells in his science-fiction novel *The Shape of Things to Come*, the term has come to mean someone who knows about money and isn't driven by strong political or ideological views. During the GFC the term has largely been used to mean senior economists who've been dragged into political roles to reassure markets that there is a grown-up in charge: the best example was probably Mario Monti, who during his brief tenure as prime minister of Italy in 2012 was popular with markets but not electors. Once upon a time the term "bureaucrat" would have been used instead of "technocrat," but bureaucrat sounds old-fashioned and anti-entrepreneurial, whereas technocrat sounds more up to date, because it's got "tech" in it.

tournament The word has a particular, rather interesting meaning in economics: it's a structure in which a number of contestants compete for a prize, and the rewards are allocated not according to how productive people are but according to who does better

at the tournament. In the words of the original 1981 paper pro-
posing a theory of tournaments, by Edward Lazear and Sherwin
Rosen, the tournament applies to "compensation schemes which
pay according to an individual's ordinal rank in an organization
rather than his output level." That might sound boring, but tournament theory is responsible for the system in which pay at the
CEO level of big firms has got so insanely high. The idea is that
because winning the tournament brings grotesquely dispropor-
tionate rewards, people are willing to work extremely hard to win
the tournament: so although you have a CEO who is overpaid in
relation to what he (usually a he) does, you have a hundred other
executives jockeying for position to be in line to be the next CEO,
so the incentive effects of the high pay spread through the organization. That's a tournament.

This might sound as if it's bullshit because nobody thinks like
that, but I've spoken to at least one City person who does. He said
that when he hit thirty-five and was by most standards already very
well-off, he sat down to think about what he wanted from work. He
realized that the only thing he didn't have that he would like to
have would be a private jet. In order to have one, he reckoned he
would have to rise to be CEO of his (or somebody else's) company.
He thought that if he worked 50 percent harder than he currently
did for ten years he would have a 33 percent chance of being a CEO
and getting his jet. He concluded that the odds weren't worth the
extra effort and lack of personal life, so he decided he was happy
where he was. In this context, he decided not to take part in the
tournament. (This is also an example of someone performing a
cost-benefit analysis.)

Examples of tournaments include the process of becoming a
partner at a law or accountancy firm, where many young people
work thousands of hours, to the huge benefit of the firm, in order
for only one or two of them to be made partner. The stagiaire system in restaurants, in which ambitious young chefs spend several

months at a time working for free in leading kitchens, is another example, maybe—though it's also a way in which people acquire valuable experience they couldn't get any other way. In fact, high-end restaurant kitchens are dependent on this pool of unpaid skilled labor.[75]

traders, analysts, quants People not in banking tend to regard all bankers as being more or less the same, but the tribal divisions inside the profession are strong. The stereotypes would be that traders are aggressive and testosterone fueled, analysts are earnest, mergers and acquisitions types are smooth and corporate, and quants are nerdy mathematicians with no social skills. The divisions and mutual incomprehension between the different tribes and their different activities is one of the things that make the big banks resemble, in the words of the Manchester anthropologist Karel Williams, "loose federations of money-making franchises."[76]

"The Tragedy of the Commons" A highly influential 1968 essay by the economist Garrett Hardin, on the subject of how to share common land, when it's in everybody's interest to maximize his or her own use of the land at the expense of everybody else. His central insight was that when a resouce is communally shared, individuals have no reason to protect other people's interests in the resource, and every reason to maximize their own use of it. If something is owned collectively, it makes sense for you to grab as much as you can for yourself. As a result, the communally owned resource is certain to be exploited to the point of ruin: hence, the tragedy of the commons. Hardin's ideas had a big impact in the study of how people use scarce or finite resources. They haven't gone unchallenged, though, and the anthropologically minded economist Lin Ostrom won a Nobel Prize for her 1999 work "Revisiting the Commons: Local Lessons, Global Challenges," which extensively studied the reality that, in practice, human beings often do a very good job of collectively managing collective resources. (Of the seventy-eight Nobel laureates in economics, she's the only woman.)[77]

trail commission Something that drives investors nuts, when they know about it, but because it's often a hidden feature of financial transactions, they often don't. It's a commission to a financial adviser for recommending a product, but unlike an obvious up-front commission at the time of purchase, it keeps on being paid. So the guy who recommended the product to you keeps on earning, say, 0.5 percent of its value, forever. Trail commission has been banned for new products in the UK, but existing trail commissions are still being paid. Interestingly, the UK has banned the payment of commission for financial advice, a step no other country has taken: now if you're taking advice you have to pay for it up front. The change is a legacy of the fact that many of the big financial scandals of the past few years, in particular the endowment mortgage and PPI scandals, were caused by financial advisers' having had an economic motive to give wrong advice.

triple dip A recession followed by a brief recovery followed by another recession (that's a double dip) followed by a brief recovery followed by yet another recession—the third one being the triple dip. The UK came very close to experiencing the first triple dip in its history in the first quarter of 2013. During the previous quarter the economy had shrunk by 0.3 percent, and there were concerns that the next quarter's number might come in negative, which—because that would have been two negative quarters in a row—would have meant the economy had reentered recession. It turned out that the actual number was 0.3 percent growth.

troika The name of the group that formed a committee to address the EU sovereign debt crisis: the European Commission, the European Central Bank, and the International Monetary Fund. Don't wander around Athens loudly talking about how much you love the troika.

tulips A prominent feature in the history of financial bubbles and manias, because by general consent the Dutch tulip craze was the biggest and maddest bubble of all time. At its peak in 1637, a single tulip bulb was worth more than ten years' pay, and the record price was to exchange a tulip bulb for twelve acres of land. Note that the prices were futures contracts for tulips rather than the bulbs themselves—so the tulip bubble was also the first-ever financial crisis linked to derivatives.

Believers in efficient markets, who don't believe in bubbles, have come up with two lines of defense against the story of the tulips: (1) it didn't happen, or the data are too thin to prove that it happened, and (2) insofar as it did happen, it was economically rational. These arguments under (2) are inadvertently funny, because the people arguing that it made sense for prices to go up because there was a shortage of demand, or because there was an inherent volatility to flowers futures prices, or whatever, are obviously in the grip of something resembling a mystical belief in efficient markets.

The general rule with bubbles after they've popped is that if you take a moment to think about it you can usually see that beneath the craziness there's a phenomenon that really is of general importance: as investors say, a "story." Railways and electricity and the Internet and overseas trade were all phenomena that changed the world, even if they did also trigger gigantic bubbles that involved enormous destruction of capital. It's much harder to do that with the tulip bubble. And this was before the Amsterdamers were allowed to smoke dope!

two-speed economy An economy in which different sectors are performing very differently at the same time. The clearest example I've ever seen was in Australia in 2012. At the time it was clear from the data that Australia was the most successful developed economy in the world: it was the only one not to have experienced recession in the aftermath of the credit crunch, and at that point its GDP growth number was higher than that of the entire G7 added together. (Perhaps one of the reasons Australians refer so chirpily to the GFC—Global Financial Crisis—is that they escaped it.) As I got off the plane, I was expecting visible evidence of prosperity stretching all across the continent's wide horizons . . . and instead saw a much more varied picture. The Australian success story had mainly to do with commodities—basically, digging things out of holes in the ground and sticking them on a boat to China. Everything connected with that was booming, and the states most involved in mining, Western Australia and Queensland, had annual growth rates of 12 percent and 8 percent, respectively—not just a boom, a proper gold rush. You heard all sorts of stories about the crazy money that was being made by miners. Elsewhere, the picture was much less cheery. I spent a day driving around parts of Sydney that, when I lived there in 2001, had seemed the most affluent and chic parts of the entire country, and that now were visibly struggling, with significant numbers of boarded-up shops. Mining was going like gangbusters, but retail, manufacturing, wholesale, utilities, food, and accommodation—in short, pretty much everything else—was having a hard time. The government was much less popular than you could have conceived possible from the headline summary of economic data. This was described as a "two-speed economy," the implication being that one part was going fast, the other slow. In truth, it seemed at the time to be more like a two-direction economy, one sector moving forward and the other back. It was also a lesson in the fact that the reality of a place is usually a lot more complicated than the numbers tell you.

tyranny of sunk costs One of several gloomy economic ideas that come in useful in real life. It means that once you have sunk a significant quantity of costs into something—not necessarily money costs; they can just as easily be costs in terms of effort and time—it becomes harder to walk away from the thing. The costs you've sunk exert tyranny over your decision making: hence the name. Funnily enough, I've found this a helpful idea in relation to writing novels: the more time you've spent thinking about a character or plot or idea, the harder it is to accept that it's wrong. Having a label for this problem makes it easier to work with, I find.

venture capital Investment in a shiny new business whose prospects for actually making money are some way off, whose costs are real and in the present, and whose future earnings potential is, the venture capitalists hope, very big. Venture capitalists invest at an embryonic stage of the business in return for a share of the equity. Venture capital is an especially important actor in the world of technology, where scrambling to attract attention from it is a crucial stage in the life cycle of a new company. It provides a good way of both making and losing a lot of money. The venture capital industry in the USA is light-years ahead of that anywhere else.

volatility index The VIX is a number that measures the general levels of expected volatility in financial markets—which in turn means it tracks the general sense of insecurity and anxiety in the market. As a result it has been a very important number in recent, anxious years. The VIX is sometimes called the "fear index," which is catchier than its full title, the Chicago Board Options Exchange Market Volatility Index. The VIX is based on options prices for the next thirty days, in other words, on how much people are expecting the market to move. After a long period of being at historic highs, the VIX has more recently been going through a period of noticeable lows. If this was a Western, John Wayne would be standing on the rampart of a fort looking into the middle distance and saying, "It's quiet . . . too quiet . . ."

Volcker rule A rule proposed by Paul Volcker, who as chairman of the Federal Reserve between 1979 and 1987, under Presidents Carter and Reagan, was more responsible than anyone else for breaking the high inflation that was stagnating the American economy. President Obama brought in Volcker after the credit crunch to make suggestions for reforming the financial industry, and his main suggestion was a ban on banks' trading on their own behalf. This came to be called the Volcker rule. He argued that banks making huge bets on their own behalf was not helpful to the wider economy and introduced unnecessary amounts of risk to the financial system. Since Volcker is nobody's idea of a hippie outsider criticizing the financial industry from a basis of ignorance, his proposals had an unusual force—especially as the big banks hate the idea. The banks and their lobbyists are very, very good at stalling things they don't like. So guess what happened? The rule is due to come into effect in 2015, a mere five years after being given the go-ahead by President Obama. Volcker's view of the delay is that "it's ridiculous. There's no reason why the Volcker rule should take three years to write." The rule is about as complicated as it's possible to imagine, weighing in at more than a thousand pages of immensely compacted legalese. Since one of the lessons of history is that complexity creates opportunity for the people in banks who want to bend the rules, this is bad news, and there is a possibility that the rule is just too complicated to do what it's supposed to.[78]

VOSL Imagine for a moment that you are an engineer building a bridge. You've done everything you can to make the bridge safe, and you're confident that it is super-duper-mega safe; but that doesn't mean it's impossible to do anything more. There are some extra features you could add to make it even more safe: a high-up guardrail, say, in a place where nobody is supposed to climb. But the guardrail would be expensive and might never be used. You reckon the chance that it would ever be used is one in a million. But in that one-in-a-million event, it would save someone's life. So the question is, is it worth adding the rail? Even more helpfully, would it be possible to work out exactly what it's worth spending on the extra guardrail, without wasting money?

Enter the value of a statistical life, or VOSL. This is the theoretical amount that a life is worth, as implied by exactly these kinds of calculations of risk and cost. Different industries use different ones: in US transport and road safety calculations, the VOSL is $6 million. So our guardrail has a one in a million chance of saving $6 million; so the VOSL tells us that it makes sense to spend $6 on our guardrail ($6 x 1,000,000 = $6,000,000), whereas spending $7 would be too much, and spending $5 would be a bargain. There's something beautifully chilling and amoral about the VOSL.

Washington consensus One name for the neoliberal economic model, as imposed on developing and emerging economies by the big international economic institutions. It was crisply summarized by the Indian writer Pankaj Mishra as "the dominant ideological orthodoxy before the economic crisis of 2008: that no nation can advance without reining in labor unions, eliminating trade barriers, ending subsidies, and, most importantly, minimizing the role of government."[79]

wealth The term is not precisely defined in economics, but the crucial point is that it refers to accumulated assets rather than to earnings. Rich people are wealthy, by definition, but you can be wealthy without being, in practical terms, rich: an elderly person living in a big old family house is wealthy, but may also be short of usable cash. "Net worth" is a synonym for wealth.

Where Are the Customers' Yachts? A highly illuminating and not-at-all dated 1940 book about Wall Street by Fred Schwed Jr. The title comes from the "ancient story" that provides the book's epigraph: "Once in the dear dead days beyond recall, an out-of-town visitor was being shown the wonders of the New York financial district. When the party arrived at the Battery, one of his guides indicated some handsome ships riding at anchor. He said, 'Look, those are the bankers' and brokers' yachts.' 'Where are the customers' yachts?' asked the naïve visitor." This exchange is to be borne in mind by anyone having any dealings with the financial services industry. It's one of the deepest and most important secrets of that business that, as old pros say, "You make more money by selling advice than you do by following it."

World Bank An institution founded by the Bretton Woods agreement, at the same time as the International Monetary Fund. Its brief was to target poverty: in its current formulation, the bank's mission is to "end extreme poverty within a generation and boost shared prosperity." Funfact: the World Bank's first loan, made in 1949, was to that impoverished and struggling Third World economy, France. If the IMF is the bad cop, cracking its knuckles and saying, "Well, I'd love to lend you this $100 million you're asking for to meet your debts, but first, you're going to have to close down all your child health programs," the World Bank is the good cop, doing things like—to cite examples from this year's report—improving irrigation infrastructure in Afghanistan, making 39,000 microfinance loans to people in Mongolia, saving 15 million cubic meters of water from an aquifer in Yemen, and helping 17 million out-of-school children in India enroll in primary education for the first time. [80]

yield A term with particular relevance to bond investing. The whole point of bonds is that they pay out a regular amount of money. The official amount they pay out is listed on the bond itself and is called the "coupon." So you might buy a $1,000 government bond with a coupon of 3 percent, paying out annually. That means you'll get $30 a year for ten years, guaranteed, and at the end you'll get your $1,000 back, also guaranteed. What happens, though, is that the rate of 3 percent will have times when it seems too low, because you can do better elsewhere, and times when it seems attractively high—that will usually be when the risks of looking for a higher rate seem too great. When the 3 percent looks poor, the value of your $1,000 bond will drop, and if you want to get rid of it you'll only be able to sell it for $900, say. When the 3 percent looks good, the price of your $1,000 will go up, and you'd be able to sell it for $1,100. But wait! That means, if you've bought it for $900, you are still getting your guaranteed $30. So the payout isn't 3 percent any more: it's now 3.33 percent. This number is known as the yield: it's what the coupon on the bond is worth once you allow for movements in the bond's price.

Note that in the example where the bond moves the other way and the price goes up, the coupon payout of $30 now represents a yield of 2.73 percent. So the yield goes up when the price goes down, and vice versa. Or, in economist-speak, the price and the yield are inversely correlated. This is an important principle, but it's one that people who speak money know so well they zoom over it at great speed, assuming that everyone understands it, saying things like "The yield on Italian debt has spiked today, causing the ECB to announce crisis measures . . . ," which leaves nineteen out of every twenty people listening to the news saying, "What? Isn't going up a good thing?"

The inverse correlation of bond prices and yields is one of those principles that is difficult to get your head around, and I find myself reexplaining it to myself almost every time I come across it. From the point of view of listening to the news, the thing to remember is that yields going up means the debt is being seen as more risky.

yield curve The yield projected into the future. If you lend money, the general rule is that longer you're lending it for, the more your money is at risk. This means that longer loans should offer a higher yield: more risk means the yield has to be more tempting to get you to lend money. The graph of time plotted against risk is called the yield curve, and over time, it goes up, as the risk and yield go up. Sometimes, though, when things are weird and the economy is hitting hard times, investors think that the long-term rates currently on offer are better than the ones they'll be getting in a few months' time. They pile into long-term debt, taking the opportunity to get these good rates while they're still available. The price of those long-term debts goes up. Because price and yield are inversely correlated, the rising price makes the yield on those debts go down: that can mean that the longer-term debt ends up with a lower yield than short-term debt. This is known as an inverted yield curve, and it is a sure sign that the market thinks there is severe trouble just ahead.

yuan and renminbi Observers of China refer to both the renminbi and the yuan in talking about the country's currency. They're the same thing: renminbi means "the people's currency," and it was the name given the new currency at the foundation of the People's Republic of China in 1949. Yuan means "dollar" and is the unit of the currency; so renminbi is like sterling and yuan is like pound. In practice, Mandarin-speaking Chinese tend to use the colloquial *kuai*, roughly the same as the American "buck."

ZIRP A zero-interest-rate policy, in which a government or central bank holds interest rates at zero. This effectively reduces the cost of borrowing to nothing, and is a desperate measure, since under most circumstances it would certainly lead to sharp inflation. The exception is when the economy is in so much trouble that the government or bank has to use every tool at its disposal: a ZIRP is what it would use after it had already used the kitchen sink. In the United States, where interest rates have been at a record low of 0.5 percent for years, the situation is very close indeed to a ZIRP.

zombie bank A bank with so many dud assets on its books that it no longer functions as a lender, and at the same time is too big or politically important for anyone in power to admit the truth about its real position. Its condition is a form of living death, hence the name. In the debate between fast and slow zombies, zombie banks are as slow as it gets.

Afterword

S o what are we going to do with these tools, with this economic language? Where are we heading?

The answer: it's up to us. The future direction of the world economy is not written in stone, and the same goes for those in the US and the UK and in the developed world more generally. Economics is a tool kit, and tool kits are used to make things and do things. We have choices and options. That might sound banal, but I would argue that it's actually a very important point. The neoliberal consensus in economics presents itself as consisting of self-evident laws. Low tax rates, a smaller state, a business-friendly climate, free markets in international trade, rising levels of inequality and an ever-bigger gap between the rich, especially the superrich, and the rest—these are just the facts of economic life, if you want your economy to grow and your society to be richer. But this is a con. This system is intellectually coherent, and it's the one we've been living with for more than thirty years, but it is not the only way of organizing the economic order. It is not a given. In the words of Tony Judt's posthumous masterpiece *Ill Fares the Land*:

Something is profoundly wrong with the way we live today. For thirty years we have made a virtue out of the pursuit of material self-interest: indeed, this very pursuit now constitutes whatever remains of our sense of collective purpose. We know what things cost but have no idea what they are worth. We no longer ask of a judicial ruling or a legislative act: is it good? Is it fair? Is it just? Is it right? Will it help bring about a better society or a better world? Those used to be *the* political questions, even if they invited no easy answers. We must learn once again to pose them.

The materialistic and selfish quality of contemporary life is not inherent in the human condition. Much of what appears "natural" today dates from the 1980s: the obsession with wealth creation, the cult of privatization and the private sector, the growing disparities of rich and poor. And above all, the rhetoric which accompanies these: uncritical admiration for unfettered markets, disdain for the public sector, the delusion of endless growth.

We cannot go on living like this. The little crash of 2008 was a reminder that unregulated capitalism is its own worst enemy: sooner or later it must fall prey to its own excesses and turn again to the state for rescue. But if we do no more than pick up the pieces and carry on as before, we can look forward to greater upheavals in years to come.

And yet we seem unable to conceive of alternatives.[81]

Judt was right. Having spent the better part of a decade writing and talking to people about economics, I've noticed that the most common shared political feeling is a sense of bafflement, alienation, impotence, and passivity. People feel as if there's nothing they can do. The weight of money is a weight pressing down on their lives from above. At the individual level, I'm sorry to say, this is sometimes at least half true. If you're buried under a mountain of debt, there isn't much you can do about it except go bankrupt or pay the debts back. Either is a laborious and painful process, with no short cuts. It isn't that you have no agency: it's just that you don't have many choices, and you have no pleasant ones. People lose jobs all the time, for no good reason and through no fault of their own—it's just the way economic things are. But what is true at the individual level is not true of societies as a whole. There are voices keen to tell us that there is no alternative to the economic order, that we have to accept things the way they are; but that isn't true. Marx was right when he said that "men make their own history, but not under circumstances of their own choosing." Both parts of that are accurate: we didn't create the world we inherited, but we also don't have to leave it the way we found it.

So here's how I see things. I'd like you to take a moment to think about what you think is humanity's greatest collective achievement—the single best thing we have all done together. Please take a few seconds to think about that. One leading candidate, perhaps most people's top choice, would be the collective enterprise of modern science and medicine. We haven't evolved in the last 20,000 years: so it's especially astonishing that the same brains that were functioning as hunter-gatherers and then as neolithic farmers are now stepping into scanners that analyze the activity of those very brains by means of positrons, the antimatter form of electrons—and one could pick thousands of other examples of science and technology that would have seemed miraculous to our ancestors. That sense of the miraculous is appropriate: we're too quick to move past wonder at what we have achieved. So that's one candidate. Another would be the development of societies that offer care and protection to all their citizens from cradle to grave, and the general phenomenon of the modern liberal democracy, the most admirable form of human society that there's ever been (not least because it is so insistent on noticing its owns flaws, and trying to rectify them). Or the collective enterprise embodied in the arts, what Michael Oakeshott called the "conversations" of humanity through literature and music and visual art: conversations that give us the ability to talk to and listen to ourselves across generations and indeed entire cultures. Consider the fact that we can read Homer, whose two-and-a-half-millennia-old work has survived the collapse of two entire civilizations, and still be amazed at its freshness. As somebody said, "If you want to see how much life and people have changed, read Homer. If you want to see how little life and people have changed, read Homer."

And now I'm going to propose another candidate for that greatest-ever achievement. On 29 February 2012, the World Bank announced that the proportion of the planet's population living in absolute poverty—on less than $1.25 a day—had halved from 1990 to 2010. That rate of poverty reduction, driven by economic growth across the world from China to Ghana, is unprecedented in global history.* Just imagine: in twenty years, there are half as many absolutely poor people. And the success story of improvement in our collective living conditions doesn't stop there. Consider child mortality, which for any parent is the most important number there is. (It's pretty important for any child, too.) This has been the subject of a precipitate decline. In 1990, 12.4 million children were dying every year under the age of five. Today that number is 6.6 million. That's obviously 6.6 million child deaths too many, but it is 16,438 fewer child deaths every day. I know I've mentioned this fact already in the lexicon, and I apologize, but then again I don't apologize much, because that's 11 children's lives being saved every minute. Does any other achievement in human history match that? Child mortality has a meaning beyond the number of lives lost and saved. It's used as a proxy for a whole set of things, to do with level

---

* The definition of absolute poverty was moved from its initial figure of $1.00 a day to $1.25 a day in 2008, on the basis of the World Bank's view that this number took account of higher-than-expected prices in the developing world.

of medical and technological development, strength of social ties, degree of access to care for the poor, a society's acknowledgment of the needs of strangers, and so on. If you want to measure a level of a society's development, and can only choose one number with which to do that, child mortality is the one to pick. A world undergoing a sharp decline in child mortality is a world that is rapidly and inarguably becoming a better place.

This focus on the numbers for people living in absolute poverty, and on child mortality, forms part of the Millennium Development Goals, announced by the UN at the turn of the new century. The MDGs set targets for 2015 from a starting point of 1990, with the books slightly cooked by setting the starting point ten years in the past—in other words the world gave itself a bit of a head start. The targets are in eight areas:

1. Eradicate extreme poverty and hunger
2. Achieve universal primary education
3. Promote gender equality and empower women
4. Reduce child mortality*
5. Improve maternal health
6. Combat HIV/AIDS, malaria, and other diseases
7. Ensure environmental sustainability
8. Global partnership for development

There are a number of points to make about that list: the goals might sound a bit vague in themselves, and it is hard to put specific and incontestable numbers on things such as sustainability and "global partnership for development." When you look into the detail, though, most of the MDG aspirations are attached to specific numbers and metrics. Even the wooly-sounding, tree-huggy "part-

---

* The MDG target for child mortality is not just to halve it but to reduce it by two-thirds. It will be missed.

nership for development" has aims that it's hard to disagree with, and it is significant that the burden of debt on developing countries has decreased by 25 percent since 2000. As for protectionist barriers on the part of the rich world, it's interesting that 83 percent of all goods exported by the developing world enter the rich world free of any duty.

Other targets are even clearer. The goal of eliminating hunger, for instance, comes attached to the defined objective of halving the proportion of people suffering from hunger. (The UN says that that objective will be met on schedule.) One of the specific targets for gender equality is to equalize access to primary education between boys and girls—which has been achieved, and which in turn emphasizes the disparity of access in secondary education. Many of the targets overlap: the higher the level of female education, the lower the rate of child mortality; so, to cite one example from the latest MDG report, a program to target hunger in Yemen has the effect of keeping more girls in school, which in turn has a positive impact on a whole range of other metrics. Greater access to AIDS education and treatment has a huge effect not just on mortality statistics but also on those for poverty and hunger. This is particularly the case in sub-Saharan Africa, where one in ten children still dies before the age of five. For instance, Botswana has a terrible life expectancy of 31.6 years, but if you remove the impact of AIDS that goes up to 70.7 years.

What distinguishes this achievement from any other is its speed—twenty-five years—and also its extraordinary scale. Small countries can get rich fast, because a spike in economic growth in one area quickly lifts all the statistics across the board. It's harder for big countries to do that, and as for the whole planet doing that, it would once have been thought impossible. We had thought that the industrial revolution was the benchmark for rapid transformation in people's lives—the most important economic event since the domestication of plants and animals in the neolithic revolution.

But not even the industrial revolution halved poverty and child mortality in twenty-five years. The MDGs have seen 700 million people move out of absolute poverty. In 1990, 47 percent of the population of the developing world was below this threshold, a number that by 2010 had fallen to 22 percent. The proportion of the developing world's population living in hunger fell from 23.2 percent to 14.9 percent. That still leaves 870 million hungry people, which, on a planet with the resources to feed all of them, is 870 million more than there should be. In addition, although the proportion of poor and hungry people in sub-Saharan Africa has gone down, the population has gone up, so the actual number of poor and hungry people has in fact increased. Nonetheless, the world has made progress, and let's not confuse progress with its opposite. Put it all together and, as I said earlier, I don't think there is an achievement in human history that matches this: it's the greatest thing we have ever done.

Two main questions arise from the progress we've made towards the Millennium Development Goals. The first is "How have we done this?" The second is "Why don't people pay more attention to it?" I think the answer to the second question is partly contained in the answer to the first.

Perhaps the single worst feature of the contemporary intellectual landscape is the way in which it is divided along such predictable and partisan lines. As the Gérard Depardieu character says to the Andie MacDowell character in Peter Weir's romantic-comedy *Green Card*, "You get all your opinions from the same place." That's depressingly accurate. Most of us do indeed get our opinions from one single place, and if you know what somebody thinks about any one issue (SUVs in the city, Michelle Obama's childhood obesity drive), you know what he thinks about everything else too, up to and including how he votes. The polarization of modern intellectual life is a large and understudied subject, too broad to tackle here; but it is a fact that in these heavily polarized circumstances, ideas tend to get allocated to one side or the other, and to stay the property of that camp, irrespective of changes in circumstance and external reality. Sometimes the allocation of views to particular sides of the political debate is not easy to understand, looked at from a distance and with a cold eye. Conservatism has, as its name suggests, a strong emphasis on conserving and preserving the legacy of the past; it isn't that hard to imagine a conservatism that took a strong stand against the prospect of sweeping, irreversible change offered by global warming, and made the "precautionary principle" of acting to prevent disaster a central part of its mission. This was once less of a counterfactual than it might now seem, since the first global leader to mention climate change in a speech was Margaret Thatcher, who in 1989 said in an address to the UN, "We are seeing a vast increase in the amount of carbon dioxide reaching the atmosphere. . . . The result is that change in future is likely to be more fundamental and more widespread than anything we have known hitherto."[82] She had moved some distance to get to this point. Her first reaction on being told about climate change, by the government's chief scientist Dr. John Ashworth, was "Are you standing there and seriously telling me that my government should worry about the weather?" But over time she got it. Thatcher was and remains the only British prime minister to have had a degree in science. She saw the question as a scientific one rather than an issue of ideology. Conversely, since globalization and trade are the single biggest factors raising GDP in the developing world, we might expect the left to be in favor of them, and the right, which historically has had a strong protectionist streak, to be against. But it didn't work out that way: climate change is owned by the left, globalization by the right, and there's an end to it.

The single biggest factor in reducing levels of absolute poverty is economic growth in the developing world: over the period in question the main locus of that growth has been China. The Chinese story is a bizarre hybrid of ultra-free-market economics, high levels of state control, and a total lack of democratic accountability. It's not a model that you're going to find in any textbook, but it's one that has been extraordinarily, unprecedentedly effective at quickly raising the living standards for hundreds of millions of people. Who in the Western world can claim that one as an ideological win? Well, the right, broadly speaking, since it's a form of capitalism, and not just any old capitalism but the hyper-free-market variety, which has achieved the progress. As it happens, though, the particularities of Chinese Communist Party–mandated capitalism are so odd that nobody on the political right is willing to claim China's progress as evidence for the virtues of free markets. So credit for the biggest economic achievement in the history of the world is in effect lying unclaimed on the table, like a weirdly toxic form of poker winnings.

As for the other component of the story, no ideological camp is claiming credit for that either. This other component is to do with aid. Writers such as William Easterly (*The White Man's Burden: Why the West's Efforts to Aid Have Done So Much Ill and So Little Good*) and Dambisa Moyo (*Dead Aid: Why Aid Is Not Working and How There Is Another Way for Africa*) give powerful critiques of the way in which aid encourages dependency and corruption. Broadly speaking, this objection to aid is becoming a popular position on the political right. This school of thought doesn't just argue that aid doesn't work; it argues that aid is actively counterproductive, since it has distorting effects that prevent the development of indigenous solutions to problems. Critics also point to the fact that a huge amount of aid is stolen by elites in the target country, and that it often contributes to conflicts continuing longer and causing more damage than would otherwise be the case.

And yet, progress towards MDGs shows that aid can indeed have powerfully positive effects. The key provision is that it is targeted and specific, and designed to maximize positive consequences, such as the example of the Yemeni hunger program mentioned above. (Since 2007, parents enrolled in the program have been given wheat and vegetable oil in return for keeping their children in

primary school; and because more than 60 percent of the children
not going to school are girls, the program has the effect of improving women's education. The illiteracy rate for adult Yemenis is 60
percent for women and 21 percent for men.) Another example is
an irrigation project in Malawi, targeting 2,800 families who live
in areas affected by flash flooding; the project teaches improved
farming techniques to increase the families' abilities to look after
themselves, with obvious consequences for the metrics on hunger,
poverty, and child mortality.

This kind of aid has a number of qualities. It is based not on
generalized good intentions but on precise goals, usually with
an emphasis on nutrition or health. It seeks to make measurable
progress towards a defined numeric target. It is difficult to do this
kind of aid—for just how difficult, look at Nina Munk's entertaining book *The Idealist*, about Jeffrey Sachs and his attempt to establish "Millennium Villages" in Africa. Perhaps the most effective
aid is designed by people who have taken on board the criticisms
of the anti-aid lobby, and who try to design their programs so
that the possibilities for the various forms of negative outcome—
corruption and dependency prominent among them—are avoided.
It is, for instance, difficult to see how teaching Malawian farmers
techniques for harvesting their crops in winter (which is one of the
main tricks of the Naamasalina program) offers potential for theft
by the elite, or increases the farmers' dependency on anyone. This
is wary, precise aid giving, and it is strongly informed with a desire
to measure things. In the 2013 edition of his charity foundation's
newsletter, Bill Gates spoke about the importance of this:

> Unlike so many vaguely worded international resolutions,
> the MDGs came with concrete numbers. You can use the
> goals to measure progress around the world and in specific
> countries. . . . And the measures apply to things that everyone
> can rally around, like saving children's lives and preventing

maternal mortality. I've been writing about measurement a lot this year, because I've found that measuring progress is the only way to drive lasting success.[83]

This is the kind of thing you'd expect Gates to say; but that doesn't mean he's wrong. As it happens, the precise impact of a lot of aid is difficult to quantify, since there is a huge difference between outcomes (i.e., what happens) and impact (i.e., the specific difference made by a specific piece of aid). To truly measure the impact of something you have to quantify the difference between what happened with the aid and what would have happened without it. This is very difficult to do, and most charities don't bother to even try, since it isn't in their interest to come up with numbers that in many cases will make the impact of their interventions look smaller. But it is difficult to disagree with programs that aim to eradicate polio or provide sanitation for the proportion of the world's population without proper toilets: 51 percent in 1990, 36 percent today. Consider the story of the guinea worm, a horrible illness-causing parasite, once endemic through parts of Africa and Asia, which today is on the verge of being eradicated. This would be the first eradication of an illness since the defeat of smallpox in 1979. The vehicle for the eradication hasn't been some expensive drug or corrupting, incentive-distorting aid program, but education and improved hygiene. It's going to be the first disease to be wiped out through changes in people's behavior. Given that this disease had 3.5 million new infections as recently as 1986, this is an amazing feat.

Perhaps this, taken all together, is why we don't hear as much about the amazing achievement of humanity in the last two decades. The right is embarrassed by the fact that the economic growth that it would normally boast about has taken place mainly in a communist country; the left is nervous about claiming success for aid programs that have been so vociferously criticized, whose fund-raising has an emetic overlap with celebrity culture, and that

don't ever seem to make visible progress. And so we've achieved
something that in terms of mass material progress exceeds the
feats of classical civilization, the Renaissance, and the industrial
revolution—and yet we hear very little about it.

The media are rubbish at reporting good news. Part of the reason is that we humans seem hardwired to pay attention to stories
of disaster and distress. Also, we are hardwired to like stories about
individuals, about heroes and villains. A good news story about systemic progress is a difficult-to-impossible sell. Look at the example
of flying. I'm completely terrified of flying—when I say "terrified," I
mean I can't get on a plane unless I'm zonked on prescription tran-
quilizers. But even I can see that that's an irrational fear, because
contemporary commercial aviation is extraordinarily, uncannily
safe. The experience of flying is so ghastly—the nasty airports,
the multiple queueing, the intelligence-insulting security theater,
the cattle-car in-flight conditions—that we tend to forget what an
astonishing success the air industry has made of its safety record.
Do we even notice? No, not really—what we notice are the crashes.
Maybe the story of aid is a bit like that. If 16,438 children died today
in a single disaster, it would dominate every news media outlet in
the world for weeks. The fact that they aren't dying isn't news.

Perhaps there is, to go with the politically uncomfortable nature
of the news, and its nondisastrous, nonpersonal nature, a third factor behind our lack of interest. What makes it so difficult to take
in the news about the extraordinary progress being made in large
parts of the developing world is the fact that here in the developed
world things can at best be described as flat. Added to this is the reality that whole categories of work are disappearing, and seem likely
never to come back. I have friends in journalism who have lost their
jobs and who have no serious prospect of ever finding comparable
work again. They aren't duffers: these are people who are really
good at their work. It's just that the work doesn't exist any more.
Print journalism is dying, and among people who work in it, con-

versations around the subject don't turn on what's going to happen, or whether it's going to happen; they turn on how long it's going to take before newspapers in their current form disappear and everything is digital-only. But digital-only can't sustain the same number of jobs and the same level of investment in quality and research and the expensive stuff—good writers, foreign reportage, in-depth pieces that take a lot of time, risky and drawn-out investigative journalism. The jobs that are going away are not coming back.

Some exciting things are going to happen in journalism, and I'm not even a tiny bit Luddite about digital media. But because people won't pay for it, or not as much, the new journalistic models can't sustain the same kind of cost base. Something comparable is happening in publishing. A young American writer said to me a few years ago, shaking his head, shrugging, frowning, and crying into his beer more or less simultaneously, that "advances are down by an order of magnitude." That's a drop of 90 percent, and it's the difference between an advance that could pay for somebody to write a book, and one that can't. Again, the underlying shift has all the appearance of being a permanent historic one. Pressure on bookshops has put many of them out of business, and without bookstores backing writers and hand-selling them and giving an initial platform at the beginning of their working lives, many writing careers would never get going. I speak from experience, because that is exactly what happened to me. But now that first stage just isn't there any more, and a landscape is being created in which the spotlight is brighter than ever before, but the dark around it is so black that anything in it is hidden, invisible. The big is bigger than ever, and the small feels as if it doesn't exist.

There are consolations and complications even in this bleak portrait; the very fact of the big getting bigger sometimes leaves all sorts of interesting ways open for being creatively small. Digital journalism may yet surprise us all, and digital forms of distribution may well end up with writers being paid more than they currently are. But the positive kinds of changes are some way off, while the negative consequences are right here, right now. I mention this not because journalism and publishing are the most important industries in the world but just because I've seen at first hand some of the disruption that is coming down the pipeline to entire swaths of the economy. Musicians, journalists, and writers are middle-class canaries in the coal mine of economic change.

Equivalent phenomena have happened many times in manufacturing, so the basic historical phenomenon of fundamental change in the mode of work isn't unusual. Indeed it's a story we've seen many times over, in forms as different as the mechanization of cotton picking, the factory mass-production line, and the disappearance of electronics repair shops (in that case, because goods got so cheap it was simpler just to chuck a faulty item away and buy a new one). Some change is cyclical, and some isn't. But as the world is getting flatter and more digitized, the prospect for what once were comfortable and secure means of making a living is much bleaker. We look ahead at the prospect of ferocious competition, remorseless downward pressure on pay, the constant prospect of outsourcing, and the incessant press of technological change threatening to disintermediate and—to use the cant term beloved of Silicon Valley—"disrupt" traditional forms of employment. Flat living standards, flat median income, the disappearance of secure employment. We are told, in the title of a lively recent book by Tyler Cowen, that "average is over." But most of us in our hearts know that in most important aspects, we are average. That's the whole basis of prosperity in our societies: it provides good livelihoods and life prospects to the ordinary citizen. The notion of its coming to an end is terrifying. It's no wonder people can't get all that excited about the fact that out-of-sight poor people in the developing world are having a slightly less horrible time than they used to.

What we're looking at here is the prospect of the world doing the splits. Here's a strange fact: during the two decades when the number of absolutely poor people was halving, inequality was growing in two-thirds of the world's economies. We are moving at a brisk rate towards ever-increasing levels of inequality. This, in my view, is certain to dominate discussion of politics and economics over the next decade.

The problem is that the current world economic order is based on the theory that high levels of inequality at the top of the income distribution don't matter as long as general levels of prosperity increase. Unfortunately, in the countries that have been following this policy in its purest form for a third of a century—mainly the Anglo-Saxon economies, which have been the most fully liberalized and open to the idea of the devil-take-the-hindmost free market—it's becoming clear that if these policies were going to work, they would have already worked by now.

The problem is compounded because there is a provable link between inequality and heritability. In plain English, the more unequal a society, the more likely you are to inherit your life chances from your parents. The United States and the UK and China are all increasingly unequal societies, and they are also societies where the economic prospects of the parents are passed directly on to their children. In the ringing words of Tim Harford,

> This is what sticks in the throat about the rise in inequality: the knowledge that the more unequal our societies become, the more we all become prisoners of that inequality. The well-off feel that they must strain to prevent their children from slipping down the income ladder. The poor see the best schools, colleges, even art clubs and ballet classes, disappearing behind a wall of fees or unaffordable housing.
>
> The idea of a free, market-based society is that everyone can reach his or her potential. Somewhere, we lost our way.[84]

Extrapolated over time, this trend offers the prospect of reinventing feudalism. It means that your life chances are your parents' life chances; you stay stuck in the station of life you were allotted by birth. People sometimes argue about the precise meaning of "fairness" and point out that you can challenge the idea from more than one direction. The notion that talented people should be rewarded according to the measure of their talents and individual achievements has force: fairness doesn't automatically mean everyone ends up in the same circumstances. But even people who believe in a right-wing version of fairness can see that feudalism is not the way to go.

In addition, societies with high levels of inequality will always tend to have broken and antidemocratic political systems. The rich will almost always have more power than the poor. But it's a question of degree. When the poor have a voice and a vote—or when the vote is the voice—there are factors at work in favor of a benign equilibrium. The rich can't advocate policies that will enrage the poor too much, for fear of inciting class war, and the poor can't expropriate the wealth of the rich, because they need the good things that are bought by the taxes the rich pay on their earnings. This equilibrium can be threatened, however, when the gap is widening between living standards at the top and everywhere else. The rich have got richer since the neoliberal order really took hold; this process went on for three decades, and has continued to go on since the credit crunch. During the recovery, such as it is, incomes have risen—but 95 percent of the rise in total income has been captured by the top 1 percent. Elsewhere, living standards are flat at best. In 1989, using real money (i.e., adjusted for inflation), the median American family earned $51,681. In 2012 the same family earned $51,107. In other words, in the richest and most powerful country the world has ever seen, the average family is slightly poorer than it was a quarter of a century ago.

As the gap widens, the rich have less and less in common with the rest. They're barely inhabiting the same spaces. The consequences can become toxic. In the words of the economist Angus Deaton,

The political equality that is required by democracy is always under threat from economic inequality, and the more extreme the economic inequality, the greater the threat to democracy. If democracy is compromised, there is a direct loss of well-being because people have good reason to value their ability to participate in political life, and the loss of that ability is instrumental in threatening other harm. The very wealthy have little need for state-provided education or health care; they have every reason to support cuts in Medicare and to fight any increase in taxes. They have even less reason to support health insurance for everyone, or to worry about the low quality of public schools that plagues much of the country. They will oppose any regulation of banks that restricts profits, even if it helps those who cannot cover their mortgages or protects the public against predatory lending, deceptive advertising, or even a repetition of the financial crash. To worry about these consequences of extreme inequality has nothing to do with being envious of the rich and everything to do with the fear that rapidly growing top incomes are a threat to the wellbeing of everyone else.[85]

This issue just isn't going to go away, and I would add that it is a problem not just for the Western world but for the emerging world too, perhaps especially for China, which had historically gone a long way towards abolishing inequality, at what must be admitted was a very high price, but has now taken a long stride towards prosperity, at the cost of greatly increasing inequality. The danger facing China comes from the fractures caused by that inequality. We already see rising tensions between this new urban workforce, the new Chinese middle class, and the rural poverty it's leaving behind. In addition there is friction between the coast and the center, between the factories and the farms, and increasing problems with corruption and maladministration. All this matters for the

rest of the world, because of China's centrality to the world economy as a producer of so much and increasingly as a consumer too,
especially of luxury goods.

I would love to have some magic solution to the problem of rising
inequality or, failing that, to have some magic piece of advice about
how to navigate the turbulence that is going to ensue, but all I can
offer instead is a complete certainty about two things: that arguments about the economy are going to dominate the next decade,
and that arguments about fairness and inequality are going to be at
the heart of those debates. This one isn't going away, anywhere—and
that in itself is a strange and new thing, because we face the prospect of a world in which, arguably for the first time, every political
dispensation, from Communist China to mixed-economy India to
free-market America to the resource producers of South America
to the welfare state capitalist societies of northern Europe, everybody, is for the first time, arguing about the same issue. In Beijng or
Rio, Sydney or Paris, New York or London, it's about the inequality,
stupid.

So where do we go from here?

The two biggest "known unknowns" are those of inequality and
crises in relation to resources. We simply can't know how these
issues are going to play out over the next few years, even though we
can be sure that the subjects are going to be at the top of the global
agenda. I think there we're likely to see a gradually increasing distinction between the developed and the emerging worlds, in terms
of their attitudes to wealth and in particular to public displays of
wealth and conspicuous consumption. Bear in mind that there are
few areas where fashion is a more important factor than in that
area; and bear in mind, too, that in the Western world, the current
has been running in the direction of money and display for three
decades. The last time there was a strong countercurrent in this
area was in the 1960s with the hippie movement and in the 1970s
with punk rock.

When the financial crisis struck in 2008, I thought we might see, as the full scale of the downturn became apparent, and also the full extent of the time it was going to take to emerge from it, a cultural reaction towards embracing financial restraint, opposing displays of wealth and consumption, and conscious and voluntary choosing of lower levels of discretionary spending. Napoleon once said that to understand a man, you must understand what the world looked like when he was twenty years old. I've always thought that a very interesting observation. When we think about what the world looks like to a twenty-year-old today, I think we get a glimpse of some trends that are going to become important. There are glimmers of anticonsumption attitudes, particularly where you'd most expect to find them, among the self-conscious and well-educated and relatively affluent young. Just anecdotally and personally, I know several young people who pride themselves on their ability to live on tiny budgets and minimize their consumption of resources and also their spending. They're enthusiastic about "freecycling," handing on used stuff, and "freeganism," living off food they've obtained without payment. I suspect that this trend has quite some distance further to run and may well become a generationally defining movement, much in the way that the hippie counterculture once was, as young people react to the prospect of a world that is worried about overconsumption of resources, and at the same time offers more limited immediate prospects than they were taught to expect when they were growing up.

As for resource shortages and the impact of climate change, that's too big a topic to sum up here. But it is clearly not going away, and will have a defining impact on polities all across the world. A 2013 paper in *Nature* by a team of climate scientists based in Hawaii predicted that rises in temperature would put the climate of cities in the tropics outside all known historical ranges— "climate departure," it's called—as imminently as 2020. Since this would obviously involve large population displacements, and probably the total breakdown of order, not just in the cities affected but all around them, this study is in effect predicting the end of life as we know it, sometime this decade. Let's hope the Hawaii team is wrong; but for sure this counts as a "known unknown."

A third "known unknown" is that the world is likely to look more and more like a genuinely multipolar place. For a long time we lived with two superpowers, then with one; now there will be several sources of global power and influence. We haven't had a world that looks like that for a long time, and it is likely to have many surprising features. When we turn to history for a comparison, the relevant one is from just over a hundred years ago, with a multiplicity of competing global empires, high and rising levels of inequality, competition over resources, and technology making the world economy an increasingly globalized place. A century ago those trends ended in the First World War, which is a discouraging comparison.

The world is getting younger, too. The median age of us humans is twenty-seven. So 50 percent of the world's population is under the age of twenty-seven. The majority of those young people live in cities—that also is a new thing. As recently as 2007 the majority of the world's population was living in rural areas; that has now changed, and the trend is for the proportion living in cities to increase. The UN predicts that the population of the world's cities will hit 5 billion by 2030. That's probably a good thing, for all sorts of reasons. As the UN puts it, "In principle, cities offer a more favourable setting for the resolution of social and environmental problems than rural areas. Cities generate jobs and income. With good governance, they can deliver education, health care and other services more efficiently than less densely settled areas simply because of their advantages of scale and proximity. Cities also present opportunities for social mobilization and women's empowerment. And the density of urban life can relieve pressure on natural habitats and areas of biodiversity."[86] So that is an optimistic prospect, with one small catch: it isn't clear whether there is going to be enough work to sustain much of this population. In the next decade, 1.2 billion young people are going to enter the labor market, world-wide. That's a big, big number: 1,200,000,000 youngsters looking for work. Projections at the moment are that growth in the labor market and retirement of the working population will open up 300 million new jobs over that same period. That's a huge gap, 1.2 billion workers chasing 300 million jobs, and it points again back to the theme I have mentioned already, that of a world doing the splits. Over this coming decade the distinction between winners and losers is going to be sharper than ever, and more visible than ever, and I say again that this will be a truly global theme—I don't think there is a society anywhere in the world where this issue will not be acted out.

The main economic model that has been used by international institutions over the last three decades is a set of policies that I've been calling neoliberalism. These policies have been effective at growing GDP, and equally or more effective at growing inequality. By now, the neoliberal agenda has taken us to a place where, for many people in the developed world, life offers the prospect of an interminable squeeze on prospects and living standards. The good years of open-ended, more or less frictionless growth that we in the developed world have all, broadly speaking, enjoyed since the end of the Second World War are over. That doesn't mean we can't have higher than ever standards of material well-being; it doesn't mean we can't have unprecedented levels of general prosperity; it doesn't mean we have to stop trying to be better societies that offer better lives, year after year, to all citizens. It just means that we aren't going to achieve those ends by pursuing the same agenda and using the same tool kit. The years around 1979 and 1980s saw a historic swing of the pendulum away from consensus-based postwar politics. At that point, inequality had been decreasing all through the twentieth century. Since then, it's been increasing. Both of those things are conscious choices on the part of the society; we decreased levels of inequality and increased levels of opportunity before; we can do it again. As the political historian David Runciman recently wrote,

> The world that fell apart at the end of the 1970s had begun to unravel much earlier in the decade, in the succession of crises that included the demise of Bretton Woods, the Arab-Israeli war, the consequent oil shock and a world-wide recession. That confused and confusing period turned out to be the dawn of neoliberalism, though it wasn't until much later that it became clear what had happened. Now that neoliberal order is stumbling through its own succession of crises. We are barely five years into the unravelling, if that is what is taking place. . . . [W]e shouldn't be surprised if we can't yet spot who is going to make the difference this time round. What we're waiting for is the counter-counter-revolution, led by progressives who have learned the lessons from the age of neoliberalism and are unafraid to make use of its instruments in order to overthrow them. Plenty have started trying. Someone will get there in the end and maybe by the end of the decade we will discover who.[87]

How would this happen? Well, we're starting to see straws in the wind. They come from all points of the compass—which is necessary, because a change of direction along these lines would have to be international, in the same way that the neoliberal turn crossed the Atlantic and spread around the world. The world's two leading centers of finance are New York and London, and coming up behind them on the rails is Switzerland. In New York, Bill de Blasio won the mayoralty with a campaign openly focused on the question of inequality: the first politician to win on a platform like that in the United States in living memory. One of the signature proposals of his campaign was to raise taxes on the most affluent New Yorkers, those earning over $500,000 a year. That's irrespective of the fact that New Yorkers already pay some of the highest rates of tax in the United States. In Switzerland, they've just had a referendum to limit the multiple between what a company pays its CEO and its least well-paid worker. The proposed multiple was twelve. It was defeated—but more than a third of the population voted for it, and this was the second Swiss referendum in 2013 on the subject of executive pay. Just for reference, across the 500 biggest companies in America, the current multiple is that CEOs are paid 204 times more than their average employee.[88]

In the cheap seats, we're often told that though people are increasingly furious about rising inequality, the most important thing is not to scare the "wealth creators," because if we do, they'll all move to places like London and Switzerland. But hang on: London and Switzerland are starting to have the same sorts of conversations that are happening in the USA. So where then would they go? The answer, I suspect, is that most of them wouldn't go anywhere. A few bankers might head off to places like Singapore and Hong Kong, but that certainly wouldn't be the end of life as we know it. When I was growing up in Hong Kong, top-rate tax in the UK was over 90 percent, whereas top-rate tax in Hong Kong was 15 percent, and there was no mass exodus of the rich then, just as there wouldn't be one now. Most of the talk about the flight of the bankers is self-serving. The ones who are going to be driven out have already gone. As I say, Wall Streeters already pay some of the highest rates of tax in America. The more important question is whether a society should arrange itself primarily for the convenience of its richest citizens and its richest, most powerful economic sector, irrespective of the consequences of that for everyone else. A robber baron's castle can be an amazing thing, full of art and color and life and music, with the most beautiful tapestries, and the highest standard of living, and the best food and drink for hundreds of miles around. The cutlery is gold, the glasses are crystal, the jewels are fulgent. But the robber baron's castle glitters so brightly precisely because it devastates the landscape in which it sits. Its glory comes at the cost of the desolation it causes. The City of London is a robber baron's castle.

The move away from neoliberalism is likely to involve higher rates of tax at the top end, dramatically increased education spending, and perhaps a rethinking of some of the ways in which capitalism can be inflected away from shareholder value towards models that include owners, managers, workers, and the surrounding community—a model that has been successful in, for instance, Germany. The provision of employment and training for apprentices is an explicit part of this. There will need to be a sharp increase in levels of social housing. The role model here is Singapore, which as well as consistently being voted the most open economy in the world—a beacon to free marketers everywhere—has the highest level of state and social housing in the world. The world capital of the free market is also the world capital of council houses. Not all the lessons of Singapore are about free markets. More generally, there will need to be a focus on material well-being in the round, and broader measures of quality of life than the mere narrow focus on GDP. In Denmark, a judge earns more than a cleaner: two and a half times more.[89] How does that work out for them? The Danes report the highest level of life satisfaction of anyone in the world.

Some readers may be disappointed that I am not advocating more-explicit alternatives to capitalism. I might well advocate one if I could see one that seemed to be working. The candidate that was touted more than once in the first decade of this century was the socialist countries of Latin America, but the problem with that as a model for elsewhere is that all those countries were benefiting from gigantic commodity booms, especially in the case of Venezuela and its oil. No big Western democracy has an equivalent prospective source of largesse. But this doesn't mean that no new model is ever going turn up. In the meantime, it may be that we have to settle for a world that is mainly getting richer, whose citizens are living longer, and whose richest countries are enjoying slower growth, but also a more equal, more satisfying, more mindful way of life. When people say, "It can't go on like this," what usually happens is that it does go on like that, more extendedly and more painfully than anyone could possibly imagine; it happens in relationships, in jobs, in entire countries. It goes way, way past the point of bearability. And then things suddenly and abruptly change. I think that's where we are today.

Acknowledgments

Portions of this book appeared in the *London Review of Books* and *The New Yorker*. I am grateful to the editors for their help and support. I'd particularly like to thank Mary-Kay Wilmers at the *LRB* and Henry Finder at the *The New Yorker*.

I would like to thank Matt Weiland and Sam MacLaughlin at Norton, and Julian Loose and Kate Murray-Browne at Faber, for their help with this book. As always, my agent Caradoc King has been an invaluable source of advice and support and succor.

For off-the-record chats over the years I would like to thank my friends in the world of finance, especially those who'd prefer not to be publicly thanked.

Further Readings

One of my ambitions for this book is that it will make readers want to go and read more about money and economics. I'd come close to saying that the whole point of my writing it is for people to be able to go on and read more. . . . The good news is that the standard of writing and reporting in this area is high, ranging from books to the business papers and pages to the blogosphere. The tricky thing is knowing where to begin, and there's no better place to start than the business pages of the newspapers. After that, it's a question of what areas within the field seem most interesting.

For a very good general overview of the field today—what amounts to a framing of the current political and economic world order—a good place to start is *The Great Escape*, by the Scottish-born Princeton economist Angus Deaton. Then you could go in several directions. For a look at the foundational technical questions of economics, *Economics for Dummies*, by Sean Masaki Flynn, is good. *Naked Economics*, by Charles Wheelan, is an excellent primer. John Kay's *The Truth about Markets* is a brilliant, wide-ranging explanation of the power of markets in many areas of life. From there, it is a short move towards the politics of economics, maybe beginning with Ha-Joon Chang's *23 Things They Don't Tell You about Capitalism*, a highly effective account of the arguments and evidence against neoliberal free-market orthodoxies. A number of very good recent books look at the effect of these policies in terms of their impact at the top end of the income distribution, and the consequences of that inequality for everyone else: Chrystia Freedland's *Plutocrats*, Robert Frank's *Richistan*, Jaron Lanier's *Who Owns the Future?*, and George Packer's *The Unwinding*. Spring 2014 saw the publication of Thomas Piketty's masterpiece *Capital in the Twenty-First Century*, an important, powerful, and densely argued study of the shift in the balance of power between capital and labor.

There is a notable gap in the market here: there are attacks on the existing neoliberal order, but there doesn't seem to be a powerful popular counternarrative. It's not as if there are no arguments on the economic and political right, and no one who believes and indeed acts on those arguments; but they aren't well represented in book form. Maybe neoliberal capitalism is so well entrenched it doesn't need defenders or advocates.

Where there's been a publishing boom instead is in the field of microeconomics. Tim Harford is a riveting expositor of the field, lively and fair-minded, and his books *The Undercover Economist* and its macroeconomic companion piece *The Undercover Economist Strikes Back* are excellent places to start, both because they are so interesting in themselves and because they give a good initiation in how economists think and study these sorts of questions. *Freakonomics*, by Steven D. Levitt and Stephen J. Dubner, is a highly successful study of a number of contentious political and social questions from a microeconomic perspective. The work of the Chicago school of economists on areas such as rational choice is worth a look too, perhaps starting with Gary Becker's Nobel Prize lecture, "The Economic Way of Looking at Life." Behavioral economics, which has a particular interest in how people think and act, has grown out of microeconomics. *You Are Not So Smart*, by David McRaney, is an introduction to cognitive mistakes—though that makes it sound a lot drier than it is. The unchallenged masterpiece in the field is *Thinking, Fast and Slow*, by Daniel Kahneman.

Readers interested in finance are also spoiled by the quality of the writing. There's no better place to start than with the work of Michael Lewis, perhaps beginning with his first book, *Liar's Poker*, an account of his job working as a bond trader at Salomon Brothers, and then skipping forward to *The Big Short*, a riveting description of the shenanigans behind the credit crunch. His most recent book, *Flash Boys*, is an account of high-speed trading that will make your hair stand on end, if it hasn't all fallen out from worry by the time you've finished reading it. Alice Shroeder's *The Snowball*, a biography of Warren Buffett, is very different in tone and texture, but it brings in a lot of stories and information from the world of finance, as does Sebastian Mallaby's *More Money Than God*, a (suprisingly and convincingly positive) study of hedge funds.

Some of you may well be thinking: but how is any of this going to help me become rich? If you are, here are two books for you: Burton Malkiel's *A Random Walk Down Wall Street*, which explains efficient-market theory for the ordinary investor, and John Kay's *The Long and Short of It*. Kay's book is the best book ever written for the British individual investor, by a country mile. Ben Graham's *The Intelligent Investor*, the first book written on the subject, remains one of the best.

One of the liveliest areas of argument in this field concerns the poorest people in the world, and the question of how best to help them. There are two camps, one in favor of aid and one not: the powerfully argued work of William Easterly stands out in the anti-aid field, thanks to his books *The White Man's Burden* and *The Tyranny of Experts*. Damibisa Moyo's *Dead Aid* is strongly argued too. A considered argument from the other side of the debate is Paul Collier's *The Bottom Billion*, and the annual letter from the Gates Foundation is indispensable reading for anyone interested in the question.

The internet offers many superb resources on economics, as

well as lively debates that respond to news and data in real time. There is no better place to begin than Twitter: I would start by following Tim Harford, Tyler Cowen, Aditya Chakrabortty, and Paul Kedrosky.

Finally, I would urge anyone who's interested in the subject but hasn't read *The Wealth of Nations* to give Adam Smith's masterwork a go. Smith was a great writer as well as a great thinker, and his book is still fresh and still readable, as well as being a serious candidate for the most influential work of the humanities ever written.

Notes

1 Grayson Perry and Brian Eno, "How the Internet Has Taught Us We Are All Perverts," *New Statesman*, 7 November 2013.

2 Daniel, quoted in Michael Lewis, *The Big Short: Inside the Doomsday Machine* (New York: Norton, 2010), p. 206.

3 You can read the original *Fortune* article at www.awjones.com/images/Fortune_-_The_Jones_Nobody_Keeps_Up_With.pdf.

4 See http://www.awjones.com/historyofthefirm.html.

5 Frédéric Bastiat, *Economic Sophisms,* trans. Patrick James Stirling (Edinburgh: Oliver and Boyd, 1873) , p. 83.

6 See David Graeber's *Debt: The First 5,000 Years* and Felix Martin's *Money: The Unauthorised Biography* for more on this.

7 John Kenneth Galbraith, *Money: Whence It Came, Where It Went* (Boston: Houghton Mifflin, 1975), p. 5.

8 John Maynard Keynes, "Alfred Marshall, 1842–1924," *Economic Journal* 34, no. 135 (1924): 333.

9 Stephen Dubner and Steven Levitt, *Freakonomics: A Rogue Economist Explores the Hidden Side of Everything* (New York: HarperCollins, 2006), p. 13.

10 Alfred Marshall, *Principles of Economics* (London: Macmillan, 1890), p. 32.

11 Daniel Kahneman, *Thinking, Fast and Slow* (New York: Farrar, Straus and Giroux, 2011), pp. 231–33.

12 Ibid., pp. 231–32. Kahneman came up with the process in 1955. To this day the Israeli army uses the same process: six structured point-scores, and then "close your eyes."

13 Marshall, as quoted in Keynes, "Alfred Marshall," p. 342.

14 John Maynard Keynes, letter to Roy Harrod, 4 July 1938, in *Collected Writings*, vol. 14 (Cambridge: Cambridge University Press, 1978), p. 295.

15 Charles P. Kindleberger, *Keynesianism vs. Monetarism and Other Essays in Financial History* (New York: Routledge, 1985), p. 2.

16 See annualletter.gatesfoundation.org/#nav=Section2_Video.

17 Available at www.unicef.org/publications/files/APR_Progress_Report_2013_9_Sept_2013.pdf.

18 Gladwell's article "Clicks and Mortar" is available at gladwell.com/clicks-and-mortar/.

19 See www.telegraph.co.uk/finance/financialcrisis/10024209/Bank-of-Cyprus-executes-depositor-bail-in.html.

20 James Buchan, *Frozen Desire: An Inquiry into the Meaning of Money* (London: Picador, 1997), p. 68.

21 The index is at www.economist.com/blogs/graphicdetail/2013/07/daily-chart-10.

22 See imagine.gsfc.nasa.gov/docs/ask_astro/answers/danger.html.

23 Lewis, *The Big Short*, p. 25.

24 See www.berkshirehathaway.com/letters/letters.html.

25 Kingsley Amis, *The Old Devils* (Penguin Books: London, 1986), pp. 133–34.

26 See www.youtube.com/watch?v=tO5sxLapAts.

27 See www.bbc.co.uk/news/business-23070728.

28 See http://www.ons.gov.uk/ (though they have replaced this helpful explanation with a new, worse one).

29 See www.thephatstartup.com/about/.

30 See www.imf.org/external/pubs/ft/weo/2013/update/02/.

31 John Meynard Keynes and others, *Times* (London), 17 October 1932.

32 For the Japanese case, see www.guardian.co.uk/business/2005/dec/09/ japan.internationalnews; for the German case, www.telegraph.co.uk/ news/worldnews/europe/germany/10114011/Snoozing-German-bank-clerks-222-million-euro-fat-finger-error.html.

33 See http://www.federalreserve.gov/faqs/about_12593.htm

34 See www.bankofengland.co.uk/banknotes/pages/about/history.aspx.

35 See uk.mercer.com/press-releases/holiday-entitlements-around-the -world.

36 See www.forbes.com/sites/scottdecarlo/2012/09/19/cost-of-living -extremely-well-index-our-annual-consumer-price-index-billionaire-style/.

37 John Maynard Keynes, *The General Theory of Employment, Interest and Money* (Macmillan: London, 1936), p. 79

38 See economics.uwo.ca/news/Davies_CreditSuisse_Oct12.pdf and www .gov.uk/government/topical-events/uk-presidency-of-g7-2013.

39 The full list is at https://www.cia.gov/library/publications/the-world-factbook/rankorder/2172rank.html. Note that the CIA uses the percentages up to 100 rather than a coefficient up to 1.

40 Gini's article is available at www.jstor.org/discover/10.2307/2142862?ui d=3738032&uid=2&uid=4&sid=21102724064461.

41 See https://www.cia.gov/library/publications/the-world-factbook/geos /xx.html.

42 Available at www.transparency.org/.

43 Graham, *The Intelligent Investor: A Book of Practical Counsel* (New York: Harper & Row, 1973), p. 277.

44 See www.wired.com/business/2012/08/ff_wallstreet_trading/all/.

45 See www.capgemini.com/resources/world-wealth-report-2010.

46 Jaron Lanier, *Who Owns the Future?* (Allen Lane: London, 2013), p. xii.

47 See www.gartner.com/technology/research/methodologies/hype -cycle.jsp.

48 See cdn.budgetresponsibility.independent.gov.uk/2013-FSR_OBR_web .pdf.

49 John Maynard Keynes, *The Economic Consequences of the Peace* (London: Macmillan, 1919), p. 118.

50 See www.forbes.com/sites/luisakroll/2011/04/22/just-how-rich-is-queen -elizabeth-and-her-family/ and http://www.guardian.co.uk/artanddesign /2006/apr/20/art.monarchy.

51 Here's the actual napkin: http://web.archive.org/web/20110503200219/ http://www.polyconomics.com/gallery/Napkin003.jpg.

52 See www.cdc.gov/nchs/data/hus/hus12.pdf#017.

53 See media.bloomberg.com/bb/avfile/rJ5Q_k_NsIk8.

54 Available at www.marxists.org/archive/marx/works/1852/18th-brumaire/.

55 The study, called "When Choice Is Demotivating," is available at www .columbia.edu/~ss957/articles/Choice_is_Demotivating.pdf.

56 See www.theguardian.com/commentisfree/2013/jul/30/obama-grand -bargain-speech-middle-class.

57 At www.un.org/millenniumgoals/poverty.shtml.

58 See www.businessinsider.com/most-miserable-countries-in-the-world-2013-2?op=1.

59 Graham, *The Intelligent Investor*, p. 108.

60 Nassim Nicholas Taleb, http://www.bloomberg.com/news/2010-10-08/taleb-says-crisis-makes-nobel-panel-liable-for-legitimizing-econo mists.html.

61 See www.oecd-berlin.de/charts/PIAAC/.

62 See www.ft.com/cms/s/0/cb2bfb08-0e06-11e0-86e9-00144feabdc0 .html#axzz2acmNJdUy.

63 Burton Malkiel, *A Random Walk Down Wall Street* (New York: Norton, 2007), p. 119.

64 Joseph Stiglitz, "A Tax System Stacked against the 99 Percent," *New York Times*, 14 April 2013, available at opinionator.blogs.nytimes .com/2013/04/14/a-tax-system-stacked-against-the-99-percent/?_ r=0.

65 Originally published in the *Economic Journal* in 1965, the article is available at www.apec.umn.edu/grad/jdiaz/A%20theory%20of%20Alloca tion%20of%20Time%20-%20Becker.pdf.

66 Marshall Jevons, *The Fatal Equilibrium* (New York: Random House, 1985), pp. 102–3.

67 See boxofficemojo.com/alltime/adjusted.htm.

68 See this riveting piece, "Prince Alwaleed and the Curious Case of King-dom Holding Stock," at www.forbes.com/sites/kerryadolan/2013/03/05/prince-alwaleed-and-the-curious-case-of-kingdom-holding-stock/.

69 See en.wikipedia.org/wiki/List_of_countries_by_GDP_sector_compo sition.

70 Ben Bernanke, at http://www.federalreserve.gov/newsevents/speech/bernanke20131108a.htm.

71 Milton Friedman, "The Social Responsibility of Business Is to Increase Its Profits," *New York Times*, 13 September 1970.

72 Adam Smith, *An Inquiry into the Nature and Causes of the Wealth of Nations* (Oxford: Clarendon Press, 1976), pp. 26–27.

73 There's a list of current government spreads at markets.ft.com/RESEARCH/markets/Government-Bond-Spreads.

74 See www.theguardian.com/money/2013/apr/03/student-loan-debt -america-by-the-numbers.

75 The original 1981 article founding tournament theory is available at www.jstor.org/discover/10.2307/1830810?uid=3738032&uid=2&uid=4&sid=21102713625541.

76 Karel Williams, quoted by Joris Lukendijk in the *Guardian* at http://www.theguardian.com/commentisfree/joris-luyendijk-banking-blog/2013/jun/19/banking-britain-beyond-control.

77 A brilliant article by Tim Harford about the two thinkers and their work is available at timharford.com/2013/08/do-you-believe-in-sharing/.

78 See online.wsj.com/article/SB1000142412788732383820457900062389 0621830.html.

79 Pankaj Mishra, "Which India Matters?," *New York Review of Books*, 21 November 2013.

80 For what they're up to at the moment, have a look at web.worldbank.org/WBSITE/EXTERNAL/NEWS/0,,menuPK:141310%7EpagePK:49567%7EpiPK:139209%7EregionMDK:119222%7EtheSitePK:4607,00.html.

81 Tony Judt, *Ill Fares the Land* (New York: Penguin, 2010), pp. 1–2.

82 Margaret Thatcher, http://www.margaretthatcher.org/document/107817.

83 The newsletter is available at www.thegatesnotes.com/Features/
    MDGs-Dream-with-a-Deadline.

84 Tim Harford, "How the Wealthy Keep Themselves on Top," *Financial
    Times*, 15 August 2013.

85 Angus Deaton, *The Great Escape: Health, Wealth, and the Origins of
    Inequality* (Princeton: Princeton University Press, 2013), pp. 213–14.

86 UN, https://www.unfpa.org/pds/urbanization.htm.

87 David Runciman, review of Christian Caryl's *Strange Rebels*, in *London
    Review of Books*, 26 September 2013, available at http://www.lrb.co.uk/
    v35/n18/david-runciman/counter-counter-revolution.

88 See www.bloomberg.com/news/2013-04-30/ceo-pay-1-795-to-1-multiple-
    of-workers-skirts-law-as-sec-delays.html.

89 Patrick Kingsley, *How to Be Danish* (London: Short Books, 2012), p. 17.